NO ORDINARY TOURIST

Richard, First Duke of Buckingham & Chandos 1776–1839

NO ORDINARY TOURIST

The Travels of an Errant Duke

Jonathan Roberts
&
Gerard Morgan-Grenville

Milton Mill Publishing Ltd

Published by Milton Mill Publishing Ltd
Milton Mill, West Milton,
Bridport, Dorset DT6 3SN

First published in 2006

Typeset and colour reproduction by stormcreative ltd, Radstock
Printed and bound in Singapore
by KHL

This book is printed on StoraEnso Matt paper, an
environmentally-friendly paper, using only pulp from
sustainable forest sources. The paper is bleached without
the use of environmentally hazardous chemicals.

ISBN 0-9540570-1-5
ISBN 978-0-9540570-1-5

A CIP catalogue record for this book is
available from the British Library

To Anne and to Margaret
whose combined contribution to this
book has proved vital to its publication

Acknowledgements

The authors are deeply indebted to Mary Robertson, Librarian at the Huntington Library for her unflagging cooperation and wide knowledge of Stowe and the Grenville family history; to Michael Bevington of Stowe School for advice and help in providing photographs and for reading the draft manuscript; to George Clarke for his enthusiasm and comments on the draft; to Professor John Beckett for pointing us in the right direction on the Grenville archives; to Hugh Robinson for copy-editing the text; to David Burnett, Sara Hudston and Nicky Bowden for sundry advice on printing; to Storm Creative of Radstock for setting the book; to the ever-helpful staff of the London Library; to Professor N A M Rodger for information on where to look for the registration certificate of the *Anna Eliza*; to Louise Pichel, archives assistant at the Lambeth Palace Library; to David Gladstone for a photograph fo the Buckler painting; to Joanna Corden, archivist of the Royal Society; to Roger Peers for information about early images of Christ; to Colin Anson for steering us safely through the Grenville family portraiture; to our respective wives for keeping us focussed on a project which offered continuous temptation to digress; and especially for Margaret Morgan-Grenville for her patient computing expertise.

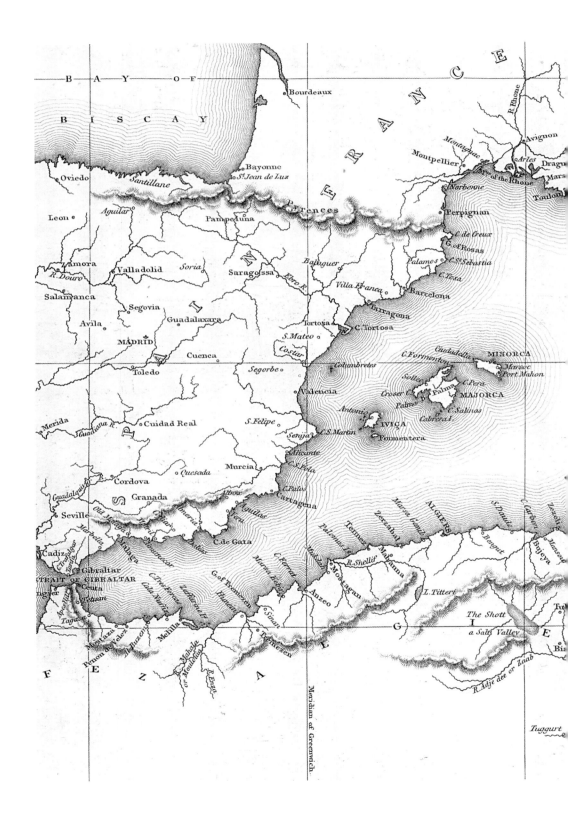

Abbreviated Family Tree

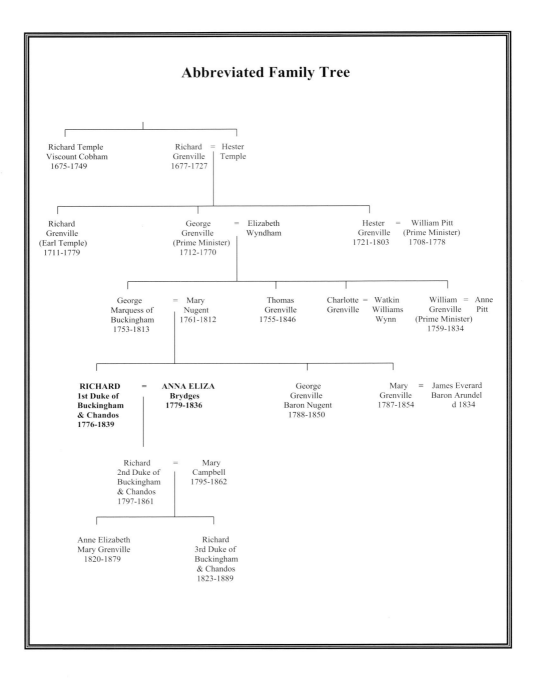

Richard Temple
Viscount Cobham
1675-1749

Richard = Hester
Grenville   Temple
1677-1727

Richard
Grenville
(Earl Temple)
1711-1779

George = Elizabeth
Grenville   Wyndham
(Prime Minister)
1712-1770

Hester = William Pitt
Grenville   (Prime Minister)
1721-1803   1708-1778

George = Mary
Marquess of   Nugent
Buckingham   1761-1812
1753-1813

Thomas
Grenville
1755-1846

Charlotte = Watkin
Grenville   Williams
Wynn

William = Anne
Grenville   Pitt
(Prime Minister)
1759-1834

RICHARD = **ANNA ELIZA**
1st Duke of   **Brydges**
Buckingham   **1779-1836**
& Chandos
1776-1839

George
Grenville
Baron Nugent
1788-1850

Mary = James Everard
Grenville   Baron Arundel
1787-1854   d 1834

Richard = Mary
2nd Duke of   Campbell
Buckingham   1795-1862
& Chandos
1797-1861

Anne Elizabeth
Mary Grenville
1820-1879

Richard
3rd Duke of
Buckingham
& Chandos
1823-1889

Introduction

There are certain unread books on the shelves of my library which emit a feeble but constant signal demanding to be removed, dusted off and at the very least, glanced through. For a good half-century the three leather-bound volumes which chronicle my great-great-great grandfather's dramatic flight to the Mediterranean have been tirelessly claiming my attention. Two years ago they won. Thumbing through uncut pages, redolent with place names of great allure, the idea of retracing his travels seemed, on a grey winter's day, to hold much promise and one which took shape when my neighbour Jonathan Roberts was found to share my enthusiasm. Agreeing to write a biographical account of this voyage (if I would attend to illustrations) it was not long before the first *espresso* lay before us in the wintry sunshine of Palermo.

In the matter of illustrations I was lucky in that, by the purest chance, Mary Robertson, the diligent librarian of the Huntington Library in Los Angeles happened upon a file marked 'No illustrations' which actually contained (all?) the sketches which the Duke had made on his voyage. That this file was but one of the 350,000 documents which were acquired by this American library when the contents of Stowe were sold soon after the Great War, demonstrates the magnitude of this luck.

These sketches, in spite of their naïve amateurishness, succeed in conveying an immediacy to the scenes and events he describes. Clearly he worked hastily, with an extremely limited palette, and must have been greatly disadvantaged by the rolling of his ship, humidity and salt-spray. Yet they – and other paintings executed around the same time – afford a glimpse of the seemingly untrammelled world less than two centuries ago, a world we can now scarcely recognise. Tracks are become dual carriageways, villages are become towns and towns become cities. Travel seldom exceeded ten miles an hour and old people sat at their doorsteps and talked with passing travellers.

The Duke was a controversial character. He lived in circumstances that obliged him to lead a life that was probably untrue to his nature. He was knowledgeable and observant, with a keen interest in the sciences, and it is possible that this voyage enabled him to be more in tune to his true nature than perhaps at any other time of his deeply troubled life.

Stowe, my family home until 1921, is now a famous public school and the great house is being restored by National Heritage funds. The landscape gardens, the finest in Europe, are being brilliantly restored by the National Trust.

Gerard Morgan-Grenville

Prologue

That morning, June 24th 1828 in the southern Mediterranean, was unusually hot. On the little island of Pantelleria, the Governor had insisted on giving the Duke a farewell tour of the island's capital town: La Citta, as he proudly called it. In reality it was little more than a squalid village, and the heat and smells in the narrow streets seemed to the Duke almost intolerable.

The Governor, a short, pompous man dressed in a major's uniform with a cocked hat, had recently arrived from Italy, and trailed at his side a curved sabre longer than himself. He was thrilled to show off his island prison to someone as important as the Duke.

> So we waded in filth unutterable, and heat inexpressible, up one vile alley and down another, with all the mob of the town at my heels, curious to see whether an English signor was made like other people. I then embarked almost exhausted, and returned to my vessel.[1]

The Duke rested in his cabin during the hottest hours of the afternoon, then embarked in the *Anna Eliza*'s barge to go for a swim before dinner. Ten of his sailors, one to each oar, rowed him to a rocky cove about a mile from the *Anna*'s anchorage.

> I had had a bathing apparatus and tilt attached to the awning of my barge over its stern, which made a very comfortable bath like a machine in England, only not upon wheels. This was made to hoist or let down and take off at pleasure, and this was the first time I have ever used it. I had a delightful bath, but, a heavy swell coming on, I was obliged to anchor and bathe in deep water. The place was very romantic.

By the time he returned to the *Anna* the swell had increased. The evening came on gloomy, with a vague, indefinable feeling that all was not well. An official boat arrived from La Citta with his passport, yacht's bill of health and his English charts of the island briefly borrowed by the Governor, who sent a message apologising for not returning them in person: the swell would make him sick. Also in the boat were some political deviants, tame enough to be allowed the freedom of the island, and, now, to tour the *Anna*. Their eyes lit up when the Duke said that he'd be sending a boat ashore the following morning to buy provisions before his departure, and could take letters home to their families at Naples. One of them whispered that they were forbidden to communicate – they hadn't been able to do so for years – and that writing-paper was unobtainable on the island. The Duke fetched a quantity from his cabin. It was quickly hidden under a coat. When they left, some of the convicts were in tears. They all blessed his generosity.

As darkness fell, the wind rose. There were heavy gusts from the northwest, the quarter from which their anchorage – the little rocky bay below La Citta – was least protected. The Duke was anxious. They had foul ground beneath them – flat shelves of volcanic rock with infrequent holds for an anchor – and were uncomfortably close to the black, jagged, basaltic shore. The *Anna Eliza* held by a single bower-anchor, attached to a chain-cable: a hemp cable would have been cut to pieces by the sharp rocks in no time. Her master, Captain Wilcox, ordered the top-gallant masts and yards to be taken down on deck, and a second bower-anchor to be dropped beneath their bows, as a belt-and-braces precaution. The seas were already too big for the barge or jolly-boat to row out another anchor ahead of their bows.

When the big wind came, in the middle of the night, it came from the south, from Africa, and was so hot that the first sailors to run out on deck thought the *Anna* was on fire. Then, in an instant, it swung round into the north, and turned bitter cold. It had begun to blow what the Duke called in his diary a *Gregale*, or 'Greek' wind, which generally blows during a Mediterranean winter, from the north-east. It can last several days. This one was from the north-west.

Daylight, on the 25th June, revealed the full extent of their danger. Their main bower-anchor wasn't taking the strain properly – it seemed to have dragged in the night – and they had drifted in to within a cable's length of the lee shore, over which huge seas were breaking up to the height of their main-top. The *Anna*, very sharp forward, was ducking merrily under the waves like a seagull, but from marks taken on the shore it was evident that she was slowly, foot by foot, drawing in towards the rocks. To reduce wind-resistance, their top-masts, spanker, driver and jib-boom were all taken down on deck, leaving only two lower-yards to take sea-room advantage of any shift in the wind. They secured all hatches and ports, shipped the jolly-boat, and pulled in the barge to a short length of painter astern. A brave young sailor, Seymour, seeing their stern light-buoy being washed away, made a flying leap into the barge and managed to grab it before it disappeared.

Thus closed in the night. We, of course, did not take off our clothes, as, had our chain gone, very few minutes would have been allowed us to attempt our escape in, and we retired to our cabins with the knowledge that, had one link of a chain given way, there was no salvation for us – but in another world.

Between one and two in the morning, as the wind howled through the rigging and the seas hurled themselves over the *Anna*'s decks, the Duke lay down in his cabin and tried to get some sleep. He thought of his family, left behind in England and not seen now for over a year: his Duchess, Anna Eliza, after whom the yacht had been named; his only son, Chandos, who irritated him; his two adored grandchildren, Richard and Anne, both aged under ten; his two political Grenville uncles, William and Thomas, who'd been begging him to come home. Above all,

The Duke's yacht Anna Eliza

perhaps, he thought of Stowe, the great Buckinghamshire house, landscape garden and estate that he'd inherited from his father, the first Marquess of Buckingham, in 1813. He loved Stowe. Stowe meant more to him than almost anything, or anyone. *Hic puer illusit.* Here he played as a boy.

CHAPTER ONE

Ave atque vale.

'Oh lead me to the wide-extended walks,
The fair majestic paradise of Stowe
Not Persian Cyrus on Ionia's shore
E'er saw such sylvan scenes.'
James Thomson *The Seasons*, 1744

July 5th, 1827. The Duke's private diary:

> In the evening I drove out with my poor wife, and remained out until ten
> o'clock at night. She bade adieu to every scene, of every former favourite
> haunt. In silence we drove up and down, until at last, after the moon had
> risen upon us, we came to the flower garden, and sent home the carriage.
> She burst out into a violent fit of tears, in which I participated without
> saying a word. In this manner she went through the two gardens, and left
> them in silent sorrow. I gave her a rose which I gathered out of the garden
> as we passed, and I know that she treasured up the last gift. I never
> thought she loved this place enough to make her grieve so much about
> leaving it.

Richard Grenville, first Duke of Buckingham and Chandos, and his
Duchess, Anna Eliza, were saying goodbye to his principal seat, Stowe
House, a few miles north of the county town of Buckingham in central
England.

The landscape garden which they toured in their carriage was, and still
is, the most beautiful ever created in England, if not in Europe. One of
its key designers, William Kent, was the first to leap the gate, as it were,
and treat all Nature as a garden. Stowe's elements are English grass,
water and trees, and within these elements stand revealed, like visions in
a dream, temples and columns, arches and bridges, alcoves and obelisks,
pavilions, grottoes and towers. Many of them are neo-classical in style.

The Gothic Temple

Although they take their inspiration from Italy, they seem oddly English, of a piece with this part of rural Buckinghamshire.

The Duke and his Duchess said goodbye to them, one by one: the Temple of Concord and Victory, largest of them all, built in 1747 when the Grecian valley was added by Kent's young assistant in charge on the spot, Lancelot 'Capability' Brown; the Bourbon Tower and Lord Cobham's Pillar from whose belvedere, it was said, he could see five English counties on a clear day; the Queen's Temple, dedicated to Queen Charlotte, the devoted nurse-wife, during his 1789 illness, of George III; the Season's Fountain, Cook Monument and Shell Bridge; the Temple of British Worthies, designed by William Kent to accommodate

Stowe, the east wing of the South Front

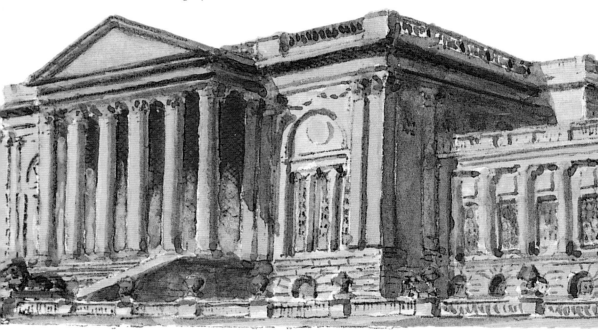

The Temple of Ancient Virtue

George, Marquess of Buckingham,
the Duke's father

the busts of Whig heroes (Stowe was a whiggish redoubt for those who rejected Stuart absolutism, and rejoiced in the 1688 Revolution and constitutional government); the Gothic Temple up on its hill in Hawkswell Field; the gorgeous Palladian Bridge, a 1738 copy of a prototype built a year earlier by the Earl of Pembroke at Wilton; the Temple of Friendship, Pebble Alcove and East Lake Pavilion.

Here the coachman might have paused a moment, for the Duke and Duchess to look south to the Corinthian Arch that starts the Grand Avenue leading to the town of Buckingham in the distance; then back north across the Octagon Lake to the extraordinary view of their home, Stowe House, with its 1,000-foot-long South Front that had evolved, over the years, from the designs of some of the most famous architects of the day: Vanbrugh, Gibbs, Kent, Borra, Adam and Soane. Stowe was a statement of almost regal majesty, of dazzling dynastic success. The name of the Grenvilles would live forever.

There were other sad farewells, too, on their carriage-drive home from the Eleven Acre Lake; so many favourite haunts; so many memories.

It cannot be claimed that the Stowe Grenvilles were England's most popular family in the 18th century. No-one denied their talent, energy and ambition, but they were notorious for a certain cold hauteur, a distant reserve of manner, which, coupled with a very lively sense of their own importance, outsiders found disconcerting.[2] The Duke's father, George Grenville (1753–1813), who became the first Marquess of Buckingham after 1784, had a reputation of being one of the touchiest noblemen in England. Twice Lord Lieutenant of Ireland and, until his resignation in December 1783, Pitt the Younger's Secretary of State for Foreign Affairs, he was often threatening to quit over trivial matters that somehow, in his view, affected his dignity. In 1788, as Lord Lieutenant of Ireland, he took violent exception to the Home Secretary of the day addressing him as 'Irish Lord Lieutenant' and gave Pitt, who was his first cousin, much grief about it. In February 1806, when his younger brother, Lord Grenville, was struggling to get his Ministry of All the Talents off the ground, he threatened to withdraw all Grenvillite support (the Marquess was *de jure* head of the family's Grenville Connection, which could muster up to 36 votes in the Commons) because he hadn't been named an assistant mourner at Pitt's funeral.

Poor King George III was once heard to complain, during one of his bouts of madness, in November 1788: 'I hate nobody. Why should anybody hate me?' Then he paused for thought and added: 'I beg pardon, I do hate the Marquess of Buckingham.'[3]

George Grenville, the first Marquess, inherited Stowe from his childless uncle, Richard Grenville, second Earl Temple (1711–79). Lord Temple, said to have been the richest man in England, was responsible for the final evolution of Stowe House into the building that we see today.

Temple's predecessor at Stowe, the principal creator, with Kent, of the landscape garden, and founder of the feast for the Grenvilles, was another childless uncle, Sir Richard Temple, later Lord Cobham (1675–1749). He came to prominence as a successful general in the Marlborough wars, then evolved into a wealthy and influential Whig politican. When he died in 1749, Stowe passed to his nephew via his widowed sister Hester, who, in 1710, had married into the Grenvilles, a Buckinghamshire family of shire gentry, respectable but fairly obscure. They were sheep-farmers in the 17th century, and lived at Wotton, some 14 miles from Stowe.

Where did the money come from? From marrying heiresses, and from what was known at the time as 'place-hunting'. The 18th-century Grenvilles were consummate place-hunters, truffling after Government pensions and sinecures which they came to regard as inalienable family possessions, rather like the King his crown. Originally intended to reward ill-paid public servants and provide for their wives and children, the sinecures became, as Britain grew richer, a goldmine for their owners, who hired underlings to do the actual work and paid them a fraction of the income derived. The richest seam of all, amid a

Wotton House in 1816, prior to the great fire of 1820, from a painting by Buckler

conglomerate of sinecures spread thick throughout the Grenville clan, was one of the four Tellerships of the Exchequer, obtained in 1764 by George Grenville, the then Prime Minister, for his son George (later the first Marquess). For every £100 paid out to the army, the Marquess received 7s. 6d; to the navy, 8d; to the ordnance, 12d. From all service pensions and annuities, he creamed off 2.5%. This was all very well in peacetime, before the American and Napoleonic wars, when his Tellership income averaged about £3,000 per annum. But in wartime it shot up out of all proportion. In 1808 the Committee on Public Expenditure reported that his share that year of the Tellership was £23,000. His average yearly take between 1793, the beginning of the French wars, and 1812, was £14,471 (about £1.5 million today).

Unpopularity resulted, as night follows day. There was even a phrase coined for it: *Odium Grenvillium*. The broadsheets caricatured the Marquess as so weighed down with sinecures that he could hardly walk. Sheridan and Fox attacked the sinecure system in general terms in Parliament in 1797, with some success, and the Marquess finally agreed, from April 5th, 1813, to return a third of his Tellership, about £8,000 a year, to the public purse. But he died that year, and his Tellership died with him. It would prove the tipping point in the fortunes of Stowe, and

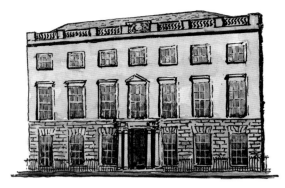

Buckingham House, Pall Mall, from a design by Sir John Soane

of the Temple-Grenville family that lived there.

By July 1827, 14 years later, when he made his farewell tour round the landscape gardens of Stowe, the first Duke's political ambitions lay in ruins, and he had run desperately short of money. More than run out money: he was deeply, dangerously, perhaps irreversibly, in debt.

The expense of maintaining Stowe and Buckingham House[4] in London's Pall Mall, and of his family's leading position in English society and politics, with all the expenses involved in nursing his six pocket boroughs in Buckinghamshire, Hampshire and Cornwall, had finally proved too much for him. His advisers were recommending him to let Stowe out, or put it into mothballs, for an indefinite period. He could either live abroad for a while, or retire quietly with his wife, Anna Eliza, to another smaller house – perhaps her own family home at Avington in Hampshire.

Even now, though, when he had made his final decision to leave Stowe, he could hardly bear to go through with it. A quiet life at home with his wife at Avington didn't, on the whole, appeal. On the other hand, if he

A sketch in oils, of Avington Park, near Winchester (Grenville)

Anna Eliza, as Marchioness of Buckingham

went abroad, he'd have the opportunity of realising an ambition that he'd nourished for many a long year: to set out on a prolonged Grand Tour of the Mediterranean, like his son, father and grandfather before him. For him, it would be a rather late Grand Tour, in a double sense: he was a middle-aged, 51-year-old politician who had failed to make it as a statesman; and the glory days of the Grand Tourists had been before the Napoleonic Wars, not after them. But it would be a huge relief to leave England and his creditors behind. His poor battered estates would have a chance to recover their financial health, and his personal health – he was a martyr to corpulence and gout – could only be improved by exposure to southern heat and sun.

The Duke was about to become, in the words of his son many years later,[5] 'no ordinary tourist'.

His mood alternated between gloom and hope: gloom in the long, dark, sleepless hours before dawn; hope in the morning sunshine.

> With a little management and the blessing of God, I may yet recover and pass what age God gives me in comfort. My reason tells me all this, but my feelings fight against my reason and prostrate my strength.

Earlier that day, after breakfast, he had ridden out with his 30-year-old only child and heir, Chandos.

Richard, Marquess of Chandos (later the second Duke of Buckingham and Chandos). From a print after Jackson

I took a ride with Chandos round the park. I determine to turn all the red deer into the park, and then liberate their paddock for more productive purposes. Shewed Chandos where I wished trees to be planted in the old park.

He and Chandos didn't get on, on either a personal or political level. His son, a member of parliament for one of the Buckingham boroughs in the Duke's interest, was a far-right Tory who supported slavery and the game laws; the Duke, like his Grenville forebears, was a whiggish liberal. On one of the great political questions of the day, whether or not to repeal the penal laws against Catholics in England and, especially, in Ireland, the Duke was an emancipationist; Chandos favoured the status quo. Chandos was outgoing, with a gift with people; the Duke, again like his forebears, was a proud, tricky, introverted man to whom human relationships didn't come easily. He got on best with small children and dogs, and his interests were, in the main, intellectual and scientific. He liked pottering about in the Gothic Library that Sir John Soane had designed for his father at Stowe, and collecting pictures, fossils and rare manuscripts. He was a Fellow of the Society of Antiquaries, and kept himself up-to-date with the new ideas that were beginning to turn the established worlds of geology and mineralogy upside down. Chandos – 'Bucky' as he became known later to his cavalry friends – was more like the Duke's mother, Mary, who had died in 1812. He was sociable, fun-loving and charming, with a wide acquaintance. He loved grouse-shooting and fox-hunting, and drilling his father's yeomanry in complicated mounted rides. He was also a snob, and cold-hearted with women. Father and son did share one thing in common, though: they were both very good at spending money.

Chandos lived at Wotton, the Grenville main earth from which the family had emerged, at the beginning of the 18th century, to marry into the Temples, and inherit Stowe.

In the course of their ride, the Duke showed Chandos

A cartoon of the Duke, aged 35 (entitled 'A Temple near Buckingham')

how he planned to extend the kitchen-garden of the keeper's lodge; he would mark out its limits with Brown,[6] his head gardener, the following day. He must remember to speak to his factor, Broadway, about the new crypt he wanted built between the servants' hall and the manuscript room of the library. The main cost, a very modest one, would be cutting a window down to size.

There were so many last-minute things to attend to before he went away.

The Birmingham manufacturers had sent him samples of cutlery for presents on his travels, and he needed to make up his mind about which to choose. Two live turtles[7] had arrived for the kitchen. He gave orders that one should be dressed and potted for immediate eating, the other preserved for his trip. The Duke, in his youth as tall and good-looking as Chandos, was now a very fat man, his stones in the high teens or perhaps even low twenties. His nickname in politics was *le gros marquis*. It was essential for him to pay very close attention to what he ate.

One of his less happy duties at this time was saying goodbye to his old friend, Dr Charles O'Connor who, after 29 years as librarian at Stowe, and now suffering from Alzheimer's, was being pensioned off to live with his brother, The O'Connor Don,[8] in Ireland.

> I go down to the manuscript room to take leave of the poor Doctor. He scarcely spoke, but, beginning to talk about thanks, gratitude, &c, I stopped him, and endeavoured to speak cheerfully to him, and of seeing him again. I then kissed the old man's forehead and left him. I felt deeply the parting with an old friend. He shewed no emotion.

The poor mad old priest, who had once tutored his mother Mary and doubled his job as librarian at Stowe with that of her undercover Catholic confessor, had spent three days packing and unpacking his trunks, losing his keys, scattering his papers round his room and protesting to Broadway that there was a plot to shut him out of the kitchen and starve him to death.

> He went yesterday or the day before to Broadway, to tell him that he had been to the kitchen door, which was shut against him; that he was famished, for that I had ordered that he should have nothing to eat in the place, and therefore that he begged Broadway would give him some victuals as for himself … The poor doctor had never been near the kitchen-door, and had just been eating a hearty luncheon when he told them so.

*   *   *

The Duchess left the next day for her old family home of Avington Park on the River Itchen, near Winchester in Hampshire. The plan was for the Duke to join her there after a few days, *en route* to Southampton, when he'd finished his business at Stowe. After she left the crushing news came through from London that he'd been passed over for the job of Governor-General of India, a post that he'd coveted since the early 1820s. India or Ireland would have been perfect for him – an ideal exit-from-England-with-grace. Now his Mediterranean tour seemed the only possible option, and the next morning he applied formally to the Government for leave to make his son Chandos vice-lieutenant of Buckinghamshire during his absence, sharing the job with two other country neighbours.

> July 6: Chandos at first affronted but it went off again … I see plainly that he wishes to pick a quarrel, but could not.
>
> July 8: I receive a very affectionate letter from my wife. She wants me to sell my house to the Duke of Gordon. I offer to let it, but I know that the house will be worth at least a third more when the works are finished … My son behaves extremely ill to me, not recollecting that he put me into Budd's hands – forgets himself entirely, treats me as if I was his groom boy, and refuses to take any steps to get me out of this new difficulty. I express myself warmly on his conduct towards me, and his lordship sulks for the rest of the day. I wrote to London to endeavour to set things right.

The Duke began his coach-journey from Stowe into Hampshire on July 12th. He left behind him in Buckinghamshire not only his son and heir Chandos, but also his little four-year-old grandson who, also called Richard, would inherit the title in 1861, becoming the third (and last) Duke of Buckingham and Chandos.

> My grandchildren took leave of me, and the little girl [Anne, aged seven] was deeply affected and cried. Even the little boy repeatedly bade me good-bye. My old servants could not speak, but grasped my hand in silence as I passed; and thus I left my poor dear old residence of my fathers. Reached Dropmore[9] in the evening. I gave my grandson a prayer-book and a testament. To my little girl I gave the 'Pocket Encyclopaedia.'
>
> I found Lord Grenville well in health, and fine and sound as ever as to mind. But he is shrunk, altered and more infirm.

William Wyndham Grenville, the Duke's uncle and former Prime Minister

Lord Grenville (1759–1834) had led the Whig administration in 1806/7, known, not without irony, as the 'Ministry of All the Talents', which had banned the slave trade throughout the British Empire, then foundered on the rocks of Catholic emancipation, to which George III was viscerally opposed. Charles James Fox was its Foreign Secretary until he died five months into office, and Lord Temple, as the Duke was then known as a young man of 30, was a part of that remarkable, reforming government (though not in the Cabinet) as Joint Paymaster and Vice President of the Board of Trade, and had supported his uncle's anti-slavery bill. Those were the good times, when a dazzling career in politics beckoned, and the Duke remembered them with affection: 13 months of Whig power sandwiched between 47 long years of opposition from 1783 to 1830.

The Duke was very much in awe of his uncle, his father's younger brother. The distinguished old statesman (his political nickname was 'The Bogey') was a Greek scholar who knew *The Iliad* backwards (he read it twice, in Greek, during negotiations over the Peace of Amiens). His particular hobby was cultivating rhododendrons on the Boconnoc estate that his wife, Anne Pitt, had inherited in north-western Cornwall. He was said to be so stiff that he forbade his tailor, when measuring him, to touch any part of his anatomy. But he had a razor-sharp political brain and an even sharper tongue and pen, and had never quite forgiven his nephew for selling out the Grenville Connection to the Tories in return for a Garter and Dukedom in late 1821. But uncle and nephew were genuinely fond of each other, and the Duke promised to keep up a regular correspondence with him from the Mediterranean.

The Duke rose early the next day and pushed on in his coach into Berkshire, where he stopped off at Eton to say goodbye to his own two nephews, 'whom I duly pouched'.[10] Then he crossed the Thames at Windsor and drove to the Royal Lodge in the Great Park to say farewell

The Duke, when still Marquess, wearing robes for the coronation of George IV. This portrait, by Whittaker, gives some idea of his size

to his old friend the king. The Royal Lodge, or 'the Cottage' as it was known in royal circles, had once been home to a Park Ranger, but now the 65-year-old King George IV, ill and bad-tempered with gout and arteriosclerosis, and made even iller by huge daily doses of laudanum, claret and cherry-gin, lived there in drugged and loveless seclusion with his current mistress, Lady Conyngham. The king disliked even being seen in public. His legs and arms had swollen to twice their normal size, and, unable to walk, he had to be more or less carried about by his servants. For the sake of their old friendship, however, he mustered all his very considerable grace and charm to receive the Duke, and they spent three happy hours together, talking politics. Their exchanges followed a pattern that Englishmen have heard before.

> He then exclaimed: 'Ah! These are indeed strange times, and it is a strange political atmosphere that we are breathing.'
> I replied: 'So strange, Sir, that I cannot breathe it, and I retire to avoid it.'

The king complained that he was being bullied by the Tory far-right, led by the Duke of Wellington, who had refused point-blank to serve in the new administration formed, when Lord Liverpool died early in 1827, by the Irish liberal Tory and ex-foreign secretary, 'Slippery George' Canning. Canning's coalition of centre-ground Tories and Whigs, nick-named the 'warming-pans', was not expected to last. The Duke, between whom and Canning there was much distrust and dislike,[11] assured the king of his own loyalty and affection while he was abroad, and left the proxy of his political interest in parliament in the king's hands, to use as and when his sovereign saw fit, subject to certain provisos.

> The King thanked me most warmly, expressed his gratitude, said he should never forget it, and I then kissed his hand. His Majesty wished me my health, again expressed gratitude, and I left him ... Thus I have established myself in the King's confidence, and have made it necessary for His Majesty to call upon me the first time Canning and the Whigs come to blows, which *must* be soon. It is plain that the King does not look to the permanence of the Government.

The Duke was deluding himself. He hoped that, when Canning fell, the king would turn to his old friend and courtier to form a new administration. And the king was being disingenuous. He had no intention of offering the Duke a top, or any, job. It is sadly and painfully obvious, reading the letters[12] that passed in these years between George IV and his

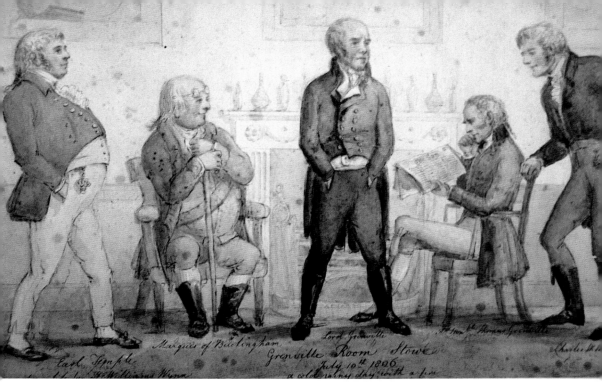

The Grenville Room, Stowe. From left to right, the Duke, his father the Marquess of Buckingham, his uncles Lord Grenville, the Rt Hon Thomas Grenville (reading the Sun *newspaper) and Charles 'Squeaker' Wynn*

ministers – and those[13] between the sharp old Lord Grenville and his nephew – that the Duke was no longer regarded by the king, or by his peers, as a serious force in contemporary politics. In late 1821, when the Marquess of Buckingham, as he then was, was given a Dukedom, the deal hammered out was a straight swap: the Grenville Connection's votes in the Commons to shore up the Tories whom the King supported, the Garter and Dukedom of Buckingham and Chandos in return. His first cousin Charles Wynn – 'Squeaker Wynn' as he was known, because of his high-pitched voice and his never-realised ambition to become Speaker of the House of Commons – who led the Grenvillites in the Commons at that time, was given the Board of Control and a seat in Cabinet. But by 1827 the Duke's erratic politics had reduced the number of committed Grenvillites to virtually zero, and throughout the 1820s he was denied all efficient office.[14]

CHAPTER TWO

Maiden Voyage

At the end of July 1827, two weeks after the Duke had his audience with the king, the fitting-out of a brig, in the shipbuilding yard of John Rubie on the banks of the River Itchen in Hampshire, was nearing completion. The *Anna Eliza* was big and fast, with two square-rigged masts: the after mast was slightly higher. Her length, from the fore part of her main stem to the after part of her stern post was 96 feet, two and a half inches, and she measured 254 tons, with a copper-sheathed[15] keel for extra speed. She had an elegant long bowsprit, a sharp prow, and a broad, 24-foot, ocean-going beam. The depth of her hold was 12 feet 7 inches.[16] She was culver-built[17]. With her square stern and six gun-ports on either side, she looked like a small man of war of the Royal Navy: very similar, in fact, to Darwin's *Beagle*, built in 1820. HMS *Beagle* was six feet shorter, measured 20-odd tons less than the *Anna*, and carried a 70-man crew.

Upon the whole, I like her, but she is certainly too sharp forward. Whether the breadth of her beam will remedy that defect it is impossible to tell until we have been at sea.

Recruiting was well under way for a 48-man crew[18] that would include a platoon of armed marines – more than enough hands to set aloft her sparkling new set of white sails, or run out in salute or anger her 10 brass six-pounder carronades[19] and two nine-pounder guns.

A month earlier, on Monday June 18th, The *Hampshire Chronicle* had reported:

The launch of the Duke of Buckingham's yacht from Mr Ruby's [sic] slip at Cross House,[20] was effected on Monday last in good style, in view of about 3000 spectators. The ceremony of naming the vessel was performed by proxy for the Duchess whose christian name (Anna Eliza) she bears. The Duke was unavoidably absent on this occasion having to attend some races at which he was the steward.

Registration certificate for the Anna Eliza

Now the yacht was being lavishly fitted out. The Duke had insisted that the main cabin should be high enough for him to stand erect, and big enough to accommodate not only his pianoforte, but also his books, his geological instruments, his writing-desk and a proper bed made up with the leather sheets he liked to travel with. There were nine other cabins for his guests and staff, and a further eight cabins for ships' officers or servants. His dog, Neptune (breed not recorded), was housed on deck in a kennel brought from Stowe.

His party of guests included Francis Lunn (1795–1839) from Lincolnshire, a 32-year-old Old-Etonian clergyman who would be his acting chaplain on board. Lunn was a distinguished geologist and mineralogist, a Fellow of the Royal Society since 1819, and had been part of the Cambridge team that had isolated cadmium from zinc in the early 1820s. Also in the party were the Reverend Robert Wilson (1801–50), Rector of Ashwelthorpe in Norfolk, and his pretty wife Emma, who was the daughter of a Buckinghamshire friend and neighbour, Colonel Piggott; his personal doctor Mr Moore; a Captain Bates; and the Vicomte de Chabot and his son Philippe. The Vicomte, another old friend, had been a member of the French court-in-exile that the Duke's father had welcomed to England, and financially supported on his Gosfield estate in Essex, at the time of the Revolution. Bates and the Vicomte had already left on the packet-boat to Le Havre, the first port of call, to buy French luxuries for their table.

The Duke's Majorcan chef, Fontara, was delighted with the steam-kitchen that had been created for him in the galley below decks; its smoking funnel would later fool some onlookers into believing that the *Anna* was one of the new steam ships[21] that were being brought into service in the mid-1820s. Space had been set aside in the bowels of the yacht for all the fine wine the Duke and his party planned to drink over the coming months.

July 20th. I finished the evening by looking over the beautiful charts of the Mediterranean, and the coasts of Greece and Italy. They are a collection of the very best Admiralty charts from the Hydrographic Office, and are corrected down to the last minute by Captain Smyth[22] himself …

July 26th. Lunn remains at Southampton, superintending arrival of instruments, &c. Ship holds more bottles and goods than I expected. My own cabin beautiful, and great height throughout.

The Duke was already confronted, however, by a tiresome and, almost as long as he could remember, depressingly familiar problem. In his enthusiasm to replace his old yacht, *Fly*, he'd spent more on the *Anna Eliza* than he could afford and was now faced with a bill[23] he couldn't immediately pay. He would have to arrange yet another loan with his London banker, Thomas Coutts. His boat-builder, of all people, was proving awkward over money.

The delays on the part of all have been abominable, and the conduct of Rubie, the builder, disgraceful. He has turned her out of hand in a state which would disgrace any dockyard. My presence has served to drive them forward, and I think they certainly will be ready to sail on Monday. Wilcox is ill – much, I believe, from vexation. I like my second officer, Radcliffe, very much.

As for Rubie's bill – and any other bills connected with the yacht – he told his secretary, Alexander, to send them to independent arbitrators. This would buy him time, and in matters of debt, as the Duke knew from bitter experience, time was everything.

An early departure from England was becoming increasingly desirable. From Avington, in the middle of July, he had written to Wilcox, ex-Royal Navy and his newly-appointed captain, a curt note.

July 17th. Receiving from Wilcox a very slack letter about the yacht, talking about 'a fortnight more' etc., I sent off Alexander to him with a letter, saying that unless he engages to be ready for sea on the 24th inst., he is immediately to give up charge to Lieutenant Radcliffe [the second officer], and understand that he is not to go with me. He tells me what I know to be lies, viz., that he has been detained for the windlass. N.B. – I have a letter saying that the windlass was on board a month ago, and for the topmost fids [*spars*]. Now, unfortunately, her sails were bent and her royals across a week ago. How could that be if the topmast fids were not come? What I suspect is this, that Rubie and Wilcox have caballed to keep me until after the regatta at Cowes, in order to shew off the yacht. Alexander returns in the evening with a penitent letter, declaring that he will be ready on the 24th. I shall keep him to his word …

The Duke of Gordon declines my house, it being too large for him. Offer it to Lord Bute …

The Duke's deadline came and went. On Saturday August 4th, nearly a fortnight overdue, the *Anna Eliza* was finally ready for sea. According to the *Hampshire Chronicle* he left Avington that day *and proceeded to Southampton where his Grace embarked on board his new and elegant yacht preparatory for his intended voyage to the Mediterranean. The Noble Duke will proceed in the first instance to Havre. The Duchess still remains at Avington.*

The Duke's version of the day's events was more down-to-earth.

All my crew dead drunk the morning before leaving Southampton: mutinous and ungovernable, and the captain doing nothing to prevent them.

Some sort of order, in the end, seems to have been established, for a steam tugboat, the *Medina*, succeeded in coming alongside and attaching a line. The *Medina* began to pull her slowly down the Itchen. The *Anna Eliza* stuck fast on a bank of mud. The crew put out an anchor and waited all night, hoping that the tide would float her off, and in the morning a second steamboat, the *Malmesbury*, joined the pull and the two tugboats succeeded in towing her down into the roadstead of Southampton Water. The crew hoisted her topsails, spanker and jib and she sailed at a brisk 10 knots out into the Solent and on to her overnight anchorage at Ryde, in full view of the British fleet anchored at Spithead, and of a visiting Russian frigate. The *Anna* flew from her masthead the Royal Yacht Club's all-white burgee, and from her stern a plain white ensign[24] with the Union flag in the top left canton.

The Duke's temper improved amid the thunder of guns. Southampton had recently made him a freeman of their town, and now the townspeople of Ryde gave him a 19-gun salute.[25] He responded with 13. The Earl of Yarborough's[26] *Falcon* was anchored nearby, nine days out from Gibraltar and still in quarantine[27], and the Duke derived much satisfaction from the thought that she looked a heavy hulk of a vessel, her lines not nearly so clean and good-looking as the *Anna Eliza*'s, either at anchor or under sail.

From his anchorage he was able to see what he called his 'poor little cottage' (it was in fact a substantial Regency villa[28]) on the seafront at

'my poor little cottage' – the Duke's Regency villa at Ryde on the Isle of Wight

Ryde. A handsome, two-storey, white-stuccoed house, it stood amid acres of lawns that gently descended to a sea-wall lined with urns and statues. Set into the sea-wall was a boathouse that could be used at high tide.

The Duke used the villa as a base for summer yachting-parties, and it held happy memories for him: lazy summer breezes on the Solent, fashionable regattas patronised by George IV and his brother the Duke of Clarence, picnics on the foreshore, dalliances after dark.

The next morning, a Sunday, dawned fine and clear. There was a brisk wind from the north-west. At 10.30 the fleet's 24-pounders thundered out a salute for the Lord High Admiral, the Duke of Clarence (he would succeed his brother George as King William IV of England in 1830) as he strolled the 200 yards from his dockyard quarters to a Communion service on board the *Victory*. They thundered out another rolling cannonade when he walked back again to his quarters, and the Russian frigate joined merrily in the shooting, probably in ignorance of what it was all about.

Shipping in the Solent, by William Daniell, 1824

The Duke was unimpressed.

This is all in singular bad taste. To announce this royal sacrifice, all Portsmouth on shore and afloat were kept from their devotions … It was understood that his Royal Highness went to church on board the 'Victory', to avoid attending Lady Grey's Dockyard Methodistical chapel. I know not who preached there, but I do really think that whoever prayed there had more chance of being heard than the Lord High Admiral of England amongst his thunder.

After the crew had eaten, the *Anna Eliza* weighed anchor and set a course for Le Havre.

It was a lovely August afternoon, and the wind remained fresh and favourable. It dropped a little as the sun went down astern over the Isle of Wight, and the Duke took a last lingering look at England; an England he would not see again for two years; and from which, in spite of his tears in the flower garden at Stowe, he was by no means sorry to depart.

A year later the Hon. Edward Fox met the Duke's sister Mary in Italy, and wrote in his Journal: *His affairs are now in such a state that he left England to avoid his creditors, and even at his departure they pursued his yacht down the river in order to seize it.*[29] Fox's story may be apocryphal, but it looks as though the Duke left England only just in time.

CHAPTER THREE

The Duke

He was born in London in March 1776. His father, the first Marquess, was twice Lord Lieutenant of Ireland, from 1782–3 and again from 1787–9, and the young Richard travelled in state to Dublin with his parents during both his father's lieutenancies. During the second, his sister, Lady Mary Grenville (1787–1845) and younger brother George, later Baron Nugent (1788–1850), were born.

Their mother, Mary Elizabeth Nugent, was the daughter of an Anglo-Irish peer, Robert Nugent, who apostasised from Roman Catholicism to advance his political career (at the end of the 18th century Catholics were still barred from all public office). His daughter Mary made up for it by converting back to the Catholic faith in 1772, three years before she married George Grenville, a diehard protestant. According to their daughter Lady Mary Grenville, also a convert to Catholicism, he so thoroughly disapproved of his wife's faith that, in the early years of their marriage, he forced her to keep it a secret, and only allowed her to see a priest once a year when they visited London.[30] Later in life, he relented, and, like his younger brother Lord Grenville, became a Catholic emancipationist. But his wife's conversion sowed seeds of religious tension within the family. The Duke was middling Protestant, indifferent either way. His sister, Lady Mary, and the man she married, James Everard, Lord Arundel, were extreme Romans. The Duke's wife, Anna Eliza, their son Chandos, and the Duke's younger brother, George, Baron Nugent, all regarded papists with horror.

The Duke was brought up in the shadow of the French Terror. To the adolescent boy growing up at Stowe it must have seemed a very dark and menacing shadow that stretched to the very doors of the great house itself, with its threshold constantly crossed and re-crossed by aristocrats, priests and nuns on the run from France. His father made it a point of honour to provide open house to the entire emigré French royal family and court. Years later his son complained that this was a contributory cause of his own financial embarrassment: the huge cost of looking after the demanding (and more-or-less penniless) Bourbons, and giving them a home on one of his estates, Gosfield in Essex. Good things came of the Marquess's hospitality, however. All his life the Duke spoke excellent French; and on his Mediterranean travels he was received with great warmth at Naples by the Bourbon king of the Two Sicilies, Francis I, whose mother had been a sister of Marie Antoinette.

Thomas Grenville, the Duke's uncle and bibiliophile. He left 20,250 volumes to the British Museum

Earl Temple, as he was then styled, didn't follow the usual family educational route of Eton and Christ Church. His senior uncle, Thomas Grenville, a charming, book-collecting bachelor much sought after by London hostesses, thought it was one of the reasons why the Duke grew up rather odd. Temple seems to have been educated privately at home, before going up as an undergraduate to Oxford's Brasenose college in 1791. In 1797, aged 21, he went into politics, and was elected MP for Buckinghamshire, a seat in his father's interest, and from which he resigned on February 11th 1813, the day his father died and he succeeded to the marquisate. But in the intervening 16 years he was an active politician, and spoke regularly on a number of topics. He was given a job as commissioner for Indian affairs in 1800, and in 1806, under his uncle William, Lord Grenville (the youngest of the three Grenville brothers), he served in the Ministry of All The Talents that abolished the slave trade in the British Empire. An 1804 portrait by Sir William Beechey, which still hangs in the North Hall at Stowe, shows him in military uniform with an arm resting on the withers of a horse: a tall, haughty 28-year-old with a lively sense of his own importance. In the same year the Revd Mr Powell, a family intimate, told the painter Joseph Farington: '*Lord Temple is not so agreeable as his father having great pride and a manner less pleasant*'.

In late 1813, as colonel of the Buckinghamshire regiment of militia, the

The Duke (when Earl Temple) aged about 28;
painted by Beechey and hanging at Stowe

(now) second Marquess of Buckingham joined his men in Bordeaux. In early 1816, after the Hundred Days, he was in Paris. On January 21st of that year, his wife, back in England, wrote sadly to Thomas Grenville: *I felt most grateful for your information respecting Lord B's plans for I have not received one line from him since the 9th till this morning ... Lord B does not name any day for leaving Paris as he is waiting to attend a masked Ball to be given by the Duke of Wellington ... I am delighted to find that we shall meet you in town as it will be some consolation for our little Stowe party being deferred. I regret Lord B did not return in time to attend the disbanding of his regiment as I know his presence at Buckingham at that moment was very necessary.*[31]

In 1827, when the Duke began his travels, his contemporaries would have perceived him as one of the richest, most powerful noblemen and landowners of England, a core member of the governing class that had done well, financially, under the English 18th-century expansion of empire; that had survived the whirlwind of Republicanism and the tempest of the Napoleonic wars.

The Duke's money was invested in land: 56,000 acres in England and Ireland, with a gross annual rent roll of some £60,000[32] (about £6 million today). There were also sugar estates in the West Indies, even though the market price of sugar was a fraction of what it had been before the French wars.[33] Six members of Parliament sat for pocket boroughs in his interest.

The Duke must have seemed rich beyond all anxiety. He could buy almost anything he wanted and never ask the price. That was how English noblemen were expected to live at the beginning of the 19th century. They borrowed money against their landed estates, and their men of business paid their bills. Senior aristocrats owed an obligation to their king and their country to live in a lavish way: to be an ornament to their age, and to spend accordingly. In the 1840s, the Duke of Bedford ran up debts of half a million pounds, the Duke of Devonshire at Chatsworth nearly a million, in order to satisfy this demand. In the 1820s, on a quiet night at Chatsworth, 40 guests regularly sat down to dinner, with 150 servants in attendance.

So the Duke lived like a prince – on borrowed money. His estate income in 1827, after costs, netted down to about £50,000 a year. Out of that, £6,000 went as an annual allowance to Chandos, and a further £4,000 a year to various other relatives[34] and family retainers, leaving about £40,000. But the debts that he'd run up over the years were becoming unsustainable. In 1827 he owed a total of £223,000 to assorted moneylenders that included Coutts and Drummonds banks, the Equitable Assurance and Westminster Life.[35] There were other debts too. He tried in vain at this time to arrange a superloan of £300,000 (perhaps £30 million in modern money) at four percent, to bring all his indebtedness under one, cheaper roof. It looks as though his real income, after outgoings and interest payments, in the 1820s may have been as little as £10,000 a year: nothing like enough to live and entertain in splendour at Stowe, or at his London home, Buckingham House in Pall Mall; barely enough, indeed, to employ the crew and support the extravagant living expenses of life on board a luxury yacht like the *Anna Eliza*.

It was Stowe, and the Duke's passion for entertaining there, adorning the palace, and improving and adding to the surrounding estate that soaked up the bulk of his cash. He ran down his other estates in England and Ireland to pay for its aggrandisement. He paid particular attention to the interior of the house, creating a Natural History museum and an outstanding collection of old prints, engravings and manuscripts, as well as adding to existing collections of Old Master paintings, books, antique sculpture and English and Continental furniture. One vast room was devoted to the engravings alone, stored in an infinite number of portfolios, and the sculptures were ranged round a large elliptical Saloon entered directly from the Corinthian garden portico on the South Front.

The Duke's taste was eclectic, but, by the standards of his day anyway, fairly serene. Elizabeth George, a tenant's daughter, visited the house in 1845, when Chandos was second Duke, and declared herself irritated by all the clutter. '*All these costly additions* [by the second Duke] *are de trop and have so crowded the apartments as to give them the appearance of a large furniture warehouse – and no space being left on the floors – you do not appreciate the noble proportions of the rooms. I never liked the house so well as during the last few years of the late Duke's life – he had put the house in complete repair, and had added a great many beautiful artistic things to the former old family collection – not merely rich furniture which money can buy at any time but things unique in themselves, and having, so to speak, a genealogy and history.*'

Did the Duke have only himself to blame? There is some evidence that, even by about 1805, money was running short. No major new building projects were undertaken at Stowe after that date. In 1804 the painter and diarist Joseph Farington reported that it took a year and a half to two years for accounts to be settled. When the first Marquess died in 1813, he seems to have handed his son a questionable inheritance, in the form of mortgaged estates. The sudden termination, of course, of the lucrative government sinecure, the Tellership of the Exchequer, was a savage blow. As the family's income declined, so its outgoings (especially when the Dukedom arrived) increased.

As a young man, the Duke had been hopelessly extravagant, the extent of his indebtedness only partially restrained by what the Marquess, his father, would say if he ever found out. In 1798, at the age of 22, he borrowed £2,000 from Thomas Coutts to buy a Domenichino, an Albani (he had a soft spot for 17th-century Italian Mannerists) and a Poussin when the French and Italian collection of the exiled Duc d'Orléans went under the hammer. By 1805 he owed Coutts £6,000. In 1813, in spite of sales of land belonging to his wife, his debt had risen to £51,500.

After his father died, there was no stopping him. Books, pictures, statues, crates of wine, porcelain, jewels, gold and silver artefacts, guns, coaches – the merchandise streamed into Stowe in an endless, expensive flood, almost

A tureen from the Royal Worcester Stowe Service

all of it bought on credit. In 1813 he ordered what has been called 'The Most Magnificent Dinner Service in the World', the 'Stowe Service' of Royal Worcester porcelain, with more than 1,000 individual pieces decorated with his own and his wife's coats of arms on a salmon-pink ground. When a neighbouring estate in Buckinghamshire, Hillesden, came up for sale in 1823, the Duke bought it with borrowed money, for £147,000. Bills piled up unpaid. In 1820 his coachmaker's account came to £465. This was, he stated with fractured logic, '*abominably high and not to be paid. When paid to discontinue employing him*'. Even now, although up to his ears in debt, he had managed to collect in his cabin a hoard of more than 1,000 gold sovereigns,[36] and the prospect of spending them and cramming the hold of the *Anna Eliza* with Mediterranean booty gave him a delicious feeling of anticipation.

It is easy to make fun of the Duke, to portray him as ridiculous and inept, a Falstaffian booby huffing and puffing and eager to cut a dash, yet liable at any moment to trip up and fall flat on his big stomach. Yet this would be unfair. Like the Prince Regent, he had considerable charm and grace. He was physically brave, with the sort of insouciant courage demanded at that time by Englishmen of his caste. He would confront some nasty moments on his Mediterranean travels without turning a hair. And he was a highly cultivated man too, in his way, a child of the 18th-century *Siècle des Lumières*, interested in, and knowledgeable about, philosophy, music, the natural sciences and the creative arts. He read widely,[37] had an enquiring mind, and loved browsing in his library at Stowe, and chatting to his old librarian, Dr O'Connor. The Duke's particular hobby was geology and he followed with understanding the contemporary debate between Neptunians and Vulcanists about the origin of the earth's crust.[38] Now the Duke was longing to see Etna and Vesuvius for himself – perhaps even make some useful contribution to the debate – and there are passages in his travel-diary that reveal him in a most sympathetic light: late at night in his cabin, by the light of a ship's lantern, poring with a magnifying glass over rock and fossil samples and trying to make some sort of sense out of the chaos on his desk. In other circumstances, he might have made a good museum curator, and it is a pleasure to think of him in that respect: a crabby, slow-to-judgement, overweight taxonomist blowing the dust off some ancient herbarium.

He was an enthusiastic amateur artist, and, given a heaving boat and a choppy sea, fairly effective. Many of the lively watercolours and pen-and-ink drawings he made during his time in the Mediterranean have survived[39] – the watercolours particularly well, having, for so many years, been stored unrecognised in the dark. But it is as a diarist that one feels he really comes into his own. On his travels he sat down daily and recorded what had happened, almost as it happened, in simple, supple, unaffected prose.[40]

The Duke's other great passion was politics and political intrigue, as one might expect of a Grenville born in the 18th century. Between 1763 and 1822 the family produced two Prime Ministers, a Foreign Secretary, a Home Secretary, a Chancellor of the Exchequer, a Lord Privy Seal, as well as adding a barony, an earldom, a marquisate and a dukedom to their family's list of titles. Stowe became a glittering, 18th-century Versailles, 'the place from which England is governed'. It was the Duke's misfortune that, unlike his grandfather George or his uncle William, he was never taken seriously as a political heavyweight.

According to the *Hampshire Chronicle*, the Duke and Duchess spent their last night together at Avington on Friday August 3rd. She remained there when he travelled down to Southampton the next day to board his yacht.

They had been married for over 30 years. During the early years they seem to have been very much in love. Even now he was still conventionally fond of her. But he had found her of late, as a companion, increasingly joyless and oppressive. She was an out-and-out Tory,[41] like her son Chandos, and had become deeply religious in a devout, Calvinistic kind of way, obsessed with hell, sin and the Devil, and filled up her pocket diaries with gloomy biblical quotes that she was fond of recycling for the benefit of her errant (as she considered them) husband and only son. She became morbidly anxious about the observances of her religion. She never travelled on a Sunday, and heaven help any of the servants if they were late for prayers in the chapel at Stowe, every weekday morning at half-past-nine sharp and properly dressed.

It had not been like that when he had married her. She was the blushing, uncomplicated child of the Duke of Chandos, heiress to a huge fortune, over £20,000 a year, and the Grenville and Brydges families had planned their connection ever since Anna was six. The couple fell in love when she was 14 and he was 18 and they went through the charade of being banned by her guardians from seeing each other until she was older. A closed shutter or a blind drawn across a London drawing-room window were signals for their clandestine meetings in Hyde Park. Two years later, in 1796, when she was 16 and he was 20, it was at last agreed that they could marry. She was dark and moon-faced, perhaps already showing signs of the religious melancholia that began to prey on her as she grew older. Her own father, the third Duke of Chandos, had died when she was nine, of injuries sustained when his Duchess accidentally pulled away the chair on which he was about to sit down to dinner. The poor woman went mad, obsessed by what she had done, and had to be certified.[42]

Anna Eliza's happiest memories probably dated from their early years of marriage when the young couple used to travel down to the estate she had inherited at Avington Park. She loved to be there for the 'Mayings' or 'Hay-diddle', a May-Day holiday for tenants and workers accompanied by feasting, dancing and dressing up, and their friend the Prince Regent liked to come and stay with them too at that time of year. He used to bring Mrs Fitzherbert with him, and he had a favourite dance called 'The Triumph' which the tenantry always put on for him. Every Christmas at Avington she sat 600 down to dinner, and she was much loved and admired in the local community for her generosity to the poor.

Her melancholia may have had something to do with the unreliability of her husband. He had a roving eye. Most notoriously he chased Anne, the wife of Admiral Hardy (as he later became) in whose arms Nelson died at Trafalgar. In 1814, when the Marquess of Buckingham (as he was then) was serving with his regiment in Bordeaux, Hardy began receiving anonymous letters accusing his wife of being Buckingham's mistress, and there was a general suspicion that Buckingham, having conceived an unrequited passion for the lady, who is said to have laughed at him, had written them himself. It all came to a head one evening at the opera in London in 1816 when Hardy publicly called him 'a great scoundrel and villain' and Buckingham had no alternative but to issue a challenge. Their seconds agreed that one pistol-shot each would be sufficient for honour's sake, and when both shots missed their mark the affair was largely forgotten about, except by the latter who continued to insist that Anne Hardy had made the whole thing up from the beginning, for a tease.

In the 1820s he began a prolonged affair with a married woman called Emma Murray Mills, who lent him £6,000 and bore him a bastard son, Eustace Grenville Murray.[43] The affair only came to light after the Duke's death, when Emma complained that no provision had been made either for herself or for her son. The family solicitor, John Robson, satisfied himself that '*she possesses undoubted proof of the duke's familiarity with her, both before and after the birth of the child.*'[44] He recommended a settlement.

Anna Eliza, the Duke's wife, and their son Richard, later the second Duke of Buckingham & Chandos. Painted by Beechey and hanging at Stowe

CHAPTER FOUR

South

At half-past nine in the morning of August 6th 1827, after a brisk overnight sail from Ryde roads, the *Anna Eliza* anchored in the little roadstead of Le Havre, on the north side of the mouth of the river Seine.

> Hoisted my banner and fired a gun: Chabot and Bates hoisted a red flag in answer. At three o'clock, PM, Chabot, his son Philip, and Bates, and the party that went on shore, returned laden with all sorts of things, eatable and drinkable.

They sailed west for Cap de la Hague and the tip of Brittany, with a stiff north-easterly wind behind them and on their quarter. During the night a following sea made the *Anna* roll and corkscrew, and queasy-looking figures appeared on deck at intervals to be sick over the side. Fontara the chef was pitched out of his berth onto his head and the Welsh cook-maid, who had never seen the sea before, blessed her stars, and wondered how it could be so sickly a place, as she had always heard of people going into its borders for their health.

> The little Norfolk dumpling of a maid casts a round face upon us like a full moon in a haze every now and then.

By dawn they were off Portland Bill in Dorset and, as the wind moderated, the sick began to gain their sea-legs and the Duke busied himself by training his crew against enemy attack. After dinner he sounded the bugle to general quarters.

> The crew and marines were exercised to their guns and small arms, and did very well. We have at least one old sailor to each gun – to some two.

The evening closed in beautifully, and as the sun set they saw the Lizard light, and England, for the last time.

They sailed south for five days. For a while two sharks followed the

Anna, one of them about four feet long. The only vessel they fell in with was an American brig out of Havana and bound for somewhere along the French coast. Exactly where, they couldn't determine, for the ships passed each other very quickly and her Yankee master was more concerned to fix his latitude and longitude – 'he guessed he did not rightly know his westing' – than give details of his destination. One of the *Anna*'s crew was ill and needed a hot dinner, and all the fires were out, and the duke proudly demonstrated the use of his 'self-acting blowpipe', as he called it – a 19th-century blowtorch – to bring a quart of water to the boil in under four minutes. There was more gunnery practice for the crew, and the marines shot at floating targets with their small arms.

On the morning of August 13th they rounded Cape St Vincent and set a course south-east for Gibraltar. Two or three fishing-boats, anchored to floating logs, lay in their way and one of them hauled up their nets which were full of pink bream and rock cod. No one on board the *Anna* spoke Spanish or Portuguese, and Captain Bates, with his head in Madame de Genlis's[45] *Manuel des Voyageurs*, addressed them loudly and sonorously as '*Amici Pescadore*' and the eight dirty fishermen in the boat looked mystified and stared.

> At last [they] pulled off their caps, believing him, I suppose, to be the Padré of the vessel, or St Peter come again to preach to the fishes. However, Bates could go on no further, even with the help of Madame de Genlis.

In the end he offered them a pigtail of tobacco in dumb show. In a trice the deal was done: all their fish for silver coin, their grapes and figs for ship's biscuits.

> Their fish … and their grapes, well washed, were excellent.

That evening, as they approached Cape Spartel, the ship's guns were cleared for action and the marines' boxes filled with cartridges and small arms doled out to the passengers, in case of attack by Barbary pirates: a very real danger at that date for any vessel in close proximity to the African coast. The pirates, Islamic terrorists of their day, had a fearsome reputation. They loved to murder, ransom or enslave any European Christian, male or female, adult or child, they could lay their hands on, and had once greeted a French punitive expedition against Algiers by firing the French consul out of a cannon at the approaching army. In the 18th century British public men had been heard to say the Barbary pirates were a good thing, a useful check on competition from weaker

European nations in the carrying trade, but by the time of the Congress of Vienna in 1815 it was generally recognised that the pirates, like the slavery they practised, were a disgrace to Europe and ought to be suppressed. In 1816 a British and Dutch squadron administered a smashing bombardment to Algiers, which discountenanced the pirates only temporarily. In 1824 the British fleet under Admiral Neal made another attempt. The great Corsair city was only finally brought to heel when the French conquered it in 1830, three years after the Duke began his voyage.

The night, however, passed peacefully away, and not a single Algerian pirate, knife in teeth, swarmed over the side of the *Anna* to murder the crew or hold the Duke to ransom. The next day, tinkering with his thermometer, he recorded 74 degrees Fahrenheit in the shady part of his cabin.

They sailed within five miles of where Trafalgar had been fought. He summoned aft the old boatswain, Carphy, who had been in the action that day on board *Britannia*, to tell his story

> ... which he did with much unction and interest. And when I bade him go below and give his mess a can of punch, and drink the healths and memories of his old comrades, the rough sailor's eyes filled with tears as he turned round, hitched up his trousers, and walked off the deck.

The Duke was intrigued by Nelson's last order – '*Anchor, Hardy, anchor!*' – as he lay dying below deck. Why had the signal never been made from the flagship to the rest of the fleet? Hardy's version – the Duke had heard it from the admiral's[46] own lips – was that most of the English ships of the line had had their anchors and cables shot away, making it difficult, if not impossible, to secure prizes. So the decision was taken to destroy them. Carphy said that he was on board a French prize, secured with jury-mast and sail, and making three knots, and in another two tacks safe within the Gut of Gibraltar, when the order came through from Collingwood, who had assumed command of the fleet after Nelson had been struck down, to burn her. For the life of them, none of her prize-crew, who stood to make a lot of money out of her, could ever understand the reason why.

> The most extraordinary anxiety was manifested to destroy the vessels which had been taken, even unnecessarily.

On the morning of August 15th, with a fine working breeze, the *Anna* weathered Cape Spartel, sailed into the Straits of Gibraltar and anchored under the New Mole.

Gibraltar from the sea (H E Allen)

I never saw a more magnificent scene than the whole passage of the Straits. We were close under the Coast of Africa, and, one knows not why, but the first sight of an enormous continent, other than that of Europe, for the first time, inspires the mind with feelings which no one can describe, but which certainly belong to the class of melancholy more than any other.

As he looked out northwards and to port, up at the great Rock and the mighty gun batteries that fringed its top and sides – King's Bastion, Willis's Point, Europe Point – the scene, although he'd never seen it before, seemed utterly familiar. As a teenager he'd pored over the pages of Captain John Drinkwater's *History of the Siege of Gibraltar*, first published in 1785. The story of that great siege by Spanish and French forces, and of its heroic, four-year defence[47] from 1779 to 1783 (in which the Duke of Clarence, the future king, had taken part as a midshipman), was written in blood and fire across the Duke's imagination.

The voyage from Le Havre to Gibraltar, some 1200 miles, had taken the *Anna Eliza* just nine days. She had averaged a respectable five knots.

CHAPTER FIVE

Sailing to Sicily

The Duke passed a pleasant fortnight in the shadow of the great Rock, the *Anna* riding quietly at anchor within the New Mole. He and his party set out on almost daily excursions by coach or ship's barge to see the local sights. In the evenings they dined on deck and listened to the music of the bands on the Alameda, pleasantly softened by distance.

Gibraltar had come a long way from the ruined fort and treacherous haven that had been captured by Admiral Rooke from the Spanish back in 1704, and ceded to Britain in 1713 at Utrecht. Now her impregnable fortress, thriving commercial port and busy naval dockyards were potent symbols of Britain's command of the Mediterranean and dominance of maritime trade: a global dominance that had been presented to her by Napoleon's intransigence after Leipzig, and his determination to waste French naval power during the Great Wars.[48]

It was the British command of the sea that now enabled the Duke to travel with such pomp, pride and, at times, arrogance; to go ashore more or less where and when he wished; to behave as if he owned the basin of the western Mediterranean. The 1815 peace treaty had quietly dropped the British 'salute to the flag' requirement that had been so contentious in the 17th and 18th centuries. There was no need for it now. Everyone knew who was king of the water.

For the Duke, British command of the ocean did not extend beneath its surface. He was fond of swimming, but not in the Mediterranean.

> The sucker, or devil-fish, which is caught here, is the most disgusting animal, and at the same time the most dangerous in the sea. His head and body are like a toad in shape and colour. His eyes [are] prominent from his head, with a head somewhat like a turtle's. The animal is in the centre of a large gelatinous web, full of suckers and feelers, and from this extends long

arms in every direction, which twist and twirl and secure their prey ... They are the great terror of bathers. Many stories are upon record of men being drawn under water by their power ... The very idea of being touched by the devil-fish would throw a swimmer into convulsions and make him quite unable to save himself, and entirely destroys all my sentimental ideas connected with Mediterranean bathing.

On August 21st, the Governor of Gibraltar, Sir George Don, a scrupulous man who worked hard to improve the sanitation of the colony since an outbreak of plague in 1805, picked him up in his official carriage from the *Anna* for a tour of the 'neutral ground', the strip of land that separated Gibraltar from Spain. The rest of the Duke's party were ferried round by boat. At three o'clock in the afternoon a single shot was fired from a six-pounder, the signal for a rolling, 101-gun salute to the Duke – who was delighted by the compliment – from all the 24-pounders in the galleries on the Rock that confronted Spain: St George's Hall, Green Lodge, Grand Battery, and so on down the line. A further single shot triggered a fire-at-will cannonade, which lasted several minutes.

St George's battery – one of those that fired a salute to the Duke
(H E Allen)

The effect was tremendous. Small parts of the rock gave way and came thundering down, and it literally is no exaggeration to say that the neutral ground shook beneath us.

The party moved on to inspect the remains of the Spanish lines, whence a Franco-Spanish assault against the Rock had been mounted on September 13th, 1782, supported by specially constructed floating batteries in the bay.

I remembered how often the present King of France, Charles X, had told my father and me the story of his being summoned to meet almost all the Catholic princes of Christendom, and all the flower of the French and Spanish armies, as to a party of pleasure, to see the 'taking of Gibraltar', where various amusements, and bull-fights and balls, were provided to while away each day of anxious expectation … So certain did they consider themselves of conquest, that dinner and a ball were prepared at Algesiras for General Elliot and his officers when made prisoners … The princes witnessed the scene from the first parallel, and the surrounding hills were crowded with the population of the country … the Queen of Spain in her chair had vowed to remain there until she saw the standard of Spain float upon the walls of the fortress she called her own. In a few hours all was dust and ashes,[49] and the few survivors among the assailants owed their lives to British generosity and humanity. On the next day the Spanish and French princes got into their carriages and returned home.

The Governor had a set of tables made out of the wood of one of the batteries, and candlesticks cast from the brass of its guns, for use in his residence on the Rock.

On August 28th the *Anna* sailed south across the Straits of Gibraltar to Ceuta on the shore of Africa. The Duke wanted to see the Spanish garrison there that doubled as a Bourbon political prison.

In the morning, about ten o'clock, I proceeded with all my party in my barge, with the British jack at the bow, to the landing-place, where I was received by a deputation of the officers of the garrison, and the clergy in their long black dresses and broad-brimmed hats. Our cook was to have acted interpreter, but one of the officers understood French … The Governor, a little, dry, withered, dark and gloomy man … paid me many deep and solemn compliments, which I returned with an equal number, shot for shot.

In the end permission was received for an inspection and the Duke's party mounted horses, and, escorted by an entourage of officers and a picquet of Spanish cavalry, toured the garrison. The Duke was enchanted by the view.

> In the deep and wide bay below, the tunny fishery was going on, and many boats marked the circle of the nets. On the other side rose in splendid magnificence the range of Mount Atlas, extending as far as the eye could reach, until the real mountain bearing that name overtopped the whole in the distance.

His reforming, English, Whiggish sympathies were less impressed, however, by the political prison of the Bourbon ruling élite.

> Here are confined in hopeless confinement what the Spanish officer called 'prisoners of opinion', which means the different victims of political opinions in all their varieties, victims of the different tyrannies which have disgraced, and continue to disgrace, the country of Spain. Here men who have fought against each other in the field, and contended in council, who have alternately saved and been betrayed by their profligate King, meet in common misery. The Spanish officer told me that they were *'fort maltreité'*, – that the Governor had his private orders respecting them, which he executed in all rigour, and that many were secreted *en cachet*. This conversation passed as we were proceeding along one of the ditches of the place; the sun of Africa reflected from the walls and the pavement, burning our feet as we trod it.
>
> I asked him, 'Ou sont ces cachets?'
>
> 'La bas,' was his reply, spreading a broad, brown hand over the surface of the bottom of the ditch; and, upon further inquiry, I learnt there were tiers of cachets below each other, even below the surface of the sea, where many lingered whose very names and existence were now unknown to all but the Governor and his immediate *employés*. All this disgusted and sickened me so much, that I was delighted when I heard on my return to the garrison that the Governor and the Bishop were enjoying their siesta, and that the moment was an unpropitious one, therefore, for a visit of adieu. I could not have seen them again and behaved with common decency.

Back on board the *Anna*, the Duke toyed with the idea of storming the prison with his crew of 48, and releasing its inmates.

> I verily believe I could have done … To them my vessel should have been with welcome open.

In the event, perhaps wiser counsels prevailed, and war with Spain was averted. That evening a party of his sailors set out from the *Anna* in the ship's barge, but only to go for a swim from a sandy beach nearby, next to a Spanish guardhouse. The barge had not returned before dark, and the Duke, becoming uneasy, hung blue lights on the *Anna* to summon it home.

> When the boat came on board, I found that the surf had run high, that one of the bathers had been afraid of coming into the boat, but had made for the shore, where he was taken by the Spanish sentries, who took him for a deserter from me, and the officer very properly refused to give him up to the boat until I sent for him in the morning.

The next day, reunited with his sailor, who had spent an anxious night in the Ceuta prison, the Duke weighed anchor, and set a course north-east for Malaga. There was a heavy cross-swell caused by stormy weather in the eastern Mediterranean. It was an uncomfortable sail.

> September 1st. After much pitching and tumbling about we reached Malaga this evening. The entrance into the Mole is beautiful. The lighthouse stands at the end of it, a plain white tower with a fine revolving light. An immense square custom-house has been building these forty years, and is yet unfinished. It is a handsome edifice, calculated to contain all the goods, all the business, and all the clerks belonging to the commerce of the island of Malaga forty years ago when the building was planned. But one quarter of it would contain all that exists now. The Spanish government pays no one, and is determined to have no revenue. Its system is one of exclusive prohibition; and even the necessaries of life, vegetables, potatoes, &c, are contraband.

The Duke was charmed, however, by the Costa de Sol, nowadays a hellish ribbon of mass-tourist development. He loved its sunny, secluded valleys filled with vines, pomegranates, oranges, figs, aloes, olives and custard apples, and delighted in, behind them, the mounting ridges of the sierra, 'like a great cauldron in a state of violent action', their summits crowned with stone pines, their slopes dotted with quintas, cottages and country seats. One derelict estate he visited, some eight miles west of Malaga, was El Retiro. It had once belonged to the Spanish royal family. The Duke rode there in a barouche lent by a friendly Malaga wine merchant, while the rest of his party followed in a hired carriage, 'exactly the counterpart of representations of the Spanish carriages in the old editions of Gil Blas and Don Quixote. They have not in the least altered the shape of their public vehicles, or the quality of their harness, or the dress of their muleteers'.

El Retiro stood amid orange, pomegranate and olive orchards, which were laden with fruit, and they spent a pleasant morning wandering in its formal, abandoned gardens shaded by oleander, vines and jasmine, and admiring the marble, spring-fed fountains and the view over the city and the sea.

> In one alcove, at the head of a canal full of fish and crystal water, we sat and ate grapes and pomegranates. The fish had got an acquired taste most creditable to their palates, for they came up in shoals and greedily devoured the pomegranate seeds which we cast to them.

Later they called at the house of the Prussian consul, about a mile away. The old man and his wife received them hospitably, showed off proudly the bananas, coffee and sugar cane grown in their garden, and insisted on them sitting down to a meal. The Duke, who hadn't expected to find the consul at home, in turn insisted on contributing a pie, an English salt-tongue and flagons of English beer to the feast. The consul enjoyed the tongue, but the beer was too strong for his taste. His Spanish concierge, though, who dined with them, thought it excellent, and was surprised that England could produce 'un vin si charmant'. Some of the Duke's party played in the consul's skittle alley, but found it hot work.

The *Anna* remained five days on her moorings at Malaga. The British consul brought news from England. George Canning, the son of an actress whom Whig aristocrats like the Duke affected to disdain (in fact, they feared him for his biting wit), had died in office only days after the Duke's departure from Southampton. In the early 1820s George IV couldn't abide Canning at any price but had latterly come to admire, even love, his Foreign Secretary, then Prime Minister, for his tact and talent. Canning's policies had made him the most influential monarch in Europe, and the king was desolated. In despair he turned to Lord Goderich, the amiable, easy-going but indecisive leader of the House of Lords, who had recently lost a much-loved daughter and whose problems frequently reduced him to tears. Goderich cobbled together a middle-ground adminstration of Whigs and Tories that the king hoped would not bother him with talk of parliamentary reform and catholic emancipation. Goderich's government would only last five months, and would be succeeded in January 1828 by that of the Duke of Wellington and the Tory ultras, who would give the king a much tougher time.

The Duke sent letters home offering to Goderich his services in government. They were ignored.

Whilst we were at Malaga, my men were one day riotous. They had been fighting each other for some time, and I was determined to put a stop to it. I therefore went forward, and, seizing the most riotous, put a sentry over him, and as he made use of insolent language to me and to Captain Wilcox, I immediately sent on shore to the English consul for a guard. They came with a corporal and two soldiers with fixed bayonets, who took my rebel off, to the great astonishment of the rest of my crew, who would not believe that I was in earnest. I had him put into prison, meaning to get another man and ship off my fellow for Gibraltar. But the accounts which I received excited my pity, at the same time that they were amusing. My men who had leave to go on shore, on passing a prison heard most piteous exclamations, and, looking up, saw their unfortunate messuali – who had been clapped into a cell by himself – sitting with his legs and arms through the bars, and his red face and whiskers, trying to get through them, imploring his comrades to intercede for him. In the loudest key of dismay he said that he should be eat up by the rats – that he had endeavoured to lay down but a rat immediately ran into his bosom, betwixt his skin and his shirt, and he should certainly die if he was left there. He implored pardon, and vowed obedience, &c.

For three days the Duke pretended to be obdurate. He sent the sailor a message that he would be put on the next ship for Gibraltar, which might leave in a month or so, and reminded his shipmates on board that the man had been put ashore at his own request, 'as he vowed that he would not stop a minute in her, run away, &c'.

I then sent an order for his release. The moment he saw the door open he rushed like a maniac through the town, never stopped until he came to the seaside, plunged into water, clothes and all, to get rid of the vermin and dirt of a Spanish prison, and then came on board, vowing he never would behave ill again if I would but take him back. He is one of the best sailors of the ship, and I have willingly taken him again, as I perceive that my point is carried – that my crew see that I am in earnest, and will not be bullied. As I am very indulgent to them all, continually giving them little articles of luxury and comfort, and above all, fruit and grog when good for them, I know that I am popular with them, and we shall be all the better friends for this little breeze.

September 4th was a day of heavy rain which, according to the Duke, ruined the local grape crop. The next day the *Anna* had to warp herself out of Malaga harbour with rope and anchor in the teeth of a stiff south-westerly and ran aground, for one anxious moment, on the end of the Mole. She beat slowly up the shore of Spain, in light airs that had backed round to the east, and the Duke had leisure to admire the view of the coast.

Whatever is not high and lofty mountain is beautiful vineyard, orange and olive groves, interspersed with flowers and high trees.

On the 7th a French corvette, part of a French squadron that was blockading Algiers, intercepted her with her guns cleared for action. As soon as the *Anna* identified herself, she was allowed to proceed.

There followed 11 wearisome days of zig-zagging into light headwinds that took the *Anna* back across almost to the African coast and over again to Spain. Her cabins were infested with flies, and there was nothing to do on deck but admire the flying-fish, bonitos and turtles that swam about her copper-bottomed hull, leaving phosphorescent trails in their wake. One day the jollyboat was launched in a flat calm and Robert Wilson, the Norfolk clergyman, succeeded in shooting, then securing with a peg and line, a small turtle, which provided them with fresh meat. In the evening the Duke sat out under the stars, and felt homesick for Stowe.

We are now approaching the meridian of Greenwich, and I contemplate with feelings of sorrow, and remembrance of times gone by, the stars which for many years I have contemplated on the meridian of my home! *Alpha Lyrae* I have taught myself to consider as the star presiding over Stowe. Night after night have I sat watching its brilliant green lustre shining over the centre of the great south portico, and here it is in almost precisely the same position over my head. When and how shall I see again the dear scenes which it looks down upon in my native land!

On September 11th, after dark, they dropped anchor north of Alicante in the bay of Benidorm, at that date a small, remote, fortified town on a rock surrounded by empty orange and olive groves and backed by mountains. The next morning Fontara the cook was sent ashore to negotiate for fresh meat and milk. The local mayor, wary of the plague, was unfriendly and venal. He set a guard with a rusty sword to allow Fontara no farther ashore than the beach, and tried to charge the Duke 24 dollars for a live sheep, and half a dollar each for hogsheads of fresh water, nearly the cost of wine; offers which were rejected with contempt. The *Anna* sailed immediately for Majorca, reaching Palma on the 16th, where they were received with great pomp by 'Il Capitan-General dellos Islos Balearos' dressed in a magnificent scarlet uniform. He gave them the freedom of the island and tactfully made no comment about the white beaver hats that the Duke and his party were wearing against the sun. They found out later that white hats, symbols of a radical party on the island, were banned by Majorcan law.

Fontara the cook had left Majorca 30 years before, and was delighted to revisit the land of his birth. He told stories ashore about Il Signor Duca and his steam kitchen, and parties of islanders, convinced that the *Anna* was one of the new-fangled vessels powered by a steam-engine,

The harbour at Palermo (Francesco Zerelli, 1830).
Note the brig flying the British flag.

came aboard to have a look. The Duke bought a quarter cask of very fine light wine, 'something like Vin de Grave, but of a much stronger body and superior flavour', and established, to his satisfaction, that the island abounded with hare, quail, partridges, and seasonal woodcock. On the 20th they sailed for the eastern end of the island, whither Mr Lunn the chaplain had travelled on a mule to geologise, and in deteriorating weather, in which Lunn's handkerchief signal from shore was invisible to those on board, just succeeded in embarking him. A course was set across the Gulf of Lyons for Palermo in Sicily, in now very lively weather. In the 24 hours from midday on the 21st the *Anna* ran 180 miles in longitude, an exhilarating sail in heavy seas, and that night, as the rollers hurled themselves against the bow of the speeding *Anna* and the wind moaned in the rigging and smacked into her sails, the Duke dreamed a weirdly prophetic dream.

As for myself, I am ashamed to say that I am more low than I should dare confess to anyone, by a dream which haunted me in my sleep, with a degree of precision which is really frightful. I was at Stowe, my dear and regretted home. All was desolate – not a soul appeared to receive me. My good dog met me, and licked my hand. Accompanied by him, I traversed all the apartments – all desolate and solitary: every room as I had left it. On my return from the state bedroom, I met my wife! She told me all my family were gone, and that she was left desolate – that even her little favourite dog, which had been her sole remaining companion, had died a few days ago. We went out at the north hall door together, and all was solitude and desertion. I awoke with the distress of the moment, and I slept no more that night. I do not like to confess how much effect this has had upon me. I have not the slightest faith in dreams, but this has strongly accorded with the feelings and tone of my mind, and I cannot shake it off. Those who will ever see this journal will, I am sure, not laugh at my feelings.

CHAPTER SIX

Palermo

'To have seen Italy without having seen
Sicily is not to have seen Italy at all,
for Sicily is the clue to everything.'
Johann von Goethe, *Italian Journey*,

September 25th. The British consul has been alongside, and is gone again to exert himself in our behalf in the matter of our quarantine … This evening we have the pleasing intelligence sent to us that there is every reason to hope that we shall gain pratique tomorrow. If this be so, we shall have had done for us what no vessel, not even a man-of-war, has ever obtained: the utmost indulgence has been to strike off the number of days occupied by the voyage. A declaration is sent to me to sign upon honour that we have touched nowhere since we left Majorca, have communicated with no ships on our passage, and have no sick. A quarantine boat rows guard round us, and has the impudence to ask of us to provision them. I refuse, telling them that I don't want their company, that those who sent them may feed them, and that they may row round us, but if they come near I will fire at them. I say this because our fresh meat hangs over our stern, and I find our guards always contriving to find some excuse for lurking about under that part of the vessel. The moment we dropped our anchor a young begging friar came off in a boat and asked for money. We told him we could only give him the plague, and he went away.

The following day, September 26th, pratique was duly granted in record time, and on the 27th the Duke and his suite went ashore and established themselves in a large, comfortable palazzo on the Marina, a wide, well-appointed avenue on the sea-shore with views out over the old port. The palazzo was owned by a resident Englishman, a Mr Lindeman, who offered it free for the Duke's private use. The palazzo would serve as the Duke's tourist base in Palermo for the next three weeks.

Palermo – Porta Felice and Marina (Leitch)

His first impressions of Sicily's capital were not very favourable. Its inhabitants seemed grindingly poor, and ground even poorer by the taxes of Francis I, king of the Two Sicilies, who ruled the island from Naples. Sicilian labourers, according to the Duke, earned just 10d a day, *if* they could find any work, and the landed caste which might have employed them was in turn impoverished by the king's penal property tax, 12 per cent per annum on the value of all land and buildings. The Duke reckoned the royal income from the island to be about a million sterling a year. (In his journal the Duke, over and again, displays a rather prurient obsession with the minutiae of Mediterranean costs and values; in view of his own precarious financial situation at home, he might justifiably be accused of penny wisdom and pound foolishness.)

The town presents a melancholy scene of splendour and misery: nothing can be finer than the fronts of the palazzi, nothing more wretched than the interior. The nobility live entirely in Palermo ... but have not the means of repairing the houses they live in. Almost all let part of them. Few keep any servants, except the footman and coachman, who are hired by the day or week, to convey them to the mansion: even the Viceroy contracts with a cook to furnish his table, at about half-a-crown English per head; and when he gives a splendid dinner he increases it to 3s 6d each. The cook enters, brings the dinner in a fiacre, warms and shakes up his casseroles, serves it up, and carries off everything again in the hackney coach the moment the dinner is over … The clergy and prêtraille[50] of all kinds swarm here, and are omnipotent.

As the days passed, however, and his eye became more tuned in to Palermo's eccentric and dishevelled grandeur, his opinion began slowly to change for the better, influenced perhaps by what he perceived as the humanity and reforming zeal of the current Viceroy, the Luogo Tenente,[51] who, in the Duke's opinion, had done much to pacify the country since the islanders' anti-Bourbon insurrection, bloodily suppressed, in 1820. Torture, police espionage and arbitrary imprisonment were – according to the Viceroy anyway – largely things of the past.

> The country is quiet – kept so, perhaps, by a firm hand – but this is surely better than being kept in constant tumult by a vacillating and unsteady one. A few years ago and no one could move across the country or into its interior without being armed to the teeth and attended by a moveable column of gens-d'armes. Now my conviction is, from all that I have heard, that anyone may walk from one end of it to the other with his purse in his hand, and without a stick in the other to defend it, and he will not be molested.

A journal-entry elsewhere shows the Duke doing his best to come to terms with the reality of arbitrary rule.

> I must do the Il Marchesé della Favare [the Viceroy] the justice to say, that his personal exertions seem to have been incessant to ameliorate the condition of the people under his charge. I am not defending the constitution or the laws of Sicily. I am, of course, ill qualified to judge of either, as nothing can be more presumptuous than for an Englishman to go into a country, and without making himself master of the tempers, the dispositions, the habits, and nature of the people, their history or their relative position with respect to other countries, condemn its establishments in a lump because it has not a House of Commons and a constitutional opposition. I believe many of the laws of Sicily to be bad; I know there is much misery throughout the land. I am sure its commercial system is very bad, and ill-suited to make the country or the King rich, or the people happy, and the tax upon the land is so heavy that much is left untilled in consequence. But because I see these faults I am not so presumptuous as to believe that we English are the only people enabled to open our eyes and perceive them, or that the governors of Sicily are not themselves aware of them. But because all is not

The Luogo Tenente *or Viceroy*
(Giuseppe Patania, 1824)

good, all is not, therefore, bad; and I do see much good already done and much doing in Sicily, implying certainly commendable activity and considerable talents of the part of the individual who is for the third time Viceroy, but is not rich, neither is he getting so ...

Since the 1820 revolution Palermo had acquired a new printing press (censored by the government, but not, as formerly, by the Catholic Church); a monthly literary journal prepared to take an independent line; a fledgling, questioning university; and a new, well-appointed and well-displayed museum of antiquities. In the Jesuits' Library in Palermo, and in the Library of the Benedictines at San Martino, the Duke found books by Milton, Shakespeare, Locke, Newton and Luther, all banned under the previous, church-dominated regime. In the mid-18th century, in the days of the first (very devout) Spanish Bourbon that ruled Two Sicilies, King Carlo, the penalty for possessing or reading Voltaire had been five years hard labour.

I know that the Government of Sicily is arbitrary, and I am not defending arbitrary power – God forbid that any Englishman should do so! – but I boldly assert that in England we know very little of the truth of what is passing in Sicily ... There is much yet to change, and much to do. But because this is so, let us not fail to do justice to those who have begun the noble work of restoring a fallen country.

Capital punishments are very few – not more than four or five in a year upon an average – in Palermo. The galley-slaves are in no very great number, are very tolerably kept, and their chains do not offend the eyes as in other places on the continent. Assassinations are but little known. The church affords no refuge to the murderer. Immediate trial and execution are sure to follow; but still the Sicilian has recourse to the knife, as the ultima ratio of men in a passion; and considering that wine is to be had at 3d English per bottle, and strong wine too, perhaps we may be allowed to think that it speaks not unwell for the police of the country, that a drunken man is scarcely ever seen, and the knife very seldom indeed had recourse to.

On the evening of September 28th he paid his first formal call: a ceremonial visit on Sicily's Viceroy, the Luogo Tenente, at the Palazzo Reale.

> Passed up a prodigious flight of stairs with marble balustrades, full of filth and bad smells; open corridors full of guards, and guard-rooms full of fellows lounging, sleeping, lousing themselves, and spitting about.

His party negotiated another two ante-chambers, hung with Gobelin tapestries and full of scuttling aides-de-camp and halberdiers being brought to attention, then were ushered into a small room where they were greeted by the Viceroy, to whom the Duke took an immediate liking.

> [He was] a well looking-man, covered with orders &c, who received me with great civility, and offered me all Sicily, assuring me that it was mine. I presented my suite; and after being seated on the edge of a sofa, and certain solemn questions, and answers, and compliments duly laboured through on both sides, he asked to stay to the Fête du Roi, which was to be on the 4th of October next. I answered that of course I should make it my devoir,

The Royal Palace, Palermo (Leitch)

and then I took my leave, he re-conducted me to the top of the stairs, and gave me notice that he would pay me a visit the ensuing evening.

The Viceroy's return visit took place as promised the following day.

Lit up my rooms, all my party dressed out in gala – marines lined the staircase, holding lights – the consul receiving him at the foot of the staircase, I at the top – ceremonies the same as I experienced at my reception. Nothing could exceed the civility and real empressement of the Viceroy.

The party then moved on to a ball at the Casino Nobile, next to the Opera House, and the Duke noted with approval that all gambling – even billiards and whist – had been banned on the island since the revolution, on the grounds that too many noble families had ruined themselves at the tables.

The ball was confined to the noblesse, none other can be admitted; and all strangers of rank, or well-recommended, receive special invitations. The ball was not very brilliant, owing to many of the noblesse being out of town – but the room was tolerably good … The dances were confined to the waltz and quadrilles. They are fond of English country-dances, but there were not women enough to make one out. There were but few pretty women; in fact, during my stay in Palermo I saw but few. All the noblesse of Palermo desired to be presented to me – and it was literally for some time, to my great annoyance, a circle; but it was all meant as a special civility … The Society in Palermo is very limited, as not only the nobles are too poor to keep open house, or to give soirées, but they are all afraid of each other. The remains of the old Queen's party still exist, and are strictly watched.

The last days of September were spent sightseeing in and around the town. He visited the King's country-house, La Favorita, built in the style of a Chinese pavilion and set among delightful olive and orange groves with a park stuffed with pheasants and game, where he was intrigued by the royal dining-table, set immediately above the kitchens.

In the table are circular trapdoors, with counterweights precisely like those used in a theatre, and upon these dishes ascend and descend on the ringing of a bell. The changes of plates, knives and forks, &c, are placed upon dumb waiters, so that the whole dinner passes off without the necessary presence of a single servant.

What really caught the Duke's attention, though, was the local loony bin, the Hôpital des Foux,[52] established by the Viceroy and superintended

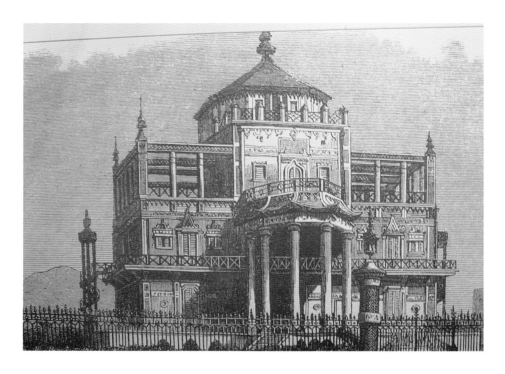

The Chinese Palace (from an early 19th century engraving)

without fee or reward, on very forward-looking principles, by a Baron Pisano, whose first action, on taking over the hospital, had been to get rid of all the medieval fetters and manacles except for one, which he had hung up on the wall as a memento. The asylum, with 300 patients at the time of the Duke's visit, was financed by the richer inmates, who lived on the top floor and paid for the poorer lunatics, who occupied the floor below.

The 'automated' table

The first thing that is done is to place the patient, the moment he is introduced, into a preparatory apartment, where he is carefully watched, and the case minutely examined into; and he is then removed into the ward appropriated to the cases under which the particular species of disease is ranked. *Every fancy is indulged*. If a man fancies himself a king he is treated with something like apparent respect due to Royalty – if a poet, he is permitted to scribble poetry, and he is told that his verses are printed and considered equal to Ariosto's and Tasso's – if the man either was or fancies that he is a soldier, he is put into a sort of uniform, and a toy musket of tin, with sham accoutrements are given him.

When I came to the door of the establishment I was astonished at being received by a drum beating 'aux champs', two sentries who never finished presenting their tin arms; and a guard of twenty-five or thirty men, all armed in a similar manner, commanded by a Suisse, with a tremendous pair of moustaches and a cocked hat, who put them through their exercise, which they performed, some facing to the right, some to the left, playing each other all sort of tricks, treading on each other's toes, but all enjoying the thing, all laughing, merry, happy – *and all mad!*

Baron Pisano gave him a conducted tour of the rooms of the 'melancholy mad', which were cheered up with frescoes of flowers, or pictures of Punchinellos and Harlequins. Then they strolled out into the tree-filled pleasure gardens and kitchen-garden where the saner lunatics worked or relaxed. The Baron, the Duke discovered, shared his own antiquarian interests, and they had plenty of subjects, beside lunacy, to chat about.

In these gardens are cells for the refractory and violent; but they even vary in their degrees of confinement. Some of them have grated gates open to the garden, where they can see their quieter brethren walk about at liberty. The cunning of madness soon enables them to see that their liberty is commensurate with their state of quiet, and they become quiet in order to be free. What, therefore, begins in a madman's cunning, leads to his health eventually, and probably to his recovery. Other cells are open only at the top, for the more violent; and others, for the outrageous, are quite dark, but mattressed on all sides, below and above, so that the maniac is in a mattressed box, and cannot injure himself. When there, no further restriction is imposed upon them, and, outside, the straight-waistcoat, which is very rarely permitted, is the only confinement.

The lunatic asylum in Palermo

Pisano, whom all the inmates addressed as 'Father' (some of them, the Duke noticed, capered and made faces behind his back), invited his guest to appear, at least, to liberate one outrageous madman, whom they heard howling and moaning in one of the cells. The poor wretch fancied himself the Czar of Muscovy, and when he was let out he was quiet for a moment and congratulated the Duke, in serious tones, on being a good Muscovite for releasing him, before disappearing into the garden, where he began roaring again and had to be restrained by his peers. Then it was time for dinner. There were two refectories – one for women, the other for men, like a double monastery – and the Duke was impressed by the delicious food provided for rich and poor alike: macaroni soup, vegetable stew, a plate of tunny fish, a side-dish of grapes, a roll of fresh white bread, half a pint of good wine and fresh, clean napkins between each course. A mad friar said grace. After dinner he was introduced to a fat lady who occupied her days in writing love-letters to Lord William Bentinck,[53] whom she had never met and with whom she was desperately in love. Her passion, in keeping with the general principles of Pisano's treatment, was kept at a high level of excitement by forged Bentinck letters in return. The Duke, who knew Lord William well, promised to convey to him, from her, a sprig of rosemary.

Thus these poor people live, happy and mad, with no appearance of a mad-house staring them in the face; on the contrary, those who are gloomy are cheered, those who are too gay are repressed, but not made gloomy. Much the greater number of the patients recover, and few stay above a year.

September drifted into October. The Sicilians, in their turn, as they grew better acquainted with the Duke, liked him more and more. His name was less and less often heard corrupted into Buckrum or Bunkingham.

The Viceroy, hearing of the Duke's antiquarian and geological enthu-siasms, sent him a bag full of silver and copper coins; a basket full of terracotta figures, all Sicilian; a box full of minerals; and a large petrified tree. The Duke, spotting an opportunity, wrote back asking for permission to dig and export. The Viceroy replied that he could give permission to dig, but that he was obliged to send to the King in Naples for permission to export, which he had duly done. In the meantime he advised that the laws in Sicily were sometimes blind and deaf.

On the evening of the Feast of San Ferdinando, October 3rd, a Neapolitan frigate in the harbour fired a salute and dressed ship, and the Duke ordered the Anna to be warped out of the Mole to do likewise. Meanwhile the garrison, a small army of 7,000 men that included cavalry, a mountain brigade with their mules and guns, and a regiment of Neapolitan guards dressed in scarlet, were paraded on the Marina outside the Duke's apart-ment and everyone started firing volleys in every direction: troops, ships and forts. The Viceroy spotted the Duke in his carriage watching the fun, and insisted on him joining the official party in the royal reviewing-stand.

The island's commander-in-chief was General Campana. He had served in the French republican army under Murat and had been out of a job, until a recent royal thaw in Naples had finally given employment to some of those, like Campana, on the wrong side during the Great Wars. In the retreat from Moscow he'd lost the fingers of his left hand. He told the Duke that all the officers, Murat included, were on foot during the retreat, except for Napoleon, who always rode in a carriage or on horseback. The men, according to Campana's account, preserved a morose silence, never complaining. There was nothing to be seen but wastes of snow and black lines of vast pine forests, nothing to be heard but the howling of the wolves. On one night of bitter cold he counted 400 of the Imperial Guard lying dead around their bivouac.

On the next day, the King's birthday, October 4th, the Duke was one of 50 guests at a banquet in the Viceroy's palace. He was seated next to the

Viceroy's wife, La Marquise delle Favare, and found it fairly hard going. The banquet, though sumputous, lasted an age and La Marquise, who tried to be civil, spoke French little and badly, and the Duke's own Italian was sketchy to say the least. Sign-language was resorted to. According to the Duke, there was a shortage of pretty women, but a profusion of green, pink and white wax candles which, mixed with artificial flowers and confectionery ornaments on the tables, made up for it by producing a pretty effect. After dinner and coffee the whole party reassembled at the opera-house, for this night only *en gala* and badly in need of a face-lift. With its blackened gilding and faded hangings it seemed a metaphor for the island's poverty and decay. The opera was *The Barber of Seville*, and the Duke thought that Rossini would have writhed in his seat to hear the *prima donna*, who, in his view, was detestable. The king's box was empty, but the Viceregal party extended to three boxes next door, and the etiquette was for anyone who had been at the banquet to present themselves sometime during the performance. The boxes were brilliant, and the ladies displayed all their beauties and their diamonds, which were many of them lent by their creditors, or withdrawn from pawnbrokers for the night. As for the Duke, he wore a scarlet uniform with a blue riband, and his garter, which, in his own view, stole the show and which the Sicilians never could make out, or tire of staring at.

For the next twelve days, there was more pleasurable sight-seeing in and around Palermo. With its Benedictine Father Abbot as his guide he toured the monastery of San Martino and inspected its school which educated the Catholic sons of Palermitan gentry in drawing, music, fencing, and Latin and Greek, and allowed them home-leave of just four days in a year.

> The first time we saw them [the pupils were] scrambling up in their black gowns the steep side of one of the rocky eminences which overhung the road, with their padré at their head, all fun and noise, perspiration and activity. The moment they saw our carriage approaching they rolled down into the road like so many black-beetles, and, ranging themselves in line, saluted their prieur as he passed, who laughed in their demure faces, and told us that he had admitted us behind the scenes. Here they remain until the age of twenty-one, when they are called upon to take their decision as to their future life, and either enter into the world or into a monastic life.

On the way home, at Boccadifalco, the Duke exchanged his carriage for a mule, and pushed on to see Le Grotté de Baida, into which Lunn

The convent of San Martino (Leitch)

lowered himself with ropes and ladders. The Duke was too fat to squeeze through the entrance (no bigger than the entrance to a fox's earth, in his judgement) and he was forced to wait outside while Lunn found enormous and beautiful stalactites within the limestone cave, and penetrated with his guides as far as he could go, until stopped by water.

Another day they headed east out of Palermo along the coast towards Capo Zefferano, beyond Bagheria, where the late King Ferdinand had a fishing-lodge. Ferdinand had been a Neapolitan lazzarone at heart, and during the tunny-fishing season liked nothing better than laying about him in the nets with spear, knife or club, and covering himself with water, blood and dirt. At Bagheria the Duke visited the Villa Palagonìa[54] with its famous rococo monsters – about 60 still survive – on its surrounding walls.

The monsters now remaining present the strangest fancies and combinations of the wigs, hoop petticoats, fishes' heads and tails, and preposterous features attached to the human form, as well as to those of birds and beasts, which a curious fancy could devise.

Two of the numerous eccentric statues at Bagheria

The easterly road from Palermo (Lojacono)

Later they visited Capo Zefferano with its flying buttresses of limestone[55] arching out into the Mediterranean and huge caverns filled with crystalline sea-water. The steep cliff at the tip of the promontory is 300 feet high or more, and two of the *Anna*'s topmen, for a lark, set off from the jollyboat to climb it, in spite of shouted warnings and prohibitions.

By the time they got some little way they had nothing left but to mount, as they could not go back.

A Sicilian village (Lojacono)

CHAPTER SEVEN

Overland to Etna

On the morning of October 16th 1827, the Duke, accompanied by his chaplain Francis Lunn, his surgeon Dr Moore, and his dog Neptune, set out south-east across Sicily to Catania, in a barouche drawn by six horses. Their baggage, bedding and provisions followed behind on five mules. The rest of his party on the *Anna*, which weighed anchor that morning, set sail round Sicily's north-east cape via the Straits of Messina. They planned to meet with him in the lee of Mt. Etna in about a week's time.

Right up until the last moment of departure the Duke was beset by custom-house officers and begging friars, to both of whom he turned a deaf ear. The Luogo Tenente, he told the customs officers, had given him clearance, and that was that.

As if to reinforce his point, he'd stuck two pistols in his belt. Everybody else travelled armed in Sicily, especially at night, but he didn't really expect to use his pistols. He'd been told that the police that guarded the roads were well paid, but deposited half their pay in a fund which became forfeit if travellers were robbed.

His first night's bivouac was on the road beyond Vicari; and roughish bivouac it turned out to be. The only *fundaco* – a miserable roadside stable with dirty, flea-infested rest-rooms adjoining and hung with ropes of onions and bunches of grapes – turned out to be full, and his bedding, with his mule train, had stopped behind him at Vicari. He elected to sleep in his carriage, wrapped in his cloak and with his pistols primed and ready to hand. Then his mules finally arrived and the landlady offered her own tiny room which she emptied of everything except its fleas.

> We put up our beds in the vacated pig-sty, and, having dressed part of our lamb by the help of our gridiron, we made up a very tolerable dinner with the means afforded by my canteen, and then went to sleep.

When he woke up in the morning, it was pouring with rain. After breakfast (hot tea without milk, fresh milk being more or less unobtainable on the road) there was a brief lull in the downpour, and they loaded up the mules and set off. Then the rain came down again, with renewed, semi-tropical vigour, and continued all day. The barouche had a leather roof and sides that could be put up over the passengers' seats in bad weather and connected to the driver's box with iron fastenings. This excluded most of the rain, but also much air and light. The Duke spent a gloomy, stifling day being jolted on damp leather. They crossed high, treeless clay country covered in stubble, which he judged, from what he could see of it, excellent ground for growing corn. He met the Viceroy travelling the other way and aiming for the *fundaco* left behind. The Duke intended to put up that night at the Vallelunga *fundaco* some 50 miles from Palermo, but when he got there he found a stream swollen into a river barring his progress and he had to wait two hours for his mules to catch him up and carry him across to the town. In the interval he took shelter in a huge barn, along with other orphans of

'the great gorge which runs between Calascibetta and Enna' (Leitch)

69

the storm – a noisy, jostling, rain-soaked crowd of mules, carriages, travellers, muleteers and beggars – and indulged himself in that most pleasurable of Mediterranean pastimes, people-watching.

One carriage there was which held a most important personage. In a richly-laced cap, dandy jacket, pantaloons, and white-kid gloves, sat a gentleman most irate. Incessant were his complaints against the weather, and loud his curses against the conducteur, who had insisted upon baiting his horses there, and then determined not to start in the rain if it were possible to avoid it, but ensconced himself in some deep recess, where he was deaf to the cries of my wretched friend. He then stalked about the hovel, cursing the man for having left him *sans mangiare*. At last he found he got wet in the feet, and then, cursing his own thin shoes, got again into his carriage, where I heard him squeaking and grumbling his complaints, and the words 'sans mangiare' were the constant burthen of his song. At length I saw him jump out of the carriage and produce out of it a live turkey with its legs tied. Producing some oatmeal and water out of a bottle, he proceeded to take off his white kid gloves to mould the stuff into little balls with his own fair hands, and regularly to cram the turkey, taking some water in his mouth and squirting it with each pellet into the wretched turkey's mouth. Feeling the animal's crop he put it into the carriage again, and, stepping in after it, put on his kid gloves, began again to curse his fate, and to sing his wretched song 'sans mangiare'.

The man turned out to be the Viceroy's cook, and the turkey was intended to be his – the Viceroy's – supper.

Every room in the Vallelunga *fundaco* had already been taken by stranded travellers, but the Duke's enterprising *lacquais de place* had somehow got a message earlier across the swollen river and engaged two apartments in the village. Here their truckle beds were erected, and an excellent supper prepared out of a chicken they had managed to buy and the remains of last night's lamb. They heated local wine – otherwise 'detestable and pernicious', according to the Duke – with water, sugar, lemon and nutmeg in a saucepan and made a delicious hot punch which they shared among themselves and their drenched, worn-out servants.

The next morning, the 18th, was warm and sunny. They did their best to dry out their sodden belongings in front of fires of vine-twigs, the only local fuel, before setting out for Santa Caterina, some 25 miles away and

70

'the occasional olive grove near a village' (Mario Mirabella)

75 from Palermo. With the sun up, they could put the carriage-hood down; and Lunn, Moore and the Duke spent a happy day geologising their way across cornlands haphazardly formed from limestone, blue clay, gypsum or red sandstone. The gullies ran turbid with yesterday's rain, and there were few trees, just the occasional olive-grove near a village. The Duke was reminded of parts of Scotland just south of the Highland Line.

> The strata dipped in all directions and to every point of the compass, in every sort of curve and fanciful shape. The effect of the whole on the cliffs bordering on the road, and on the distant mountains, was beautiful, but set all geological rules and order at defiance.

At Santa Catarina they stayed in *a loranda*, one up from a *fundaco*, which seemed like a palace compared to the hovels of the two preceding nights. It had big rooms with glass windows, and doors-that-shut, with plenty of space for them to put up their beds. The inhabitants of the town, particularly the children, seemed wretchedly poor, apparently existing on an exclusive diet of prickly pears. Here, though, as elsewhere in the island, he was struck by the magnificence of the average Sicilian male adult physique.

From Santa Catarina and its sulphur mines (not able to be visited because their mules were not to hand) to Leonforte, their next night's stop, was another 30 miles, through countryside becoming increasingly sub-Alpine. They saw vines, pomegranates, olives and oranges growing in the valleys. The hill-pastures were bright with pinks and marigolds and mauve and golden autumn crocus. Wild cucumbers fruited on the waysides. They made their way through the great gorge that runs between Calascibetta and Enna, the towns only a cannon-shot apart and perched like rookeries thousands of feet above them. They would have found it hard to credit the engineering of the A19 Palermo-Catania motorway which, today, has triumphed over the gorge. At Leonforte they met another English party on the road, a Mr Anderson with his wife and son (the former turned out to be the nephew of Sir George Don, the Gibraltar governor) and heard of two redoubtable Scotch ladies, the Misses Cunningham, who, accompanied only by a maid and a guide, were skirmishing their way across Sicily. The Duke's *lacquais de place* bought a live black lamb, which, half an hour after being killed and skinned, arrived in the form of lamb chops on their table. Another arrival was the ubiquitous Luogo Tenente, who turned up with his baggage and mule-train, and his chaplain in a cocked hat riding one of the mules. Whether or not he had been reunited with his cook is not recorded.

'they descended out of mountains into wooded valleys' (Gonzalvo Cavelli)

On the 20th, they descended out of mountains and clouds threatening rain into wooded valleys where the vines had dropped their leaves and the olive harvest had begun. Beyond Nissoria, at S Felipe d'Orgiro (the modern Agira), they had their first view of Etna, capped with snow from the recent storm, clear from base to crater. The Duke ordered his coachman to stop the carriage and, unscrewing a telescope out of his walking-cane, made a careful survey of the mountain.

> Its first appearance, owing to the extent of its base, rather disappointed me, until I recollected myself, and compared it with the objects round. I then comprehended the immensity of its magnitude, and more so as the eye fixed itself gradually upon the different mountains and forests which cling around its sides, and over which the eye at first was carried.

They were three more days on the road, skirting round the vast base of Etna, before they arrived at Catania. At Real Bucco [Regalbuto] they put up for the night in an Augustinian Whitefriars monastery, in three guest-rooms devoid of furniture. The monks – there were only 18 of them – were fascinated by Lunn, *un ecclesiastico* wearing a shooting-jacket, and their Prior made a detailed examination of the Duke's travelling plate, dressing apparatus and liqueurs. For a lay-brother verger who was desperately thin from fasting, Dr Moore prescribed a pint of hot wine and spices. The verger pulled faces at first, then, finding out what it was, settled down to enjoy it a teaspoonful at a time.

On the road to Paterno, the recent storm had washed away the road, and they were forced to take to the mules along the sides of steep, clay-sided ravines.

> The mule could only make his path by planting one foot carefully and cautiously on the side of the shelving clay, and, when he found himself established, moving a hind leg into the spot evacuated by his fore foot, and thus drawing himself over ... I shut my eyes and left him to himself, being too nervous to look at his manoeuvres.

He comforted himself with the thought that the two Scotch ladies had passed this way in a litiga (a litter carried fore and aft between two mules) only two days before. He ran across the Cunninghams later in his trip, and they confessed that they, too, on that part of the road, had not been confident of their survival.

In the plain below Paterno they saw cotton being grown. Beyond were

Regalbuto, the first of the Duke's sketches

lava-fields, left behind by the last eruption of the mountain in 1819. They reminded the Duke of Wolverhampton, the ground black and covered in

A litter. The Cunninghams, two Scotch ladies, had not been confident of their survival

cinders. Catania, when they first saw its palaces, arches and cupolas, seemed very white by comparison. They had been on the road a week, and had covered 130 miles from Palermo. Captain Wilcox and the *Anna* were waiting for them in the harbour. She had been caught in the great storm of the 17th in the Straits of Messina and had been forced to lay to. For half an hour, amid continuous crashes of thunder and forks of lightning, St Elmo's fire shone out from the two mastheads – a white electric flame of about the size and shape of a quart bottle, according to the Duke, tapering up into a blue flame. The Italian sailors among the crew had been convinced they would all be drowned.

Mount Etna from the harbour in Catania

28th. Catania rejoiced in our departure, and its inhabitants thronged to see us go; for although the Sicilians have little curiosity themselves, and scarcely ever take the trouble themselves of visiting 'La Montagna', as they style Etna, believing that it is the only mountain in the world worthy of that name, they highly honour those who do.

Their first night's halt was at Nicolosi, where the Duke presented a letter of introduction, and Lunn a self-registering thermometer sent by a mutual friend to measure winter temperatures on Etna, to Signor Gemellaro, the mountain's 'celebrated and estimable cicerone'. Gemellaro was a local judge and amateur vulcanologist who had made it his life's work to study Etna and facilitate visits by interested tourists. He welcomed the Duke's party most hospitably, and insisted that they should all stay with him at his house, rather than go to the *loranda* nearby. The Duke was prevailed upon to put up his bed in Gemellaro's library, and, having unpacked their provisions and prepared dinner in his kitchen,

Signor Gemmelaro, the vulcanologist with whom the Duke stayed

they spent a pleasant evening chatting to him about Etna: 'his wife' as he called the mountain.

The next morning, October 29th, they set out to climb it. The plan was to spend the night at the Casa Inglese (now the Osservatorio Vulcanologico), at 9,623 feet only about 1300 feet below the crater's topmost rim. The Casa had been built by subscription from English officers during their occupation of Sicily in the Great Wars. Gemellaro had been the driving force behind the project, and now held the keys, and the Duke tactfully referred to it, in his protesting presence, as the Casa de Gemellaro. Gemellaro had wanted to record the subscribers' names on a stone over the door, but the officers had demurred.

The lava field (Lojacono)

Beyond Nicolosi they crossed a fertile plain of volcanic ash cultivated with vines and figs. They saw in flower what he called Spanish broom (in fact, the famous yellow broom endemic to the mountain: *Genista aetnensis*). On their left reared Monte Rossi, from whose base lava had flowed to destroy Catania in the huge eruption of 1669. On their right, three miles up the road, they passed a Benedictine convent embowered in pine trees. Here, so the story went, a monk had been overrun by a lava-flow while washing linen at a fountain. Four centuries later he awoke, like the Seven Sleepers of Ephesus, from a long slumber and wandered down to the monastery to ask if his linen had survived the eruption.

Next they entered Il Bosco, the Woody Belt: ancient oaks and beech used as pollards by local charcoal-burners. The trees stood, in defiance of repeated lava-assaults by the mountain, amid drifts of yellow autumn crocus. The track – *la Carmina* as the guides called it – rose rapidly through the 1819 lava-field. The recent storm had done a lot of damage, creating a *malo passo* for half a mile. They hung onto their mules' neck-straps for dear life. The heavy Duke was particularly at risk.

I had no idea that such a staircase could be surmounted by beasts on four legs. I know that on two nothing would have persuaded me to have attempted the passage. The conduct of the guides is exemplary. They ride before you, and each stranger mule follows one of Etna. Where you desire it, or they themselves think it right, the guides slide over their mules' tails, put themselves at the head of the stranger mules, and by their voice and exertions carry them over places where no lowlander would think any animal not winged could scarcely venture. The result of all this is perfect and entire security. The mules never make a false step, and when they do they never fall, or hands and arms are instantly at hand to receive you. The only *real* danger is this: in coming down these tremendous passes straps are fastened to the mules' cruppers, by which you hold to prevent your plunging forward over their heads, for they have slabs of rock and lava to carry you down of several feet in depth and surface. The resting-place, when they come to it, is often scarcely large enough to hold the mule's foot, and if you check him by the bridle you prevent him from judging his distance correctly, and his foot may go over the place of safety. In going down, therefore, it is more necessary to abandon all bridle even than in going up – and here if a man is heavy he *is* sometimes in real danger, for frequently in the middle of a descent is a sharp and sudden turn with a precipice in front of you. If, therefore, your weight comes upon the mule's shoulders he topples forward and both go over the precipice. As this could not be provided against by any sure-footedness of my mule and no exertions of my own, there were literally places where two guides placed themselves before me, and, receiving me and my mule in their arms, turned us fairly round on the face of the rock.

The Casa Inglese, the Etna refuge built by a subscription from English officers during the Napoleonic wars

At the beginning of the snowline they could see the Casa Inglese high above them. The temperature – it had been hot in the Bosco – had dropped sharply, and they wrapped their cloaks tight around them and pulled green veils down over their eyes. The mules swallowed mouthfuls of snow, and a frolicking Etna dog (an endemic species, like the broom) belonging to one of the guides ate it too. Slowly, by zig-zagging traverses and in the teeth of a by now considerable, and freezing, wind, they ascended to the Casa, and arrived there just as the sun was setting.

The whole earth below was one mass of brilliant rosy purple. The sea possessed a tint exclusively its own. The white cities glittered for a moment through the purple veil, the rivers of Sicily ran in tides of silvery thread through the land. Etna was covered with a rosy tint of blushing snow. This lasted for a minute – and all was gone.

This was probably recollected, later, in tranquillity. That evening, when he dismounted from his mule, he had little inclination to admire the view. He was exhausted. His breathing was laboured in the thin mountain air, and his gouty ankle was giving him trouble. He had lost his appetite, was feeling slightly sick. He, at least, had come as far up Etna as he could go.

The mules were established in a shed next door, and his party, having dined on hot tea, mulled wine and negus,[56] went straight to bed, wrapped up in great-coats, cloaks, night-caps, and anything else they could lay their hands on to keep out the cold.

At half past two in the morning the Duke woke up to see his companions setting off for the summit. He saw them later on the rim above him amid steam and smoke, and they reminded him of chimney-sweepers perched on a roof ridge, having finished their morning's work. As for himself, he was only too happy to spend two more hours curled up in his warm bed. While it was still dark he was roused by a guide left behind. Later, in his journal, he recorded the experience of watching dawn break over Etna. He was not one to pass up the opportunity for a purple passage of prose.

I had the pleasure of setting forth ... across Il Piano de Lago, towards Monte Fuimento and the Vallé del Barile, from which glowed the queen of the night, in the clearest sky without a cloud, the stars just quenched by the morning dawn. Nothing could look more gloomy. The dark lava was most strangely contrasted with the snow which streaked it, and behind me rose the giant cone looking paley and streaky and snowy through the uncertain light. By degrees the streaks of purple, which are the first *avant couriers* of the sun, began to spread themselves over the heavens and the bosom of the sea, which lay like a vast mass of uncertain gloom, I know not how far before me. Almost in an instant, in the twinkling of an eye, shoots of vivid red ran up from the edge of the sea to the zenith, filling the sky with masses of crimson, shot with golden threads; and after I had considered this extraordinary spectacle for perhaps two or three minutes, the streaks of golden light getting momentarily more intense and vivid, giving the effect more of a golden aurora borealis than anything else, a speck of dazzling brilliance became visible on the surface of the sea; and breaking an awful silence, which had lasted from the moment we had gained the crest of the mountain, my guide exclaimed in a low tone, as if in fear, 'Ecco il Sole!'.

Syracuse from across the bay (Maria Bergler)

CHAPTER EIGHT

Finders Keepers

Hadrian climbed Etna for the view at dawn. So did the elder Dumas and William Ewart Gladstone, the latter a year after the Duke, in 1828. But the Duke's near-ascent of Europe's largest and highest volcano, for a man of his age and physique, was no mean feat. Forty years earlier in the month of May, at a date, admittedly, when the overnight shelter of the

A party of tourists viewing an eruption of Etna, at great risk to their lives (Busse)

Casa Inglese was not yet in existence, Goethe was warned off the climb by a local expert, in the plainest possible terms. '*When we asked [him] how we should go about climbing Etna, he refused even to discuss an enterprise which was so hazardous, especially at this time of year. He apologised for this and said: "Most foreign visitors are too apt to consider the ascent a trifling affair. But we, who are near neighbours of the mountain, are content if we have reached the summit twice or thrice in a lifetime, for we never attempt it except under ideal conditions … If you will follow my advice, ride early tomorrow morning to the foot of Monte Rosso: you will enjoy the most magnificent view … If you are wise, you will let others tell you about the rest."*'

Goethe never climbed *Mongibello*, as the Sicilians call it: to his sorrow, for, apart from anything else, it would have played well with his brooding[57] fans at home. Nowadays, of course, there are lifts and cablecars for winter skiers, and waymarked paths for walkers, and refuges near the summit for overnight stops. On occasion, though, the great volcano bestirs itself – as it did more than seven times in the 19th century. The biggest recorded eruption was that which destroyed Catania in 1669. In more recent memory, roads, refuges and cablecar stations have been engulfed by lava flows.

News of the Duke's climb reached England quickly. On December 8th his uncle Thomas wrote to him from London: '*I rejoiced to hear of your being stout enough to scale Mount Aetna, and trust, that, before this time, you will have taken steps enough, or your mule for you, to enable you to compare these two mountains of the older world* [Etna and Vesuvius], *and to have disserted most scientifically upon them with your learned and valuable companion* [Mr Lunn].'

The climb, in fact, took a good deal out of the Duke. For the last two months of 1827 he was ill, on and off, with fever and gout, and several times took to his bed on board the *Anna* to recuperate. The damp Sicilian winter was no help, and his natural optimism and curiosity seems, on occasion, to have deserted him.

The early days of November were taken up with sightseeing in and around Catania, especially its Greek and Roman remains, which demand a considerable talent for imaginative reconstruction; so often has Catania been destroyed by lava, war or earthquake. At three o'clock in the morning, on the night of November 4th, the Duke and his party were woken by two earthquake tremors, each lasting a couple of

The square of the Elephant, Catania (Leitch)

seconds, which made bells ring in the town, and windows rattle and beds shake.

The next day pupils from the local Benedictine school came on board the *Anna* for a visit – a great excitement for the boys as they were only allowed one day's holiday a year and had never been on board a ship at sea. One of them fell overboard, or was pushed by a companion, on the way out to the yacht. Captain Bates fished him out by his hair. They dried him out, and put him to bed on board with a glass of hot wine, before returning him to his seminary safe and sound. The visit was a huge success. *Una palazzo maritimo*, they called the *Anna*, and wanted to make Bates a Benedictine for saving their brother.

Basaltic columns on the Cyclops Isles

The Duke geologised in his barge up the coast as far as Acireale, and spent a day on the Cyclops Islands (*Isole dei Ciclopi*), chipping off specimens with his hammer and becoming more and more convinced, from the evidence of limestone strata overlaying lava, of the inadequacy of Bishop Ussher's biblical dating of the earth's origin to 4004 BC. Then, on the 10th, it was time to say goodbye. His valet, Sharp, to the amusement of all on board, was chased around the yacht by two Italian inn-keepers who wanted to kiss him on both cheeks. They sailed south for Augusta – now one of Italy's premier oil ports – where the shooters on board went ashore and walked up snipe in the marshes: a welcome variation to their diet.

On the 12th they anchored in the harbour at Syracuse, and the Duke had another of his jousts, which he so much relished, with bureaucracy. The health officers, coming alongside, demanded to see his passport before they would give pratique. He protested that his passport was the concern of the police, and had nothing to do with the health authorities. In the end he handed his passport over, into a pair of long tongs as a precaution against plague, and the health officers, having studied it carefully, said it was only for *Il Signor Duca* and for no one else on board.

> I then said that, to be sure, my own Secretary of State and the different ambassadors who had *visé* and signed my passport had not in contemplation the possibility of a boatful of signori, calling themselves the health officers and the police officer of Syracuse, not being able to read. I therefore requested them to look over my passport again for the sake of their own literary reputation, or, if they did not choose to expose it to such risk, I recommended them to send on shore for some one who could read.
>
> This harangue, slowly delivered in English, and interpreted duly to them in pure Italian, much diverted my own crew and their own boatmen, and sadly enraged the authorities, who, however, upon looking again with bent brows and spectacles and clustered heads over my passport, saw that it was for 'Il Signor Duca, e sua Sequita'.

The Duke gave them five minutes to think it over. If pratique was denied, he would weigh anchor, sail round to Palermo, and lay a formal complaint before the Luogo Tenente – who had directed all authorities on the island to assist him in every way. They promptly caved in, assuring *Sua Excellenza* that they were his devoted servants and at his orders. Immediate pratique was given, and they tried to follow on board the English Vice-Consul – or rather his representative, the English Vice-Consul being away in Malta. The Duke ordered them off. They should learn to behave with greater civility to strangers before he'd allow them as guests on his ship.

Having gained the initiative, he pressed home his advantage. He immediately went ashore and paid an official call on the Intendente of the province, and its military governor. Both greeted him warmly, and offered their homes and carriages for his free, personal use (he accepted the carriages). They sent on board presents of almond and cream cakes, and pots of jam, and local vinters gave him free samples of fine Syracusan wine, in the hope that he would put in a big order. [He did, later: a present of a hogshead – nearly 300 bottles – for each of his officers at a shilling a gallon, and permission to his servants to speculate on another hogshead to take home].

The Duke began to feel better disposed towards the town, with its narrow, clean, well-paved streets and medieval architecture magpied

Syracuse cathedral which incorporates the ancient temple of Minerva (Leitch)

from Graeco-Roman remains. He thought that the Duomo, Santa Maria delle Colonne, on the island of Ortygia, with its tremendous 18th century façade incorporating the ancient temple of Athene/Minerva, was magnificent. In classical times the temple was topped off by a huge statue of the warrior goddess with a burnished shield that returning seamen used as a beacon. Now it exhibited, thought the Duke, 'the greatest triumphs of ancient architecture over modern bad taste'. On the right, as you go in, inside the baptistery, is a huge marble bowl used as a

*The bronze lions which
so upset the Duke*

font, with a Greek inscription. It sits on seven charming bronze lions that date from the 13th century. The Duke thought them more recent, and didn't like them.

> In order, however, to ensure bad taste appearing wherever the hands of modern aid are shewn, they have put the votive urn upon pert little bronze lions, with each of them one paw in the air, as if proud and careless of the burthen they bear.

He knew his Thucydides, however, and was fascinated to find himself anchored in the same bay where, in 413 BC, the hitherto invincible battle-fleet of the Athenians had been trapped and their Mediterranean thalassocracy utterly destroyed. He visited the quarries (*latomie*) into which 7,000 Athenian prisoners had been lowered and worked to their deaths in appalling conditions, and from which – so the story goes – the only ones to escape alive were those who could recite Euripides, whose dramas the Syracusans adored.

> November 19th. This is the Queen of Naples's birthday, and there are great rejoicings on shore … At night I threw up rockets, and blue, red, white and green lights, to the great edification of the Syracusans. At night we were all invited to a ball at the Commandant's house. I could not go, from ill-health, but all the rest of the party went. They returned much pleased. They gave them English country-dances for their benefit, and a table, at which, of course, none but the Sicilians themselves played. The women were in general not pretty, but there were some exceptions.

The next day, the 20th, was warm and sunny, and the Duke, feeling a little better, was rowed by his sailors across to Cape Plemmyrium, where the Athenian army under Demosthenes and Nicias had once lain encamped. The same day a working-party of his marines began opening some of the tombs on the rocky hill above the town's Roman amphitheatre. The tombs, slab-covered and hewn out of the solid rock, were all filled with earth. In one they found a broad, pointed, iron sword, about two feet long minus the hilt, lying among four skeletons. The Duke

A greek lamp of the kind excavated by the Duke's marines

thought it might be Roman, and kept it for his collection, along with one of the skulls, which had excellent teeth. Two days later one of his barge's crew was scrambling for fossils on the cliff of Cape Plemmyrium and broke off a piece of sandstone. Underneath was what appeared to be an ancient Greek lamp in mint condition.

It was full of the sand of the cliff, and even the carbon on the beak of the lamp was fresh ... Mr Lunn at once went with the man, whom he made show him the precise spot where it was found, as the bed was one full of fossil remains, both above and below the lamp ... It appeared clear that it was on the ledge of an old working, on which the sand had fallen in and buried the lamp, that probably had been left there by some Syracusan or Athenian workman. The lamp was quite plain, but interesting because it is so perfect, and from the classical spot on which it was found.

Next he turned his attention to the ruined Norman church of San Giovanni Evangelista, in the Tyche district, built on the spot where St Paul is said to have preached in AD 61. They explored its vast network of underground catacombs, mostly early-fourth-century-AD and, today, open to the public. The *loculi* – niches for burial – had been cleaned out by robbers centuries before the Duke's arrival, but they found a marble slab, carved with Constantine's cross, commemorating a Roman lady called Fausta. Emerging into the day, he spotted among the ruins the shaft of a Gothic column sticking up out of the ground.

Making my workmen clear it out, I found a beautiful Gothic capital belonging to the old church, richly voluted ... This I brought away, both as an interesting remains and as a memorial of a place which no Christian can view without feelings of veneration.

On the 24th his marines were at work in the Roman amphitheatre, where they found another lamp and the remains of glass and mother-of-pearl ornaments. In a corridor they spotted a wooden cornice, preserved by lime carbonate, running along the crest of a stone arch. They tore out what remained of the wood, and its nails; then examined the wood and nails by burning them with a blow torch and treating them with acid. When they had finished, very little remained of the subject of their experiments. Then they returned to opening up the rock tombs above the amphitheatre.

My party of excavators, which I confine wholly to my own marines, is very successful; and having now got into the habit of distinguishing the proper tombs to open, they find every day lamps, vases, and paterae – some entire, and others broken, but all so as to be restored, and many interesting. I have, therefore, altogether made a very good collection of Syracusan sepulchral remains. So long as they were under the guidance of our cicerone we found nothing; when left to ourselves, we succeeded. We found most in the tombs of young persons and children … But we found no coins … If I had remained here longer, I am convinced that my discoveries would have been more valuable. A dolphin in pottery, sacred to Venus; a handle of a small vase, with a Greek inscription; the leaden bolts thrown out of slings, the weights used in the Grecian Custom-House, and a Saracen's head, used in later days as a weight to a steel-yard … and the sword … are very interesting. Some of the lamps, also, with sacrificial and mythological figures upon them, are equally so.

The watermill in the Greek amphitheatre at Syracuse

On December 3rd, the day before the *Anna* was due to sail north away from Syracuse, the Duke took his cutter up the river Anapas (*Anapo*) to look for the Fountain of Cyane. *Kuanos* means blue in Greek, and the spring of Cyane, set among groves of green papyrus – the only place that papyrus grows wild in Europe – still runs deep and blue. Cyane, in the Greek myth, was a nymph who was turned into a spring by Hades because she had tried to stop him kidnapping Persephone to the Under-

Papyrus growing at the spring of Cyane

world. The Duke's crew had a good deal of difficulty getting his cutter over the sandbar – nowadays there's an artificial canal for pleasure-boats – they had to pull it with ropes, or pole and paddle it, up-river for about five miles before they got to the spring. In one place the papyrus grew so thick that it overarched their heads. Today the area is a nature reserve, and a good place (although the Duke doesn't mention it) for migratory birds in winter: night-herons, many species of duck, penduline tits, red-legged stilts, falcons, occasionally flamingoes.

Arrived at the spring, the Duke considered, then reluctantly dismissed, a project that would have involved some fairly technical underwater archaeology.

> The water is so pellucid that, although its depth is above thirty feet, the fish at the bottom are clearly discernible, as well as blocks of marble and remains of pottery, which denote a water-temple having existed here, and the bogs which surround the spring and afford no footing, have hitherto prevented the depths of this basin from being ransacked. It is not, however, improbable that, with a good barge's crew and proper implements, something might be found worth the pains of seaching after.

He contented himself with digging up some roots of papyrus to send back to England, then returned downstream by moonlight. It was very late when they arrived back at the *Anna*. The next day, they sailed north for Messina.

December 12th. This day, after a long attack of fever and gout, I once more have got into my barge. Under a warm sun I have taken a long row along the shore. Nothing can exceed the magnificent beauty of the situation of Messina. Stretched under a splendid canopy of mountains, which descend in sweeping ravines and fuimanas to the sea, it reposes, and displays its palaces, cupolas, and towers, amongst orange groves, olives, and vineyards. The lower hills, most romantically shaped, are cultivated up to the summits, and the orange trees are now glowing with fruit. A beautiful extent of palazzo-fronted buildings[58] forms the marina or esplanade to the water's edge, which is so deep that the largest ships are moored to the shore. We have twenty-four fathoms of water, and are within a hundred yards of the city.

The harbour at Messina – before its destruction by earthquake in 1908 (Leitch)

To the west, across the straits, they could see the snow-topped mountains of Calabria. The Italian coast, at its nearest, lay only two miles away, across the ancient whirlpools of Scylla and Charybdis, described so vividly in Homer's *Odyssey*. Scylla, on the Italian side, was a monster with six heads and 12 feet, and Charybdis, on the Sicilian shore, was supposed to suck in, and spew out, the sea three times a day. While anchored at Messina, they witnessed a brig lose her headway opposite the Faro Point and, twisting helplessly in the whirlpools, run ashore.

In the town, the Duke saw a convicted murderer being taken to execution, a member of the Order of Penitents on either side: grim, black-hooded figures with slits for their eyes, bawling into the wretched man's ears the prayers for the dead. He watched Messinese men ambling through the streets and thought them great dandies. They twirled pink umbrellas and wore stiff stays, pea-green gloves, and coats cut in at the waist and gathered in puckers down to the knees like watermen's jackets. He also discovered another side to the Luogo Tenente, who wasn't popular in Messina. Before he became Viceroy, he had been a spy and *agent provocateur* for the Neapolitan police, and had spent a lot of time in Messinese coffee-houses talking the language of revolution and trying to flush out political deviants.

December 25th. Today it cleared up, and allowed us to enjoy our Christmas-day. We had divine service upon deck. I then had the awnings spread fore and aft, and the deck enclosed with canvas. My ship's company had a plentiful hot dinner served to them, and my warrant-officers had another on the quarter-deck. My servants had a third. An allowance of beer was given them, as well as wine. In the evening I got two fiddles and a harp on board; a quart of warm punch per man was served out to the whole ship's company; dancing began and continued all evening. The men enjoyed themselves beyond measure. The deck was lit up with signal lanthorns, and they kept it joyfully and happily until nine o'clock, when they all turned in. In the great cabin we had a good dinner, and drank the healths of all those whom we loved dearest, and had left behind. I had found a conjurer, whom I hired to come on board to show off his tricks before the men in the cabin. In short, I did my best to make all hands happy.

CHAPTER NINE

Caccia di Cinghiale

On the morning of January 11th, 1828, three days north from Messina in Sicily, the *Anna Eliza* crept slowly and cautiously round the finger of Italian mainland that sticks out from Sorrento and Amalfi, and dropped anchor in Naples Bay. There was a thick fog. The wind was light and intermittent, off-shore, from the east, and Buckingham was reminded of Essex and the damp mists that roll up the Thames estuary into the pool of London. Naples and Vesuvius were blotted out from view. The night before, becalmed and without steerage way, he'd worried that they were drifting dangerously close to the rocks of Capri, on the port bow.

> At length, however, we got her head around, and she slowly drew off from the island.

The Neapolitans seem to have been expecting his arrival. A customs cutter came alongside, and as soon as the *Anna Eliza*'s name, and its owner, were made known, the Duke and his crew were given immediate clearance to go ashore. His books and shotguns, however, presented a problem. There followed the sort of brief, comic, bureaucratic wrangle with customs that the Duke relished.

> January 12th 1828: The Minister made a great fuss about letting me land my effects and books – especially the latter, as there is a commission of priests established to examine every book imported into the country, and there is a heavy duty per volume on their introduction. At length the Minister gave me a free order to introduce my effects free of duty, and 'seven or eight sets of books, if they were not amongst those previously prohibited.' The priests must see the names of them; and this cannot be done before Monday. Although I had the Minister's order, the douaniers had not, and they strenuously resisted the establishment of so bad precedent as the landing goods unexamined, pertinaciously insisting on

opening my writing-box. I declared they might open everything else, but that they should not open my writing-box after I had shewn them Monsieur de Medici's[59] letter. They still persisted, and I had just ordered them to quit the vessel, declaring that I would not land until they had been taught better manners, when a peremptory order came in a boat, commanding my books, effects &c, to be landed without examination; with license to shoot, and an order to land my guns. This was accompanied by a letter from the King to go into the country with him that evening to shoot.

The Duke turned down the shooting invitation of Francis I, King of Naples and Sicily ('The Two Sicilies'), in a polite letter of excuse to the King's Grand Veneur, the Duke of Sanvalentino. He excused himself on the grounds that he was still weak from his gout and fever at Messina. He would pay his respects to the King as soon as his health allowed, and the English Chargé d'Affaires at Naples, a Mr Fox, (currently absent on business in Calabria) had returned to court and was in a position properly to present him. Privately, Buckingham was only too well aware that the rendezvous for the shoot was 20 miles away, over rough roads.

> I must then have slept in a barrack-room with three or four other men, on mattresses shaken down on the floor in the wretched outhouses of a wretched place, where the King alone has a little room to himself.

The Duke, of all men, was good at anticipating, and avoiding, discomfort.

Of the Italian Bourbons that ruled the kingdoms of Naples and Sicily in the 18th and 19th centuries (until the last of them was kicked out by Garibaldi when he landed with his Thousand in Sicily in 1860), historians have found virtually nothing to record in their favour. They were cruel, despotic, pleasure-loving, mean, treacherous, lazy, ill-educated, bigoted and stupid, and committed appalling atrocities against their countrymen when they were on the up, then ran like rabbits to the safety of their Sicilian island at the first hint of trouble. Francis's father, Ferdinand IV, ran wild as a boy among the *lazzaroni*, the beggars and thieves of the Neapolitan back-streets. He affected their accent and idiom, and liked nothing better than dressing up as a fisherman and haggling over his last night's catch in the city's fishmarket. With the *lazzaroni*, at least, he was always a favourite; and when there were scores to be settled with political enemies, or atrocities to be committed, he could always rely on his *lazzaroni* to oblige. He ruled after a fashion from 1767 to 1825, with long gaps during the Napoleonic era when first Joseph, Napoleon's brother, then Joachim Murat, his dashing cavalry commander, were kings in Naples. Real power in Ferdinand's time resided, via a corrupt network of spies, informers and security police, in the hands of his wife, Maria Carolina, sister of the French Queen, Marie Antoinette. She was as foxy, neurotic and ambitious as her husband was stupid and idle, and longed to turn the Kingdom of the Two Sicilies into a Great Power that could look France or Austria in the eye. The absurdity of her ambition became apparent in 1798 when the French marched on Naples and the royal family ran for it to Palermo as fast as Nelson's HMS *Vanguard* could carry them[60]. They made a similarly rapid exit in 1806, after the French victory at Austerlitz. In both cases they crept back to Naples when French backs were turned, and exacted a terrible vengeance upon any of their countrymen tainted by republican or liberal ideas. Islands like Favignana in the Egadi, and Pantelleria off the coast of Tunisia, were filled to overflowing with political prisoners. They were the lucky ones – at least they survived. Maria Carolina was merciless. Any suspected Jacobin collaborator, high or low, was either tortured, then bayoneted or shot out of hand, or handed over to the tender mercies of the backstreets *lazzaroni*. Nelson, egged on by Emma Hamilton who was the Queen's friend and confidant, will forever bear the dishonour of having been an accessory[61] to the Queen's appalling acts of revenge.

In January 1828, when the Duke sailed into the Bay of Naples, her son, Francis I, was in his early fifties, and had been on the throne three years. When he succeeded his father in 1825, he set aside the liberal agenda he had adopted as heir-apparent, and became every bit as savagely reactionary and repressive as his parents. He lived surrounded by 12 children (the youngest at that time four months old), mistresses and Swiss guards, in perpetual fear of assassination, and took little interest in the day-to-day business of government, which he turned over to favourites and secret policemen, who, so long as they protected him from Carbonari assassins, were allowed to carry on more or less as they wished. The Carbonari – in Italian 'charcoal-burners' – were members of a secret society active in France and Italy in the early part of the 19th century. Dedicated to the cause of freedom, independence and constitutional government, they were the heirs of Rousseau and the Enlightenment, and forerunners of Garibaldi and his Risorgimento. In 1820 they infiltrated several regiments of the Neapolitan army, and stirred up a mutiny against the king. Ferdinand agreed a constitution, which he swore on the altar to observe; then, true to form, as soon as help arrived in the form of Austrian troops, he broke his oath, tore up the constitution and set about hanging, shooting and exiling as many liberals and mutineers as he could lay his hands on.

Francis's son, Ferdinand II, who ruled the Two Sicilies from 1830 to 1859, was known as 'King Bomba' because he ordered the shelling of his countrymen in Sicily's main cities in retaliation for their 1848 uprisings. His son, Francis II, who became king in 1859 and was ejected from Naples by Garibaldi in 1860, was the last of the reigning Italian Bourbons. Today the family, and its claim to the throne, lingers on in the person of HRH Prince Ferdinand, Duke of Castro, Grand Master of the Dynasty Order and the Orders of Knighthood of the Bourbon Two Sicilies, Knight of the Order of St Umberto of Bavaria, of our Lady of the Annunciation, of the Crown of Wurttermberg etc; and of his son, Crown Prince Charles, Duke of Calabria.

The Duke had no sooner set foot on Neapolitan soil than an Irish priest, Abbé Campbell, introduced himself, with messages from friends and acquaintances. The Abbé, who attached himself to the Duke like a leech, was the sort of gossippy, ingratiating Mr Know-it and Mr Fix-it of which most expatriate communities boast an example, and with whom new arrivals engage at their peril. He claimed to have an inside track to the king's Prime Minister, the Chevalier de Medicis, and was rumoured to take an impression of every seal that passed through the city's post office. Very probably he did some useful espionage work on the side; it made little difference to him whether it was for the English, Austrian or Neapolitan governments, so long as he was paid. The Duke found him useful.

> He was considered a bore, and a bit of a hanger-on. But I still found him
> very active and civil, and he did many things for me which I could not have
> well done without him. He told me all the gossip of the place, and put me
> au courant as to all that was passing.

Rooms in an inn on the sea-front were quickly engaged, of reasonable comfort. The Duke had his eye on something grander: a '*piano*' (floor) of a house overlooking the fashionable Riviera di Chiaia, perhaps, just

The Riviera di Chiaia, the promenade of Neapolitan society

back from the harbour, where Neapolitan high society liked to promenade in the evening, and where he could sit on his balcony and watch the pretty girls walking or driving past in the street below. Several such pianos were available.

That evening he took a box at the Teatro di San Carlo, a short stroll from his sea-front lodgings, and saw an opera and a ballet, both new productions. He didn't think much of the opera, but liked the ballet. He thought the German ballerina very handsome and that she danced beautifully. The opera-house, which opened in November 1737, was – and still is – one of the biggest in Europe, with nearly 3,000 seats. Today it faces out onto the city's busiest, noisiest traffic intersection, the Piazza Trieste e Trento, where you can sit of an evening and admire the death-defying manoeuvres of Neapolitan drivers. In those days the piazza outside must have been a quieter, more sedate affair, filled on opera-nights with carriages and coachmen and hansom-cabs. Inside the theatre, though, all was hubbub and inattention. During a performance the Neapolitans liked to stroll from box to box and greet their friends, men and women, not with demure English handshakes, but with smacking kisses that resounded round the house. They gossiped and booed and spat orange peel, and paid attention only to a favourite aria or dance. If they were bored, they disappeared into one of the gambling rooms adjacent to the auditorium. Singers needed powerful voices to make themselves heard above the din.

The Duke enjoyed his evening, taking equal delight in what he saw off-stage as on: the fashionable dresses of the women, the gala suits of the men, the glittering uniforms of regimental officers, the wax torches that illuminated the great auditorium with a smoky, flickering light.

The San Carlo theatre where the audience strolled from box to box

The king was there – he had clearly changed his mind about going shooting – accompanied by his wife, his brother the Duke of Sorrento, and a gaggle of their more grown-up children. The Queen, Maria Isabella, daughter of the Bourbon King of Spain (Charles IV), appeared to him very fat, coarse and red-faced. She was rumoured – no doubt by the sly-tongued Abbé Campbell – to be beaten regularly by the king for her infidelities, but was said to prefer his beatings to his kisses. The royal boxes were on the same side of the house as his own, and the Duke flattered himself that he saw the king and queen leaning forward to try and get a glimpse of him, once they'd heard he was there. He was surprised and rather shocked that only polite applause greeted the Royal entrance, and silence their departure: in England, he thought, it would have been reckoned a very cool reception. He bumped into some acquaintances from Sicily, who asked him to a ball after the opera, but he turned the invitation down. He was feeling knocked up after a long day, he explained; anyway, it would have been bad manners to accept a private ball (at which he knew the king's brother would be present) without first paying his respects to the king.

By the next day, the fog had lifted. Vesuvius was still capped in cloud, but the bay was clear.

> The effect of the sunlight upon the whole range of Naples, its towns, villages, palazzi, and villas, all along the mountain's brow, and up its lava-encrusted side, was beautiful beyond expression.

He had been presented with a perfect excuse for temporary social withdrawal. His aunt, the Margravine of Anspach, born Elizabeth

The Bay of Naples – 'beautiful beyond expression' (Francis Towne)

Berkeley in 1750, had suddenly died in her villa at Chiaramonté on the city's outskirts, and he was forced into mourning at least until after her funeral. The old lady was a keen gardener, and only three weeks before had been energetically forking over her borders and enjoying her wonderful view out over the Bay of Naples. But digging on a cold wet day had been the death of her. She caught a chill which developed into a terminal fever. In her day the redoubtable Margravine had been a great beauty, much admired by Horace Walpole, who published her play 'La Somnabule' in 1778 and wrote poems to her. A stipple engraving of her by William Ridley shows her aged about 24 and looking long-necked and ravishingly pretty. In 1780 she left her first husband, Lord Craven, whom she had married as a young girl and couldn't abide, and when he died in Switzerland in 1791, she married her lover, the Margrave of Anspach, within a few days of getting the good news. After the Margrave's death in 1806 she settled in Naples and became a leader of expatriate English society there. An independent, lively-minded woman who loved music and poetry, she was the author of several books, including accounts of travels to Constantinople and the Crimea, and in Russia and France just before the Revolution.

The Duke, arriving at her villa just too late to find her alive, was asked by her son, Keppel Craven, to witness the opening of her will, which he duly did. The will was complicated by the fact that, in 1792, the

The Duke's aunt, the remarkable Margravine of Anspach, 'ravishingly pretty'
(from an engraving by Ridley)

Margrave had sold his principality to the King of Prussia and settled in Hammersmith (Brandenburg House) and Berkshire (Benham Park), but the deal had never been fully honoured, and the Margravine was still waiting for payment when she died. The Duke, with all his experience of debt, advised Keppel to write the money off. Four days later he was in the slow procession that followed her coffin. It was covered in red velvet, on a barouche drawn by her four grey horses, and the cortège wound through the streets of Naples to the English cemetery.

> It is a very quiet, good burying-ground, shut in by gates and surrounded by a high wall.

The old lady, matter-of-fact and Protestant, had left strict instructions that her body should be buried in her adopted city, and was on no account to be carted all the way across Europe, to lie beside her second husband, the Margrave, in Berkshire. Something of the sort (being carted across Europe) had happened in recent memory with the unhappy corpse of the Duchess of Devonshire.

On February 3rd, a fortnight after the funeral, the Duke finally had an audience with the king. He turned up at the Palazzo Reale, not far from his lodgings on the sea-front, at 11 o'clock on a Sunday morning, in evening dress. The king's small private apartments, he discovered to his dismay, were as far away as possible from the Palazzo's entrance, and he had to puff his way up five flights of stairs, and through endless corridors and galleries full of 'frotteurs, garçons, peruquiers, restaurateurs, women selling oranges, priests, and soldiers idling about'. In the end he asked for help from a private of the guard, who showed him the door of the

The Royal Palace in Naples. The Duke had to climb to the top floor in great heat and full regalia to meet the King of the Two Sicilies

The King's family paying homage to his father

anteroom to the king's apartments. They overlooked the medieval, five-towered, heavily-guarded Castel Nuovo next door. A covered passage from the Palazzo led to an arsenal on the harbour-front, where his yacht was kept on permanent stand-by, ready for sea at a moment's notice. Francis I liked a good exit at his back – and you can hardly blame him, remembering what had happened to his aunt, Marie Antoinette,[62] in France

The audience lasted about half an hour, and seems to have been cordial enough. The room in which he was received was tiny, about ten feet square 'and not near so good as that to my apartments at the inn'. Two chamberlains in court dress were in attendance, and various pages and servants milled about in the doorway. A few minutes after the Duke's arrival the king entered by another door from his own private apartments and the chamberlains knelt and kissed his hand. Portraits of Francis painted around this time suggest an outdoor type, a slightly dilapidated cavalry officer who has seen better days: mutton-chop whiskers turning to grey, blue eyes and a high colour, a receding auburn hair-line, a forward stoop supported by a stick. The king was ceremonious and charming. He thanked the Duke for all the help he and his family had given the Bourbon family in England after their exile from revolutionary France, and for his general support to the cause of Royalty. The Duke demurred. It was his father who had helped the Bourbons, he insisted. He had only followed his father's example. As for the cause of Royalty, he had merely done his duty as a loyal subject and citizen in maintaining the principles of constitutional monarchy. The point was not lost on Francis, who quickly changed the subject to that of gout. They were both sufferers from its agonising pains, caused by deposits of uric acid in the joints. Today the disease is thought to be hereditary, but it was generally believed at the beginning of the 19th century that lack of exercise, combined with rich food and fortified wines like port, sherry and madeira, were the culprits – the poor seemed infrequent victims – and the usual prescription was an anchorite's lifestyle coupled with a course of drops distilled from the highly-poisonous root of Meadow Saffron (*Colchicum autumnale*). The Duke had only just recovered from a bad attack, and the king regretted he hadn't made use of the special royal gout-chair that had been offered to him during his illness. Thus they chatted happily on, united in sympathy by their ailment.

The king showed off his latest toy:

> a regular room or cabinet for four people, which by a counterpoise is raised up the well of the staircase to the top, and he can stop it at pleasure at any piano he chooses. In short, it appears to me like a large parrot cage or staircase lanthorn.

The Duke was impressed by this early, royal example of a lift. They parted with expressions of lasting friendship and gratitude, and the king promised to invite him to a chasse he was planning within the next few days.

Six days later, at ten o'clock on the morning of February 9th, the Duke arrived in his coach at Lago d'Agnano, a volcanic lake (nowadays overarched by the *tangenziale* motorway out of the city) some four miles west of Naples on the road to Baia and Pozzuoli. The lake lies in a highly unstable area of volcanic activity known to the ancients as the Phlegrean Fields. Here, steam and sulphur gases vent through fumaroles, and mud pits bubble and plop. The land is gradually sinking by a process known as *Bradyseism* (a kind of long-drawn-out earthquake protracted over thousands of years). Hither, ever since classical times, gout and arthritis sufferers had come in summer to take the spa waters.

The whiff of sulphur gas, like rotten eggs, assaulted the Duke's nostrils as his carriage descended the hill to the lake. Piles of locally-grown flax being steeped and softened at the water's edge added to the potent brew. The lake's surface, he noted, was teeming with wildfowl preserved for royal sport.

Today, though, the quarry was *cinghiale*, wild boar. The king had arrived just before him. They both transferred from their carriages into waiting droshkis – low, open, four-wheel, horse-drawn carriages, good across country – in which they climbed the hill above the lake and arrived at the edge of an extinct volcano, Astroni. Its crater was about three miles round at the top and rimmed by a wall, and its deep interior was covered with a tangle of maquis underwood and mature trees, mostly oak. Half-way down the crater was an inner reserve, bounded by a high wooden stockade, about a mile and a half round, with gates that could be opened and closed at will, and at its bottom was a fair-sized pond stocked with freshwater fish. This was the king's biggest and best *cinghiale* reserve, of which he was very proud. For several days his keepers had been feeding outlying boar and deer into the inner enclosure. Now the gates were shut, and many unfortunate animals trapped within.

The shooting-party drove round the crater to the king's Casino, or hunting-lodge, where they dismounted, and the king busied himself giving orders to his keepers, and suggesting various improvements. Here he seemed to feel safe. His only guard was a dragoon orderly, whom he kept near him for carrying messages, and he allowed the local people to press close around him with their petitions. The Duke was impressed by the king's patience and politeness, and the fact that he answered them in their own tongue, Neapolitan not Italian. (It is intriguing that the Duke's snapshot of Francis at this moment denies the accepted historical view.) Then the Queen arrived, accompanied by two younger princes and her 21-year-old daughter, Princess Maria Christina, 'a very pretty, pleasing, amiable girl' who had recently – and very wisely, in the Duke's view – turned down an offer of marriage[63] from an international scoundrel, the recently-widowed Portuguese Emperor of Brazil. Others in the shooting-party included the king's younger brother, the Prince of Salerno, and Prince Pignatelli, a Sicilian nobleman who, in spite of serving as one of Murat's cavalry commanders during the French wars, had managed to ingratiate himself as a favourite at court. There were 16 guns in all, including the Queen and the Princess, both very keen shots.

The shooters took their places in a line of butts within the inner enclosure. It is unclear from the Duke's account whether the line ran across or down the slope (probably the latter, the boar being driven round the hill). Each butt was surrounded with a breast-high dead hedge to conceal the shooter, and inside were a chair and a foot-mat, and space not only for the shooter, but also for a *chasseur* and a personal servant too, one or the other acting as loader. Outside under the hedge crouched two more servants with boar spears. The Duke had turned down the offer of a loan of guns from the king, preferring his own matching pair of double-barrelled shotguns, by Joseph Manton[64] of Piccadilly, which he had landed, with his books, from the *Anna Eliza*.

The *battue* began. It seems extraordinary that no-one was killed, or at least wounded. A hot February wind, already too hot for the sweating Duke, was blowing up from the African desert, and the crater caught the sun. There were about 80 in the shooting-line, including all the servants. A battalion of infantry, dressed as peasants and armed with sticks and with dogs at heel, drove the boar towards the shooters in the line.

> The effect was very fine. The scenery was grand and romantic to a degree, and the echoes of the horns, men, and hounds, very cheering.

Rifles had been banned, for fear of ricochets off rocks, but, even so, heavy ball-shot from shotguns was soon whizzing around the crater in all directions and the Duke was understandably nervous.

> It is dangerous work, as, in spite of all our precautions, the balls flew about nearer than I thought was prudent. One cut a tree not ten yards from me. But the danger was greater for the beaters, none of whom, however, were hurt; and accidents, I am told never occur.

As soon as a boar was shot or wounded, the two men crouching by the butt with boar spears rushed forward to finish it off, thus adding to the general mêlée in front of the guns.

The boar, trapped inside the enclosure, were not so fortunate. The shooting didn't stop for three hours, and at the end of it 236 lay dead. Even the Duke, not particularly squeamish by the standards of the day, was taken aback. It was 'but tame shooting after all, and bloody work'. But he admitted that it was a magnificent sight, and that he would have been sorry to have missed it. After it was all over, the boar were laid out in a long line and refreshments were served and the various shots praised and discussed, while hunting horns snorted and tootled their tales of shooting prowess. The Prince of Salerno had killed 35, the King 25, Prince Pignatelli 21, the Duke 17, the Queen 13, Princess Christina 12 –

and so on down the line. Then the weather closed in – by evening it was blowing a gale – and the shooting-party climbed into the king's droshkis and drove away, and the sound of hunting horns dwindled behind them into the distance.

That evening, although quite knocked up, he went, at the Queen's command, to the Teatro di San Carlo to hear the final act of *Il Ultimo Giorno di Pompeii*.[65] It was pouring with rain, and the wind was blowing hard. A full house had turned up for a benefit night for the bass singer, Lablache, who was a great favourite with Neapolitan opera-goers, and the Duke was impressed by his singing, and the set which showed Vesuvius erupting. The king was not there – his gout was troubling him – but the rest of the royal family were in their boxes and the Queen pleased the Duke no end by sending a polite note, via Prince Pignatelli, hoping he was not too tired out from the day's sport.

CHAPTER TEN

Viva Il Signor Duca!

January and the first half of February were carnival time in Naples, before the rigours of Lent, and the Duke, his gout gradually improving, began to enjoy getting out into Neapolitan society and joining in the fun. Half-heard melodies are sweetest, and the Duke would have caught echoes in street and salon of the glory days of Naples before the Great Wars, when the city was the cultural capital of Europe; a rendezvous for writers, artists and musicians to exchange ideas and learn their crafts, and for Grand Tourists to be astonished by the magnificence and pageantry of the Bourbon court. Now, once again, there were banquets and carriage processions, and masked balls with many English in attendance. At one ball he counted over 100 of his countrymen. In the San Carlo, where the orchestra pit had been boarded over on a level with the Duke's private box on the bottom tier, a masker leant over and made love to a young unmarried Englishwoman in his party, giving her a nosegay and squeezing her hand in a most forward manner. He turned out to be a waiter in a local hotel. On Sundays the Naples *lazzaroni* good-humouredly pelted the carriages of aristocrats with bon-bons as they drove up and down the two principal thoroughfares, the Via Toledo and the Riviera di Chiaia, and the carriage-occupants did their best to chuck them back. On the last Sunday in January the king and queen joined the carnival procession in an open carriage drawn by two horses and accompanied by only two outriders, and the *lazzaroni* milled about them, cheering and waving wildly, delighted that their sovereigns should come among them in such an easy, friendly way.

The Duke was riding in a carriage in the same procession.

I got a very severe blow from a complimentary dragée, as big as my thumb, in the face, and it requires great skill and good humour sometimes to avoid, and to be, or to appear to be, pleased with the shot. Sometimes the mischievous boys throw stones instead of sugar-plums; but this is severely noticed immediately by the police, who are in active attendance.

At the end of February he heard that an English family were about to move out of their lodgings on the Riviera di Chiaia. The *piano* they had occupied – the entire first floor of a palazzo – had a lovely view of the bay, and was large, airy and comfortably-furnished. The Duke took it for 200 ducats[66] for the month of March to include all linen and china, and moved out of his inn. There were changes, too, to his party. Francis Lunn, his grave, high-minded chaplain and member of the Royal Society, seems to have become ill-at-ease with what he perceived as the louche society of Naples – too many idlers in the city, too much amorous intrigue – and asked to be allowed to return to England. The Duke was sorry to lose his young friend and geologising companion, but agreed to his departure, and probably used his family's influence to obtain a living for him, for the next we hear of Lunn[67] is that he was installed in 1828 as vicar of Butleigh with Baltonsborough[68] in Somerset, whose patron was the Hon and Revd G Neville Grenville. The Duke wrote to the Bishop of Norwich asking for permission to appoint the Revd Robert Wilson as acting chaplain in Lunn's place. At about this time, too, the Vicomte de Chabot and his son Philippe, who had sailed with him from England, left for Rome.

The tipping-point with Lunn seems to be have been an incident involving a young English catholic soldier of fortune called Stapleton who had distinguished himself at Navarino[69] and who was in a high state of excitement after being approached by an attractive woman at a masked ball. She spoke several languages, gave him a ring and a rendezvous, and claimed to be of high rank.

> Stapleton was fool enough to tell this to Lunn and his friends, and to spread it amongst his female acquaintance of his bonnes fortunes. Lunn told me with much gravity, and mentioned it as a proof of the corruption of morals here among the highest order &c, &c ... Lunn, if he were writing a tour, would inevitably have inserted this incident, as one happening within his own knowledge, and cite it as a proof of the manner in which all Neapolitan Principessi, without distinction, conduct themselves.

Stapleton's friends later discovered the woman was a dresser for one of the dancers in the San Carlo chorus: an excuse for much teasing.

The journal is full of shadows, dark interstellar spaces where what isn't recorded seems of much greater significance than what is. What was Lunn's relationship with the Duke? Why did he leave the cruise? Did he have reason to disapprove of his employer's conduct? Was the Duke behaving disreputably in some way?[70]

They remained, anyway, on good terms after his departure. On December 31st 1830, a year after he had returned to England, the Duke wrote to Lunn at Butleigh asking for an opinion about some Greek inscriptions on vases that Lucien Bonaparte[71] had sent him from Canino in Etruria. The Duke's handwriting in his journal and in letters to his political clients is generally a hurried, forward-sloping, more-or-less-illegible scrawl. In this letter[72] there is a noticeable improvement. The Duke has taken some trouble with his script. One gets the impression – it's only a guess – that the Duke thought Lunn rather a prude, but at the same time was a little in awe of his scholarship and integrity, and desired his good opinion.

On February 27th the Duke took the Wilsons and the rest of his party on a day's outing to the king's palace at Portici, now a part of the University of Naples, a few miles south-east along the bay towards Vesuvius. The king had given him permission to take his carriage into any of the royal parks and drive wherever he wished, at any time.

> The park is beautiful: the finest evergreen oaks I ever saw – the underwood myrtle and Mediterranean heath. The gardens and orangeries are beautiful, but in the Italian taste. The park is overgrown, just like an English park, with the finest views of the bay on one side, and of Vesuvius on the other, breaking in at every turn.

On a hill behind the park they visited a mock fort where the late queen, Maria Carolina, wife of the Lazzarone King, had once amused herself staging sham sieges and battles in which the loathed and feared Napoleon Bonaparte, who had ejected her from Naples in 1806, was defeated every time. In the dining-room was a table like the one they had seen in the Chinese Palace at Palermo, with lifts for dishes that went up and down. The table sat up to ten people. They examined the machinery underneath, and reckoned it would require at least four servants to work the trapdoor alone – more fuss and bother than the thing was worth, in the Duke's estimation.

The day was drawing on. Where to eat? Their choice, a folly in the park, proved embarrassing, but the Duke, mixing bravado, good manners and rapid French, managed to save the day.

Swiss cottages, and summer-houses, hermitages &c, are dotted about in tolerable good taste. In one of the latter my party voted it necessary, *à l'Anglaise*, to have their luncheon; and immediately, to the horror of all our Catholic conductors, who had assembled in some numbers to stare at us, an immense collection of pies and cold chicken, on *Wednesday in Lent*, was produced and attacked; and, just as every soul of us had got our mouths greasy and full, an alarm was given that the Queen was coming, having arrived from Naples.

In an instant our chicken-bones were thrown away, our baskets and scraps disappeared, and, just as we had got into decent and presentable order, I saw her Majesty and the Princess Christina at the further end of the walk. I immediately went up to her, leaving my party formed in single line, like all Englishmen and women, in a fuss, not knowing what to do with their hats, their heads, their fingers and their toes. I had to exhaust myself in apologies and speeches, in delights and sorrows, in horrors and re-joicings. She was very good-natured; asked what had become of my gout, of which it was evident she did not believe one word; asked who my party were, and desired the ladies might be presented to her, which I immediately did, with all the form of a Lord Chamberlain. We then took our leave; She told me the king was also *dans le parc*; so, as I found the groves were peopled with grand folks, we all bundled into our carriages, and drove off without ever looking behind us.

March 8th. A London druggist lodges in the palazzo where I live, and sports the fine gentleman. He gave a dinner on Thursday to twenty people, some Neapolitan officers and apothecaries amongst them. They got drunk with champagne, and in their folly broke all his china, and some of his furniture …

The same day, the Duke and his party made an expedition out to Pompeii, where the king had ordered a special *scavo* [excavation] to be made in his honour. In 1748 a chance inspection of an underground aqueduct first indicated the existence, at the foot of Vesuvius, of the important Campanian town buried by volcanic ash in the huge AD 79 eruption so vividly described by Pliny the Younger. His uncle, the elder Pliny, was the Roman admiral in command at the Misenum naval base at the time and was trying to embark refugees on the shore of the Bay of Naples when he was overwhelmed by the same ash-avalanche that destroyed Pompeii. For nearly 1700 years the town was covered by a fertile field growing vines and mulberries, with no trace of the archaeological treasures – Roman lives, art and artefacts suspended at a moment in time – that lay beneath. Haphazard excavations began in 1763, were continued in a more serious way by the French and by Murat during their 1806–1814 occupation, then relapsed into random digging under the restored Bourbons in 1815. It wasn't until 1861 that the Italian government finally got a systematic, scientific grip on the town's excavation, dividing the town into nine sections and proceeding methodically, and very, very slowly.

Pompeii. (Hannah Palones)
The excavators were not 'anxious that we should find much'

In 1828, according to the Duke's account, a typical archaeological procedure was for workmen to clear a street first; then, house by house, empty the rooms of rubbish down to within three feet of the floor.

> The workmen then leave the rooms, and the excavations are finished at leisure, either in the presence of the King or of such persons as he chooses to favour with an exhibition; but no excavation is allowed to be finished unless by his order. The first room we attacked was evidently a glass shop.

We came directly to vast numbers of lachrymatories, essence bottles, glass tumblers broken, and a quantity of glass for windows.

Scattered about the floor of another room, in a private house, they found various bronze vessels, including a basin, ewer and kettle, which suggested that the occupants had been surprised at table, while preparing or eating a meal. But the *scavo* was fast developing into a farce.

Another was then opened, and they were going on until I detected that they evidently were opening a room which had before been excavated, as there was a great dab of fresh modern plaster work in the wall, which extended from half way up the wall down to the floor. The earth must therefore have been removed to get at it, and the room probably filled up by the rubbish thrown in from other walls. Obeying their orders to give me a *scavo*, it was of little interest to them whether my time was occupied by excavating ancient or modern ground, and they naturally were anxious to preserve all that they thought best for the King ... It struck me that our *conducteurs* were far from energetic in their researches, or anxious that we should find much.

A crowd had gathered to watch the fun, and in the general hustle and bustle one of his party, a Mrs Townshend, lost a valuable watch that had been hanging at her side. The workmen spent the rest of the day in search of it, re-digging over the ground they had already dug once (or twice) before, and there was a barely-concealed suspicion that one of them might have stolen it. Mrs Townshend returned to Pompeii a week later, on the off-chance of finding the watch, and there it was lying in a corner of the forum civile where she remembered having stood.

It was a frustrating day. In the end they wandered rather aimlessly around the already-excavated ruins, then had a meal in a tent which had been erected for the Duke's party in the forum. He toured the streets in a small caleche and saw the pavement-ruts made by cart-wheels in the time of the Emperor Titus. Titus, son of Vespasian, with the reputation in the Roman world of being a cruel, profligate man, nevertheless visited the scene of the disaster in 79, and reached deep into his own pocket for the relief of survivors.

On March 13th the Duke gave a dinner-party in his *piano*, followed by dancing, and found to his surprise that it was difficult to get the Italians in the party on to the dance floor. Their king, who was devout, disapproved of the practice during Lent. So they sat and watched while the English danced. There was gossip that there had been an earthquake at Ischia in the Bay of Naples, with much loss of life; and that the police intended to arrest the son of an Italian duke who, race-riding his horse down a Naples street, had knocked over the Austrian ambassador, the Count de Figuelmont, and never stopped to apologise. It was the count's pride that was the most injured part of his person. A passing coachman who had picked him up and taken him home was locked up instead, to prevent his evidence becoming contaminated. Other gossip – this must have raised a laugh – was that the Duke had been targeted by Greek pirates with orders to take him alive. When he first arrived in Naples, he had been laid up with gout and the word had gone round that he was one of George IV's younger brothers, travelling incognito. Greek pirates had evidently got hold of the tale and were on the look-out for his substantial, and hopefully valuable, frame.

At this time, also, the Bourbon government of the Two Sicilies seems to have suspected that the Duke wasn't all that he seemed. His correspondence with England was always being opened or going astray. He complained to the king's First Minister, the Chevalier de Medicis, who promised to do something about it. He threatened going direct to the King. He even confronted the sly priest, the Abbé Campbell, whom he was sure was at the bottom of it. But nothing much changed.

March 14th. Today at twelve o'clock detonations were heard from Vesuvius, and a small aperture was formed in the centre of the great crater; fire issued with a vast quantity of smoke, and stones were thrown up. This continued all day. Nothing is to be seen from the cone but a great crown of smoke, as the flame is confined to this small aperture, and the stones and fiery matter which are thrown up are not cast high enough to be seen from the exterior.

The next day the Duke drove out to the foot of the mountain, which continued to rumble and smoke, to take a closer look. The word from the guides was that an eruption might be imminent, but that it was still fairly safe to travel on the mountain. The surest sign of its being about to burst – a sinking of the water in the wells – had not yet occurred. Ash debris was being thrown up about 50 feet within the crater, from a fiery crack ten feet wide, and the best way to see the spectacle, according to the guides, was to climb up and peer down into the crater's interior. They were delighted by the mountain's renewed activity, excellent for business. For six years Vesuvius had been asleep, with no visible fire and hardly any smoke, and word was beginning to get around that the mountain had become extinct.

Since the great eruption of AD 79, almost nuclear in its magnitude, there have been more than 100 other occasions when Vesuvius has blown its top: the last in 1944. At 4202 feet high, it isn't, like Etna, a colossus. Its position, though, looming over Naples, makes it capable of catastrophe on a colossal scale.

On March 21st, 1828, with smoke and detonations still on the increase, the Duke decided to attempt its ascent.

> I drove to Resina in my carriage, there ascended a mule and rode to the Hermitage, romantically situated in a grove of fine elms and chestnuts, within two miles of the foot of the cone … Here we rested, and here we first heard the detonations of the mountain, sounding like a loud but heavy salute of large cannon. At the Hermitage is a guard of gens-d'armes stationed, three of whom attends every party which goes up the mountain, and remains with it during its stay there; for, three years ago, a party of strangers was robbed; and the woods and roads that skirt the lower region of the mountain are not of good repute.

According to the Duke, the 1822 eruption had blown the sharp top of the volcano clean off.[73] He watched fascinated as majestic plumes of smoke, like great bales of cotton – pink, buff, pure white and deepest black – rose from its flattened apex into the blue Mediterranean sky.

> As we proceeded to the foot of the cone, we passed the small crater at the foot of the mountain from whence lava issued in 1822, and into which a wretched Frenchman threw himself, for the purpose of self-destruction, that effectually answered, for not a shred or bit of him was ever seen again …

At the foot of the cone he exchanged his mule for an open sedan chair, with a muscular porter on each one of the four shafts. They set off with him up the highly unstable, 30-degree slope, sinking up to their knees in ash at every step and often slipping backwards.

> The guides assured me they could do it; and Prince Leopold, the King's brother – a much larger man than myself – had been carried up with perfect success. The men achieved their task, but with immense fatigue, and even with great fatigue to me. The declivity threw the chair upon its back. Had

A plump tourist descending Vesuvius. The Duke needed four porters

I leant back too I should have performed an unwieldy somersault over the heads of the bearers in the rear. I was, therefore, obliged to sit bolt upright on the edge of the chair, holding on as best I could by the ropes and poles which supported me, unable to help myself, and depending wholly upon my wrists, as, had I let go, I must have turned over inevitably backwards and gone down the mountain's side. It seems absurd to talk of *my* fatigue, being thus *carried*, instead of being the *carrier*; but, I declare, I never was before so exhausted, or so near losing my senses and fainting, from exertion. The bearers changed every ten minutes; and although the ashes retired from under their steps, and immense masses rolled thus to the bottom, they at length succeeded, and lodging me upon the edge of the crater, cried out, with a cheer, 'Viva Il Signor Duca!'

The chief guide for the mountain was called Salvatore. He lived at Resina, put in a daily report to the Government about the state of the mountain, and loved gossipping about travellers who had climbed it. In 1830 he told the diarist Charles Greville that one of his toughest assignments had been helping an Englishman win a bet that he could ride relays of horses from Resina to the crater's rim in under 90 minutes (they did the five miles in 73, Salvatore on foot all the way). '*He said it nearly killed him, and he did not recover [from] it for several weeks; he is 53 years old, but a very handsome man. He said, however, that the fatigue of this exploit was not so painful as what he went through in carrying the Duke of Buckingham to the top; he was carried up in a chair by twelve men, and the weight was so enormous that his shoulder was afterwards swelled up nearly to his head.*'[74]

✳   ✳   ✳

The Duke lay down, steadied himself against a rock, and peered nervously over the edge – into a perpendicular hole some 500 feet deep, at the bottom of which were three vents, the biggest about 40 feet wide, vomiting fire, ash and blood-red molten lava. Ash and lava shot up continuously into the air within the crater like rocket fireworks, almost to the level at which he sat. He timed the descent of some of the bigger objects on a stopwatch at seven seconds. It was all very alarming. The heat was intense, the mountain never stopped shaking, and the noise was ear-splitting: in the Duke's words like a stormy sea hitting a cliff, mixed with the noise of thunder, battery-cannon and the clang of iron bars.

The Duke's energetic sketch of Vesuvius in action

Even the guides were nervous. They made him shift his ground twice, away from unstable rock at the crater's rim, and called for the attendant gendarmes when madcap members of his party suggested climbing down into the inferno on a rope. The bottom of the crater was visibly filling up with lava, and billows of choking smoke, fortunately blown away from them at the top by the wind, rolled about its interior.

Overleaf: Vesuvius by night during a major eruption (Giovanni Battista Lusieri)

The effect of this scene was at first so awful as to take away all feeling but that of dread, and all recollection save that of the scene before our eyes. It was long before any of us could speak, and longer before we could lay down at ease. We did so, however, and, wrapped up in our cloaks, remained there until eight o'clock at night, the darkness making the scene more dreadfully beautiful. At length we descended by torchlight.

Two days later, on the 22nd, the minor activity of the mountain reached its climax. Fire was clearly visible above the rim from Naples, with molten rock and ash being thrown high into the air, most of it falling back into the crater without damage. No dangerous side-vents had been reported opening up on the volcano's flanks, so far as anyone knew. At two o'clock in the afternoon an immense column of smoke arose. The Duke had a theodolite set up and ready to go on the balcony of his piano, and measured its altitude. The angle subtended was 14 degrees. Counting four degrees for the mountain, he reckoned the smoke rose 9,000 feet into the air above its summit.

On March 28th he wrote home to Thomas Fremantle, MP for Buckingham and a political fixer for what remained of the Grenville Connection in the House of Commons: 'My health which was bad in the Winter is now just re-established and I hope to be able to enjoy the lovely spring of this delicious climate. Of politics I do not like to say much …'[75]

CHAPTER ELEVEN

Beside a pumice isle.

April 1st. I return on board my yacht, tired of Naples, and glad to find myself in my own home again. My lacquais de place, Giovanni Gandolfi, excellent, finding out the oddest holes and corners in which to stick his clarionet, snuff-box and music book. I heard much objurgation going on between Captain Wilcox and him. 'You must put nothing there, I tell you. I say I won't have it!' exclaimed the former.

'Indeed, Mistere Villicock, it vill not be in no vay at all!' whined out the latter.

'I tell you it shan't be!' reiterated the former.

The Grotto at Posillipo (William Pars)

It was Holy Week. For two days from midday on Maunday Thursday the city fell silent: no bells, no carriages in the streets, the flags of Catholic ships in the Bay at half-mast, sentries with their arms reversed, the faint sound of the Miserere from distant churches. The king and queen washed the feet of 12 poor men in public, and the Host was carried about in silent mourning, followed by penitents dressed in white.

I am glad that I am on board – I dislike making sights of religious processions or ceremonies, which are contrary to my own ideas of religion.

On Good Friday he slipped away in his barge to reconnoitre the coast westwards, towards Posillipo. The tufa shoreline was a tangle of aloe, prickly pear, myrtle and tree heath, the latter bearing clusters of white, sweet-scented, spring flowers. Here and there he saw ruined villas of the Neapolitan nobility, their neglected gardens running down to the sea. Beyond Posillipo he came across the remains of a two-storey Roman villa, built on arches out over the water, through one of which he rowed into a watery hall. The roof was off. Otherwise it looked as if it had been lived in almost yesterday.

'a roman villa, built on arches at Posillipo' – was this it? (Thos Jones)

6th. Easter Sunday. Service on board, and service and the Sacrament at the British Consul's. All the Catholic world in jubilee. Every one out on the streets in their best clothes, and all rejoicing at having got rid of Lent.

The King had let it be known that he expected the Duke to attend his court at midday after Mass, for a gala reception. The Duke replied politely that Easter Sunday was just as important a festival to Protestants as to Catholics, and at midday he and his party would be celebrating Holy Communion on board the *Anna*, conducted by his new acting chaplain, Robert Wilson. Privately, the Duke had little time for the King's exaggerated Catholic piety, worked up into a frenzy, in his opinion, by a neurotic alliance of Jesuit priests and a jumped-up *valet de chambre*. The influence with the King of his first minister, the Chevalier de Medicis, seemed negligible by comparison.

At daybreak on Easter Monday morning the *Anna* slipped her moorings, warped herself into the outer harbour, and shook loose her sails. As she tacked tediously from one side of the Bay of Naples to the other in light airs, one of the new paddle steam-boats, carrying Easter day-trippers to Capri, came puffing past at 13 miles an hour. On the northern shore he spotted the remains of a villa, now a total ruin, that had once belonged to the Roman voluptuary Lucullus. A begging friar, standing among the ruins and making the sign of the cross and blessing fishermen as they passed, inspired in the Duke an Ozymandias moment. With a sinking heart he remembered Stowe, and wondered if similar devastation lay in store one day for his beloved old home.[76]

That evening the *Anna*, shadowed by a government schooner that he suspected of being a spy ship, glided quietly on to moorings under the Castle of Baia.[77] The schooner, as if by accident, moored close by. In classical times Baia was the most exclusive seaside and spa resort in the Roman world, a place where the rich and powerful took the waters, enjoyed the wonderful colour and light, and competed with each other in building ever grander and more luxurious homes. Here, so the story went, a little boy made friends with a dolphin and rode it to school every day across to the other side of the bay, and the emperor Caligula built a bridge of boats to fulfil a prophecy that he would ride his horse from shore to shore. But now the Bay of Baia was silent and deserted; the proud villas, baths and temples lay in ruins or underwater; and the Duke, remembering Stowe, was overcome by homesickness and depression.

The next day he and his party were rowed in the *Anna*'s barge to Pozzuoli, where they mounted mules and donkeys for a visit to Lake Avernus. The lake, which now stands at the foot of Monte Nuovo, a little 460-ft extinct volcano thrown up by a minor eruption in 1538, was regarded in Roman myth as the entrance to the Underworld: a crepuscular, doom-laden place where even the birds were believed to drop dead if they flew over its evil-smelling water. But the Duke saw coots and moorhens happily paddling about on its surface, and according to the guides the lake was full of tench and eels. He tasted its water and found it sweet and fresh. He counted himself lucky, however, that he was visiting Avernus in April, not August.

> No one can visit the lake in summer-time without danger – no one can sleep upon its banks, and wake again in life.

At this date it was still widely believed that malaria (literally 'bad air') was caused by poisonous vapours from hot swamps, especially at night.[78]

> A narrow path, amongst the brushwood, leads to the Sibyl's Grotto, formerly a place of interest … But an official, resident at Pozzuoli, having no right or title to the ground, or to the cave, and having no authority from the Government, still thought that he might make money of the place, and make the fabled descent into hell contribute to the income of a Neapolitan judge. So he has walled up one end of the grotto next to the Lucrine lake, and has built a door in the other, the key of which he keeps at Pozzuoli, four miles off, and will deliver to the curious only on the payment of a fee.
>
> After I had ascertained that this act was done without the authority of Government, and that the person who had done it was, in no respect, proprietor of the ground, I directed my sailors to batter down the door, which they did in an instant; and I sent my lacquais de place to Pozzuoli to the police, to lodge a complaint against the judge, to say that the door had been beat down by my orders and men, and that the guides of the place had not done it. I did this as, otherwise, the roguish judge would have visited my sins upon the wretched guides, as he had, in fact, begun to do, having issued an order for the arrest of my guide to-morrow morning. As it was, the police acknowledged the justice of my complaint, refused to receive the judge's, or to arrest the man, and sent to me to desire me, on no account, to pay him a grain for his broken door.

On the way home they visited steam baths cut into tufa cliffs on the sea-shore and attached to a prestigious villa.

At the further end is a low, arched recess, into which the moment you enter you experience the current of hot vapour, which in an instant envelopes you. If you proceed further you must, like your guide, strip yourself, taking off your shirt, and everything but your drawers. This, of course, I did not do, but others of my party did, and penetrated down into a narrow passage, at the end of which rises an immense boiling spring. At the entrance into this gallery my thermometer stood at 116 deg of Fahrenheit. In the water the mercury flew up directly the whole length of the tube, and as a bucket was drawn up full, into which fresh eggs were put, that in three minutes' time were perfectly boiled, it was not necessary further to examine the quantum of its temperature … Those who visited the spring came back the colour of boiled lobsters, with their faces and eyes inflamed, and their entire persons pouring down with perspiration. The greatest care must of course be taken to cover up most carefully and warmly upon coming out of this mass of vapour into the outer air.

That evening, back on board the yacht, his chef Fontara cooked for dinner a pair of two-foot-long *murenae*, bought live earlier in the day from an enterprising fish-farmer.

The murena is an eel, with a skin spotted in stains of light and dark-red brown, of different sizes … They tasted rich, like any other eel perhaps; and certainly the knowledge that we were tasting a Roman delicacy did not counterbalance the unpleasant feeling arising from the fact that we were eating a disgusting snake-looking animal.

On April 10th, a blustery Thursday after Easter, the Duke and his party rounded Cape Misenum in the ship's barge and on its northern side explored the canal dug out in 37 BC by Cornelius Agrippa, Augustus's lieutenant. The canal connected Lake Misenum, otherwise known as the 'Mare Morto', with the ocean. Here for centuries was moored the great battle fleet of Rome's Mediterranean empire, crewed by 10,000 mainly Greek and Syrian sailors. The Duke could see underwater the remains of their barracks, arsenals and wharves. In the Duke's day the Mare Morto was dammed up with sluices as a royal fish-farm, its fish sold at high prices to profit the King's exchequer. The banks of the Mare Morto were planted with poplars and vines, but presented, in the Duke's opinion, a dull and dreary aspect and in summer, he thought, the surrounding countryside would be a malarial death-trap.

The Duke's sketch of the islands of Procida and Ischia

Early 19th century transport in Southern Italy (Lojacono)

On the 11th they returned to Pozzuoli and rode in a carriage, then on mules and asses, to the ancient city of Cumae, a Greek colony that succumbed to Roman power in the 3rd century BC. Its acropolis sits on a hill with dazzling sea-views out to the west towards Ischia.

On the top of the mount of Cuma are the ruins of the Temple of Apollo. It is now a heap of stone and rock ... I however brought away a part of a frieze representing a winged lion, two hollow sacrificial altars in fragments, forming portions of fluted columns, and a piece of richly-worked entablature. I also brought away four very complete and perfect amphorae, found in a house in Cuma, but was obliged to leave behind much that was too heavy to remove.

On their way home it came on to rain. At Bacoli they found temporary shelter in the Piscina Mirabilis, an underground reservoir excavated from the tufa. In Roman times an aqueduct from the River Serino had kept its five, enormous, pillar-supported sections topped up with fresh water for supplying the fleet at Misenum. Farther on, in the village of Santa Anna, he sheltered in a down-at-heel chandler's shop, where he bought some minor items and doled out copper money to the proprietress's five children who were milling about at his feet. Their mother was touched by his largesse, and gravely offered him for sale her youngest, a little boy of eight months.

A view of Nicida, from a 19th century postcard

April 12th. The rain of yesterday appears to have broken up the Neapolitan winter, and to have brought on spring. This morning we weighed anchor, and sailed out of the bay of Baiae for Procida, in a most lovely day. But, before my departure, I had the satisfaction of getting an amphora fished up out of the sea, from the ruins of Julius Caesar's villa, and another from those of Cicero's. Both are covered with oysters, serpulae, and barnacles. I find the conviction here is, that I am the King of England, or, at least, his brother.

The Castle and rock of Ischia (Leitch)

His Procida charts proved unreliable, and the *Anna* had to move cautiously onto her mooring under the Castle, taking lead-soundings as she went. Ferdinand had used the fortress to lock up political prisoners, and the rest of the little island, which today retains its integrity in a way that tourist-blighted Capri and Ischia have dismally failed to do, was reserved as yet another hunting-ground for the King. Three English ladies, the Misses Wilbraham, neighbours at his Chiaia apartment and now his temporary guests on the *Anna*, spent an uncomfortable night ashore in the royal hunting-lodge and came back in the morning infested with lice and fleas. He explored round the island in the *Anna*'s barge, and they caught some rabbits on the little islet of Vivara, now connected to Procida by a modern bridge and teeming with the wild rabbits that are still very much a part of the island's cuisine. The itinerant Romantic poet, Alphonse Lamartine, came here in 1811 and seduced a beautiful fisherman's daughter. She died of melancholia when he sailed away, but achieved literary immortality in his best-selling novel *Graziella*: not much compensation for a broken heart.

On the 14th he weighed anchor at daybreak and by breakfast time had found, unmarked on any of the charts, a safe, well-protected mooring below the Castle of Ischia. The Neapolitan spy ship was no longer shadowing him, and he took the opportunity to survey the anchorage for possible future use by Royal Navy men-of-war. From a cliff nearby labourers were cutting out huge blocks of tufa for anchoring tunny nets in the forthcoming season; a single tunny net with all its tackle cost, he discovered, an astonishing 500 ducats (in modern money, about £7,500).

He was keen to see with his own eyes in the north of the island the hot-springs[79] town of Casalmicciola which had been devastated by the earthquake in February, and talk to survivors of their experience. The next day he and his party set out on mules and donkeys, the only available transport on the island.

> A donkey with a most splendid jingling scarlet bridle, with a looking-glass in front and a small horn suspended to the cheek-piece, in order to avert the evil eye, was selected to carry sa Excellenza il Signor Duca.

He was horrified by what he found at his destination. The earthquake had hit on a Sunday when most of the inhabitants of Casalmicciola were in church. There was a hissing, rumbling sound which lasted for about a second, then a deafening explosion like a mine going off beneath their feet. The church cracked but didn't collapse. When the congregation rushed out into the street, however, they saw their town flattened. Few stay-at-homes survived.

> I wish I could say anything in favour of the humanity of the Government, or even of the people of Naples; but I cannot. They have done *nothing*. The English have subscribed liberally, and the people of Ischia bless them and the English Consul, Sir Henry Lushington, who himself came over and distributed money and necessaries to the sufferers. But the merchants and

nobility of Naples did not subscribe a *doit*. The Government has not given one farthing of relief. It has offered the wretched peasantry the money to rebuild their homes for seven years, at three per cent; but not one has accepted the offer, as at the end of the seven years the houses would become the property of the Government, in default of payment of principal and interest, and an enormous rent would be imposed upon them. Not a single tax, direct or indirect, has been remitted to them … I left the poor creatures gazing upon their ruined homes and buried relatives.

On the 18th April he circumnavigated Ischia in his barge, a distance he calculated at 22 miles. He admired the resilient way in which the islanders, undaunted by the earthquake, were going about their business. The summer quail season was just beginning, with huge numbers of exhausted birds of passage, migrating from north Africa, expected to drop down on the island, and he saw nets like those he was familiar with in England for catching woodcock being set out on the cliffs to welcome their arrival. He bought some for Fontara to cook for dinner. They cost a carlino[80] each.

Wherever a scrambling islander can plant his foot, he plants a vine, and builds a wall to protect the earth from crumbling away from it. As we sailed along, we saw the peasants sticking to the faces of the precipices, making ledges in the lava, and crumbling down decomposed tufa and laporillo upon it, to make a soil and plant a garden. The poor know not what meat is. Their bread is good and cheap. Their wine is excellent, and to be had for next to nothing. During the summer they have grapes, and figs, and oranges in profusion; fish, both fresh and salted – chiefly the latter; and *agrami*, which they find growing spontaneously, such as wild garlic, asparagus, &c.

The men are the finest race of beings I ever saw – tall, robust, black-eyed, active, and always gay. The women have a beautiful cast of features; but hard labour, the climate, and precocious child-bearing, reduce their figures to bundles of clothing, and dirt makes them disgusting.

On the 17th he ended his 10-day, island-hopping cruise and sailed back to Naples, where his younger sister Mary,[81] a Catholic convert, was waiting for him. She had travelled down from Rome with her husband, Lord Arundel, to visit him and witness the annual spring miracle of the liquefaction of St Januarius's (San Gennaro's) blood. Also waiting for him were letters from his wife and from his younger brother George,

Lady Mary Arundel, the Duke's sister.
She was a devout catholic

Lord Nugent.[82] The agitation for political reform and catholic emancipation was threatening civil strife in England, and George begged his older brother to come home and help his country in its hour of need. The Duke's reply was stubborn. No, he would not. He had no intention of coming home. His political career was over.

The Duchess's letter inspired a ghost story on the ship, with its news that Muir's[83] wife had died in childbirth and that she, the Duchess, was seeing to the welfare of his surviving children. On the very day his wife died, Muir had told Wilcox, Sharp and several others on board of a dream in which his wife had come to him and announced her death.

CHAPTER TWELVE

Malta Bound

April merged into May, a glorious Italian spring emblossomed the Kingdom in the Sun,[84] and the *Anna* set off south to explore the peninsula that extends south-west, like a gnarled finger, towards the island of Capri. In the Duke's day the picturesque little havens crouching along its coast beneath sheer limestone cliffs were connected with Naples by sea alone. On land there were only *mulietera*, rough mule paths, at best intermittent: no trace of the hairpin, tarmac corniche that today conducts tourists by the busload to hotspots like Sorrento, Positano and Amalfi.

Between Castellamare and Vico Equense they saw lime being burnt, and olive-wood fuel lowered from the top of high cliffs to the seashore below. The woodcutters used a complicated arrangement of forked sticks and fixed and sliding ropes for lowering the faggot-bundles down the cliffs to the lime-kilns. From the *Anna*, standing off at a distance, their ropes were invisible and it seemed as if the descending bundles were floating down like leaves.

A Neapolitan aristocrat called Monticelli who had made a collection of minerals from Vesuvius, and with whom the Duke was slightly acquainted, had volunteered his secretary, Giuseppe Donati, to take Lunn's place as the yacht's expert in mineralogy and archaeology. Donati turned out to be both well-informed and energetic, but politically rather enigmatic. The Duke liked him well enough, and was intrigued by his politics. It took Donati a little time, though, to find his sea-legs.

> Donati has never been at sea before, and, beginning with the delights of smooth sailing, soon commenced showing the effects produced by a little swell, and his dark Italian countenance began to look very green and very yellow. At length he came up with great glee to us all, and exclaiming, 'Ho vomitato', found himself much relieved.

Donati led a party of fossil-hunters ashore and found beautiful fossil remains of a small flat fish and a sardine in a clay stratum, and made a careful record of the spot where they were found. Getting him aboard again from the exposed beach proved far from easy, however.

> The surf was so strong that we were obliged to bring our boat to a grapnel, to let her go stern forward on the beach, when the men jumped into the surf, threw one gentleman into the boat on their shoulders, and the boat was instantly hauled out of the surf by the grapnel rope.

Sorrento stood on a high cliff backed by mountains with olive and orange groves. In summer the high mountains, providing protection from the south, were said to render this stretch of coastline the coolest in the Kingdom. Their chart indicated a good anchorage inshore, but they found the rocks very steep-shelving, and dropped anchor farther out, in 20 fathoms, to allow the *Anna* to swing in towards the cliffs, and get under way if the weather turned nasty.

The Duke, exploring along the coast in a barge, tasted the local oranges, famous for their size, but thought them insipid and tasteless with thick rinds and much inferior to those he was used to eating in England. Then he landed in a cove about a mile west of Sorrento to watch tunny being caught in a net and speared from boats. The season for tunny and quail was just beginning.

Tunny fishing beneath Sorrento (the Duke)

All the cliffs are covered with nets, set between slight poles, to catch the quails, which are now emigrating from Africa to the coasts of Italy, in thousands to breed. They are sold for three grains each, and last year one net in Capri caught in the season 14,000 quails. Just before daybreak the poor birds come in, and drop exhausted on the rocks. After a few hours' rest they rise again, and fly into the interior. They may at first be picked up with ease, and the land resounds with guns; fifty or sixty shots may be got in a morning. But they are uncertain in their flight, and some mornings consecutively follow without any flights.

He landed at Mafra [Massa Lubrense] opposite Capri, and took on board wine, bread and cheese to refresh his bargemen. While they ate and drank, he sketched two convents perched above the shore, and watched a beach scene that might have been painted by a Tischbein or Cozens.

The shore was covered with fishermen and children, the latter almost naked, many entirely so, and all dabbling in the water, in which they pass the whole day. The men had finished their labour, and were waiting on the shore, chattering to each other, and romping with each other, until the evening came on and they were again to pass the night at sea. Dressed in nothing but a shirt tucked up at the elbow, a lazzaroni cap of blue or scarlet cloth on their heads, and a pair of linen trowsers tucked close up between the thighs, and leaving the half of them and all their legs and feet bare, they presented magnificent models for the painter and sculptor, A boat was unloading on the shore, and we held by her whilst our men were eating.

Having more wine than we wanted, I gave a glass apiece to the children round us; and seeing two young girls helping to unload the vessel, and bearing great weights through the sun, the boat being loaded with sand, which these girls carried in great baskets on rolls on their head, marching up-hill with them, without even supporting their burthens with their hands, I called to them and offered them some wine – but they smiled and turned away. I desired the people about me to call them, and explain to them that we would not offend them; but they said the girls would not take the wine. I asked why, and the answer was, that if they took wine from strangers they would be thought 'cattive', and that it was not modest to do so. Of course we said no more. In fact, I never saw so much decorum anywhere as amongst the lower orders of women in the country here. Both these girls were pretty, finely formed, and, from the practice of carrying heavy weights on their heads, very upright, and walked and stood beautifully. They were labouring hard, amidst a large parcel of men, and I observed that not one indecorous look, or word, or demeanour, even in play, passed between them; and they refused a glass of wine, offered without any freedom of look or voice, by strangers, lest it should be deemed immodest.

On May 3rd they returned to Naples. His brother-in-law, Lord Arundel, came on board. Mary had gone to watch the miracle of the liquefaction of the blood of St Januarius,[85] which was due to occur, regular as clockwork, on the first Saturday in May, and she had been promised a front-of-house seat close to the altar rails. The next day, when she joined them, she was in an excited state. The blood had taken longer than usual – 22 minutes – to liquefy in its glass vial, and the officiating cardinal had had to rub and shake it vigorously in his hand while the mob screamed and shouted abuse. In the end the cardinal declared '*Il miracolo e fatto!*', and the crowd yelled and clapped its delight, and a courier, ready at the church door, swung into the saddle and galloped off to Portici to give the good news to the king who was an ardent believer.

Mary said that it did not appear to liquefy entirely, but to become pasty and smeary, like red savoury jelly.

In the Duke's opinion, it was all to do with heat acting upon iron mixed with ammonia.

Capri is a paradigm of what a beautiful Mediterranean island – some say the most beautiful – was once, and what it has become. The paddle steamer that had churned past the Duke in the Bay of Naples at 13 miles an hour on Easter Sunday was hurrying towards a faster future: the Anacapri heliport, hydrofoils from Naples, despoiling speedboats, 'rubbish' written on bins in 30 languages, not an inch left for development.

When the *Anna* dropped anchor beneath its sheer northern cliffs on May 6th 1828, it was still a wild island inhabited mostly by farmers and fishermen. For a decade, from AD 27 to AD 37 when Tiberius made his home here, it had been the command centre of the Roman empire. Then, for centuries, it had been forgotten: a place of exile, settled by Carthusian monks, attacked by plague and pirates. It was impregnably fortified by Sir Hudson Lowe in 1806, then surrendered by him without a shot to Murat and the French in 1808 when they landed and scaled the heights of Anacapri behind him during the night. Lowe was later appointed Napoleon's gaoler on St Helena.

The next day the Duke rowed round the island anti-clockwise in his barge, a distance he calculated at about 11 miles. At the north-western end of the island, beneath perpendicular cliffs, they saw limestone caverns – perhaps one of them the famous Grotta Azzurra whose greeny-blue, startlingly irridescent interior, behind a low entrance, had been

The Anna Eliza's *barge exploring a cavern on Capri (the Duke)*

discovered only two years before, in 1826, by a Polish poet called August Kopisch who is supposed to have swum into it by accident.

> In one of the numerous caves which the water has formed in the calcareous rock we saw a stalactite column. We contrived to get men into the recess, and, having our geological apparatus with us, sawed it off at both ends, and lowered it safely into the boat. It was above three feet long.

They rounded the south-western tip, Punta Carena, crowned by an anti-pirate watch-tower, and gazed in awe, south of Capri town, at the Faraglioni, the three huge limestone pinnacles of rock, still home to a rare species of gull and even rarer species of blue lizard, that rise sheer out of the indigo sea.

Not only the top of every cliff, but every crag which is accessible to the foot of a Capri quail-catcher, is crowned with a net; and in the day, when the few poor birds which escape the nightly massacre are regaining strength to

Natural Arch & Cove near Amalfi—

take another flight into the interior, men are to be seen stalking with huge batfowling nets carried before them, many in a line, and each with a little dog, which is trained to beat not more than ten feet from the master's foot, and, as a quail is raised, the net is dropped upon him, and is scarcely ever missed.

The Duke bought some live quail and African doves, their condition affected by the stress of migration, to fatten for his table. The next day some of his party went ashore to sightsee, but he stayed on board to polish up his geological finds.

On May 9th the *Anna* set sail for Salerno. Two swordfish, each about four feet long, swam with her, and one of them jumped clean out of the water, flourishing his sword in the air. They lowered the cutter with a harpoonist, but the fish dived before the boat could get close enough. As darkness fell, they were still some distance from Salerno. Captain Wilcox was nervous of anchoring there in deep water in the dark with his bowsprit up against the rocks, and there was the added hazard of fouling a tunny net. He recommended they put into Amalfi for the night.

The town of Amalfi ... is the most picturesquely situated that I have yet seen; in a gorge at the foot and up the slopes of the Apennines, intermixed with foliage of evergreen oak, olive, orange, myrtle, &c ... All the slopes are covered with cultivation, either in the shape of vineyard, orange, or olive grounds, with here and there a patch of corn ground, and the whole studded

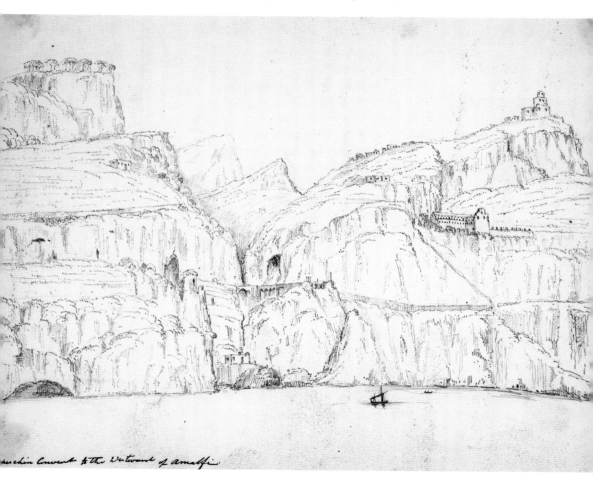

The Duke's sketch of the convent near Amalfi.
'It would require remaining a month to finish one view properly'

with villages, single houses, cottages, and convents ... We endeavoured to take sketches of the scenery here; but the size of the scenes is so large, and their details of rocks, shadow, light, buildings, and foliage, so minute, that it would require remaining a month to finish one view properly ...

They weighed anchor at daybreak on May 13th and, sailing 20 miles south down the long, flat plain of Salerno and anchoring two miles offshore, landed from the barge on a sandy beach opposite the temples of Paestum. They were all armed to the teeth and pretending to be shooting pigeons, with a guard of sailors carrying their baggage. Paestum had an evil reputation for Calabrian banditry and about three years before his arrival an English couple had been murdered there, so the Duke was taking no chances. They walked half a mile in the heat through marshland and arbutus-covered dunes and negotiated deep ditches dug around the temples to stop cattle getting in, then sat down to eat their cold dinner in the central Temple of Neptune. A party of local gendarmes seemed to be expecting him. They formed another bodyguard while he ate.

Paestum, with its three marvellous temples[86] built by colonists from Sybaris in the 6th and 5th centuries BC, was probably the closest the Duke ever came to the Greek Experience. The political and military situation in mainland Greece, whose bid for independence from the Turks had recently been brought to a successful conclusion at Navarino, was still fluid and dangerous; too dangerous to contemplate, even with his cannon and armed marines. Paestum was bad enough.

Whilst we were at dinner, surrounded by the people, who looked wistfully upon our provisions, and to whom we gave the remains of the repast, a stout dark man, dressed above the common rank, with a belt round his waist, appearing like a postilion or a courier, having a travelling whip in his hand, hovered round us. He evidently did not belong to the party which surrounded us. He was a stranger, and, after remaining some time on the skirts of our party, entered it, and, beginning with insisting on kissing my hand, became very officious and obtrusive in his attentions – endeavouring to call off the attention of my altezza to objects which he pointed out, officiously making way for me, removing stones from before my path. I saw he was not a cicerone, and by his dress he had travelled that morning. I had my suspicions, but did not betray them; yet I took care not to go with him, although he several times appeared anxious to get me away from my party, under pretence of shewing me a more convenient path and objects of curiosity.

At length, whilst we were eating, seated on the steps of the temple, I observed one of the gendarmes go up to his brigadier and whisper something in his ear. I followed his eye, and saw he was adverting to something which was passing behind me. The brigadier took a circle, and entering the temple a few yards further down came behind me. I watched him, and saw him turn out from behind the massive columns *close to me* my stranger friend, who had hid *himself behind it*. From that moment the brigadier and one of the gendarmes stuck close to me, and never let me stir from them. My friend kept hovering round us, but could never join us again. *They* suspected him, and so did I; and, remembering the public tale at Salerno occasioned by the discussions relative to the hire of carriages, &c, for me and my party, and that I unexpectedly came by sea, I cannot help suspecting – God forgive me if I am wrong! – that my courier friend had evidently come forward to see what had become of us, disappointed at our not coming by land, and curious to see whether we meant to return. The gendarmes' suspicions at least excited mine.

The Temples of Paestum (J R Cozens), where
the Duke encountered a sinister stranger

A mid-19th-century cork model of the Temple of Neptune and Paestum, probably made by the padre (private collection)

They spent the afternoon pottering about the ruins, but were anxious to get back to the *Anna* by sunset. Paestum – called Poseidonia when settled by the Greeks – had originally been sited on dry ground among pine trees. But deforestation for ship-building, and seismic activity, had gradually turned the surrounding countryside into a swamp. By the first century AD the Roman town of Paestum was in sharp decline, and in the end it was abandoned. The local padre, who was an expert on the temples and made excellent models of them in cork, told the Duke that the annual malaria-kill among his parishioners was a scarcely-credible ten per cent.

In the cool of a delicious evening they strolled back to the beach and tried to glimpse beneath the water-surface traces of the old harbour of Paestum, now silted-up.

For the next two days they sailed south in light airs towards Stromboli and the Aeolian islands off Sicily's north-east coast. Wilcox took advantage of the calm weather to scrub out and whitewash the ship's galley and sleeping-quarters, and have all hammocks and bags scrubbed too. He handed out fresh ones to the crew. A school of tunny swam alongside, and the ship's carpenter, Michelson, managed to spear a good one for their dinner. It was a welcome addition to their diet. The weather was hotter now. Keeping meat fresh for eating was difficult.

The fiery, intermittent gleam of Stromboli's volcano was clearly visible to them on the night of May 14th, but it was not until the following evening that they dropped anchor in its lee in an open roadstead. There was no harbour (the mole at Scari is modern concrete). Before the days of steam this most northern of the seven islands that make up the Aeolian archipelago was a regular stop-off for sailing ships between Naples and Sicily, and the islanders made a good living ferrying out supplies in open boats. But the place had – and still has – a bad reputation (as befits the home of the wind-god) in stormy weather, and Wilcox was ready to weigh anchor again for the open sea at the first hint of trouble. A picket went ashore for provisions, and was confronted by two nervous islanders with guns who thought the Duke's red flag and ship's cannon implied Barbary pirates. In the end they got what they wanted, including two barrels of excellent, locally-produced Malmsey wine. It was sweet, but not too sweet, with a bright amber colour. Another party rowed in the

The Aeolian Isles, with Panarea in the foreground
and twin-humped Salina beyond (the Duke)

barge to the base of the volcano's cone and watched in awe in the darkness as molten magma, ejected from the crater, rolled down its flanks and splashed into the sea. One or two boulders fell uncomfortably close, and the Duke called back into the boat some bold souls who had landed on the black beach to get a closer look.

> We got on board two large specimens, red hot, which fell on the shingle close to the boat's bow ... The greater quantity fell into the crater again, but sometimes they fell over its edge, and then came pattering down the inclined plane like a heavy ricochet fire of shot and grape.

They spent the best part of a week exploring Stromboli and the rest of the archipelago. There were two days of heavy rain. They hunted for fossils on the barley-growing and idyllic island of Panarea, the smallest of the seven sisters and now a holiday resort of the Sicilian mafia; saw sulphur, ammonia and alum being extracted from the ever-smoking island of Vulcano; tried to shoot from the barge shy rock-doves flying out of the sea-caves that honeycombed the shore-line; and bought snow imported to Lipari every day from Etna, some 50 miles away, to cool their wine. There were nervous moments when they finally set sail for Malta in choppy seas. They lost headway beneath Vulcano's sheer cliffs and tried to tow themselves out of danger with the barge and the cutter. Two fishing-boats saw they were in difficulties and hurried to the rescue. Just as they arrived, the wind got up again and blew the *Anna* to safety. The Duke nevertheless tipped the fishermen handsomely, to encourage them to do the same for someone else.

CHAPTER THIRTEEN

Daughter of the Wind

Malta lies in the central channel between the eastern and western basins of the Mediterranean, 60 miles from Sicily, 180 from Africa. From the dawn of maritime trade its possession has implied domination of the indigo sea. Nelson captured the island from the French in 1799. Its natural harbour, Valletta, soon evolved into the headquarters of the British Mediterranean fleet.

The Grand Harbour, Valletta, with, probably, the Anna Eliza *(centre left)*

The *Anna* sailed into the Grand Harbour before breakfast on May 27th, beneath, on Fort St Elmo, a Union flag billowing out in a hot, dry, enervating, south-west wind. The scirocco had been blowing for a month. She anchored beside three British frigates. At two o'clock the island's Governor welcomed the Duke with a 19-gun, siesta-busting salute, and asked him to dinner. The *Anna*'s guns thundered her reply. They were the opening salvos of a relentless, 14-day round of dinners, opera-visits, dances, receptions and reviews, at which the Duke made new friends, and became reacquainted with some old, including a sad Dowager Lady Errol, a friend of his youth, who was taking a leaf out of the book of the late Queen of Naples, Maria Carolina, by destroying herself with opium. He had a long talk with the Commander-in-Chief Mediterranean, veteran of Trafalgar and the Glorious First of June and now victor of Navarino, Admiral Sir Edward Codrington. The old salt had arrived home off patrol unexpectedly one evening, having been rowed into Valletta in his barge ahead of his becalmed flagship the

As befitted a Royal Yacht Club member, the Duke was comfortable drawing ships. This is HMS Asia

143

The marina in Valetta (H E Allen)

Ocean, and had walked into a dinner-party that his wife and daughter were giving for the Duke. He was introduced to Captain Wilcox, who was thrilled to meet such a naval celebrity.

Codrington complained that his instructions from Government, while Canning was alive, were always precise and clearly-defined; after his death in 1827, muddled and contradictory.

On June 6th the Duke gave a party on board to all those who had been civil to him during his stay.

We had turtle soup and beef steaks (the latter a favourite luncheon dish here), and all the rest cold. We sat down at two o'clock, and afterwards had a dance on my quarter-deck. We contrived to have fifty people, who found ample room; and all parties were in high good humour. I dressed the ship, manned the yards, and cheered the Admiral when he came on board; and when the General and he left me, I saluted them with thirteen guns each. At eight o'clock I went and dined with the Admiral, where I met some of my morning's party. But everybody was dead tired, and went to bed. I introduced Signor Donati to Miss Codrington, who danced with him, and he was in the highest heavens. I also took him on board the man-of-war when I went, and his ecstasy was extreme. He had never been in an English man-of-war before.

*　　*　　*

The *Anna* left the Grand Harbour at dawn on June 10th, and put into the neighbouring island of Gozo, where the Duke mounted a donkey and rode off to explore the Stone-Age, megalithic temple of Gigantia, four miles away on top of a hill. He took measurements of the huge upright stones that form the temple's circle, and set his sailors to work excavating down to the base of a column he identified near the central altar. He would, perhaps, have liked to remove the four-foot-high, priapic column, but it proved too deeply embedded. Before he left Gozo, he did his best to persuade the island's Governor, a Major Bailey, to use his hard-labour convicts to carry on his excavations.

On the 13th, departing from Gozo, they saw on the horizon the sails of Admiral Codrington and his Mediterranean squadron heading east for Greece and the Peloponnese. Their own course lay north-west, and after a brisk overnight passage the *Anna* moored within the little fishing-harbour mole of Agrigento, half-way along Sicily's southern coast, and settled down to wait for the port's health officer to row out and give them pratique. They were all keen to see the magnificent remains of the sixth-century BC Greek colony of Akragas, in the (nowadays so-called) Valley of Temples below the town. But the health-officer, in a land of officialdom, turned out to be the most officious the *Anna* had ever encountered. He referred everything upwards to his boss, the Intendente of the town. Tempers frayed. Radcliffe and a party of sailors were arrested on shore and had to be rescued by the *Anna*'s armed marines; a gendarme was assaulted; a letter of complaint to the Intendente was contemptuously kicked off the jetty back into Radcliffe's cutter. As soon as he had his precious papers back on board – clean bill of health from Malta, passports and Viceroy's letter – the furious Duke weighed anchor and sailed west to Marsala, where he was given immediate pratique and whence, to the Viceroy at Palermo, he dashed off a passionate letter of complaint about his outrageous treatment. He had missed, at Akragas, seeing some of the finest temples on Sicily.

The next day a Mr Barlow, partner in the local wine-house of Woodhouse and Co, came aboard with samples of his Marsala wine. The winery had been founded in the 1770s by John Woodhouse from Liverpool, who spotted that the local wine, sweet and strong, was very like Madeira, then popular in England. In 1798 Nelson, his fleet anchored nearby, put in a large order and made it fashionable in his wardrooms, and by the time the Duke arrived the firm was exporting

The temple of Juno Lucina at Akragas (Ferdinand Waldmüller).
The Duke's visit was aborted after a potentially fatal scuffle with the Health Officer

3,000 pipes (about 32,000 gallons) annually, mainly to America, and the British Mediterranean fleet at Malta was still a loyal customer.

But the Duke was not a buyer.

> The wine is good in itself; but it is, to my mind, very much injured by the quantity of brandy which they put into it.

The Agrigento affair, which he seems to have taken as a personal insult, was still affecting his mood. The Marsala windmills grinding salt on the saltpans around him, and the reedy marshes and inlets haunted by night-herons, sea-birds and flamingoes, gave him no more pleasure than the local wine.

The coast is extremely flat and uninteresting … In the evening, the smell of the marshes was very distinctly appreciable on board, and perfectly explains the malaria. There is nothing to be seen here – no antiquities to be collected, and no temptation to stay.

How wrong he was. In 1979 the marvellous statue of a young man, over life-size, fifth-century BC, Greek, without arms or feet, was discovered on the island of Motya, a few miles north of where the Duke was moored. Called the Fanciullo di Mozia, and on display in Motya's museum, it is one of the finest pieces of Greek sculpture ever found in southern Italy, on a par with the Riace bronzes in the museum at Reggio Calabria. The sensuous way that the diaphanous marble pleats of the young man's tunic seem to caress his muscles beneath is truly amazing.

He sailed north the same day for Trapani, where he was given a much better reception: immediate pratique, and a guide and the loan of the Intendente's carriage to tour the town. To the west he could see the Egadi islands and Favignana, yet another grim island prison for anti-Bourbons. The Chevalier de Medicis, current prime minister at Naples, had spent an uncomfortable time there at the turn of the century, locked up by Maria Carolina for collaborating with the French.

The north-west corner of Sicily with Favignana island in the distance (Lojacono)

June 20th. At six o'clock this morning I proceeded to Segestum. The road is a very good one, and is the new communication from hence to Palermo. You pass along twenty-two miles of it until you come to a red house, which is a station for the persons having the care of the road. You then must walk, or take a mule, to the temple, which lies amongst the hills. There was no such thing as a carriage and post-horses to be hired at Trapani. A friend of the English consul lent me a *caleche*, in which we crammed four people, and from four persons more we collected four horses; another equipped us with a coachman who had never driven, and a sixth with a postilion who had seldom rode in his life. We set forth.

The Intendente offered me an escort of gendarmerie, which I positively refused, and was very near regretting my magnanimity, as I found rather late in the day that thirty galley-slaves had escaped from the neighbourhood of Trapani, that part only had been retaken, and the rest infested the neighbourhood.

His companions were Radcliffe, Giovanni Gandolfi his *lacquais de place*, and probably (although he doesn't mention him by name on this occasion) Donati. At first progress was slow, through open corn land that reminded him of Dorset. They were held up by one horse kicking, another shying, a footboard and a trace breaking (its leather was rotten) and their postilion dismounting every mile to ease his aching muscles. Later, though, they picked up speed and reached the red house by nine o'clock. The Duke was irritated to find that his mule, booked for the whole day, was already at work with two or three others treading out corn. It was unmuzzled.

The consequence was, that my poor mule got his feed by the sweat of his brow, instead of enjoying it, as he ought, in quiet in his stable; my rogue of a muleteer, besides his bargain with me for the whole day, pocketed the little extra job gained by the mule's extra exertion, and I had to pay for the feed, which the mule never ate, besides.

The temple, they were informed, lay only a couple of miles away, so they left their refreshments behind at the red house to await their return. The distance turned out to be five miles at least, through rough hill-country desiccated by a scirocco wind that seemed to be blowing out of an oven, drying and caking their lips and skin. They were lucky to find a working roadside well.

Liquor passed down the throat and gave a momentary coolness as it passed, but it did not quench an incipient thirst, and produced no refreshment. Those who walked lay down and panted like dogs, and, I, who rode, could scarce sit upon my mule. We had some water in a bottle which we brought from the last spring, but it was hot and frothy ere it reached the temple.

The first, distant view of the Doric temple of Segesta, squat and eremitic in its wilderness, has astonished many a traveller down the ages. The Duke proved no exception.

After rounding one hill after another, and crossing many a dried-up and rocky river bed, we at length swept round the base of a rocky knoll, and on a height above us to our right stood, magnificent in its magnitude and frowning in desolation, the Temple of Segestum.

Lawrence Durrell was another who saw it suddenly from a distance: 'standing there so quietly in the vale, wise as an elephant with the world on its back'.

'magnificent in its magnitude and frowning in desolation,
the Temple of Segestum' (the Duke)

They spent the rest of the morning, and part of the afternoon, sketching the temple and measuring it like a tailor for a suit: overall length and width; number, diameter and circumference of columns; intercolumnar spaces; height of pediments; and so on. The Duke had no sextant with him, and roughly calculated the height of the columns by standing one of his party, whose height he measured, beside a column on one side, then, from the other, marking off a piece of paper held out in front of his eyes and making the appropriate calculation. He suspected, rightly, that the temple had never been finished – no roof nor inner sanctuary nor columnar flutes were ever added. Even its dedicatee is unknown, although Verres, the rapacious governor of Sicily in Cicero's time, is supposed to have made off with a statue of Demeter. The building persists, sturdy and mysterious, defying earthquake, revolution, conquest, time itself.

The rock on which the temple stands ends abruptly in a steep cliff overlooking a garrigue-covered ravine. A boy who had attached himself to their party told them of a miraculous cave in the cliff with corridors and chambers and an underground river, and a white marble statue holding an iron club. It had been discovered, he said, by a shepherd looking for a lost goat. Radcliffe and Giovanni Gandolfi went off to look for it, guided by a now less-than-willing boy. The cave, he warned, was haunted.

> They came to a steep precipice, and found they could not get at the cave that way. They went into the ravine below and saw its mouth. They separated in their course and lost sight of each other. The boy guide remained with Radcliffe. Giovanni advanced his own way. He stopped to strike out with his hammer some agate rock for me, and as soon as his hammer struck he heard a shrill whistle, and, looking up, beheld two men in the dress of the lowest peasantry, but armed with guns, creeping on their hands and knees out of this *unapproachable* cavern, and then dive among the brushwood. He hallooed to Radcliffe, to warn him of his danger, and at that instant the boy ran away from and left him, never appearing again, not even to ask for a reward for having guided him.

Gandolfi returned to the Duke's side, but Radcliffe, in spite of the other's shouted warning that the men were armed, climbed up to the mouth of the cave and crawled inside. Someone had been there before him; the smoke of their torches had blackened the roof. He could dimly discern tunnels off the cave, but the interior was pitch-black, and, having no light, he very sensibly beat a retreat.

Back at the temple, they considered their case. The Duke had sent his guides and mules back to the red house to bring up their provisions. The temple, apart from their own party and three more small local boys who had somehow materialised out of nowhere, was deserted. There wasn't a house in sight. Their only arms were the two pocket pistols that the Duke carried in his belt. If the two men, assumed to be galley-slaves, attacked with their superior firepower, the Duke's party could be rushed with ease. He primed and readied his pistols. There was nothing to do but stick together, hope, and wait.

They waited for three hours. There was no attack, no sign of the two men. In the end help arrived in the form of mules, guides and provisions from the red house, but it had been an anxious time. They returned exhausted to Trapani at ten o'clock at night, on one of the hottest evenings the Duke had ever experienced. The next day he put in a report to the Intendente, who said that the two men were almost certainly galley-slaves on the run. He'd send out an immediate search-party. The cave was quite well-known, and was often pointed out to tourists, although some of its recesses had never been fully explored. They – particularly Radcliffe – had had a very narrow escape.

On June 21st the *Anna* was at sea again, heading for the little black volcanic island of Pantelleria, some 80 miles away to the south south-west. The weather was still very hot and humid, but the scirocco, to everyone's relief, had ceased. In the shade of the Duke's cabin, the coolest part of the ship, his thermometer read 89°F.

> I have been writing this journal on the deck, until the paper got so wet that I could write no more. Our decks and clothes are as if they had been sprinkled with water.

Why Pantelleria? A Sicilian contact had told him that it was very interesting from a mineralogical point of view, and more or less unknown to science. It was also, at that date, a political prison, and it's clear from his diary that institutional life, whether in monasteries, asylums or prisons, held a particular fascination for the Duke.

> So little is the place known, that Monticelli, at Naples, desired Donati to ascertain whether the island is 'vraiment volcanique'. It is nothing else.

They anchored the next morning in a little bay on the north-west point of the island. He didn't like the look of the town of Pantelleria[87] above

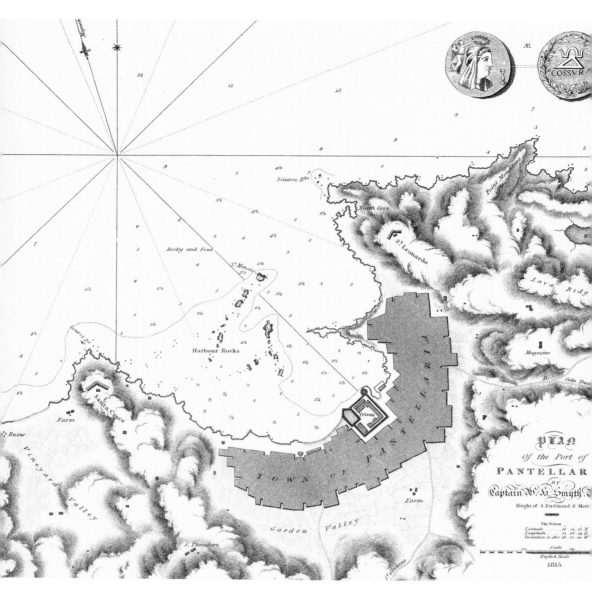

Smyth's chart clearly showing the rocks that nearly wrecked the Anna Eliza

him, with its frowning Spanish castle-prison, clutch of churches and mean white huts; any more than its anchorage below, open to every quarter except the south-west to south-east and with a rocky bottom that would tear a hemp cable to pieces in no time.

As soon as we dropped our anchor the health-boat came out to us, and gave us pratique; advising us, however, to haul further out, as we were in foul ground, and if wind set in strong [from] the north-west or north-east we should inevitably be on the rocks. We took their advice, and hauled out into seven fathoms water, but in the worst anchorage ever laid down for vessels. Smyth's[88] sketch of the town is very correct.

Today, Pantelleria remains one of the Mediterranean's most unusual islands, with its fertile red soil, dry-stone walls, white-domed *dammuso* houses and little vineyards growing *zibibbo* grapes, all girt by a black basalt coastline. The island still retains a flavour of the agricultural Middle Ages, in spite of the best efforts of tourist developers to suppress it. The Arabs were here for centuries, and called the island 'Bent el rion', 'the Daughter of the Wind'.

That evening the Governor came aboard, and the Duke gave him coffee, rosalio wine and a tour of the ship. He was a short man wearing a major's uniform and gold-laced cocked hat, trailed a sabre longer than himself, and was fascinated by the Duke's local charts. As he left, a thick fog descended, obscuring the bowsprit of the *Anna* from her stern.

The Duke was up early the next morning, at six o'clock, to set out on his customary island-circumnavigation, which he always so much enjoyed. The fog had lifted. They went round the island anti-clockwise. His barge was rowed by ten sailors, one to an oar, and he hoped to get the barge's sail up on at least some points of the compass, but the wind shifted against them round every headland, and his sailors had to row all the way: a distance of about 25 miles. South-west by south they came across a small cove with fishing-huts, where fish were being salted for sale in 'La Citta', as they called Pantelleria town. They tried to buy some for their dinner from a fishing-boat they overhauled, and the terrified fisherman, thinking they were Barbary pirates, clasped his hands in prayer and begged them to spare his life.

> It was now past noon, and the heat was intense … It was impossible for the men to row longer under such a burning sun, as the awning only smothered them, and I anxiously looked out for a place where they might lay by during the hottest hours … The air was like a quivering furnace, and the sea like an expanse of hot molten steel.

On the inaccessible 'Dietro Isola' or so-called 'back of the island' they found a cave[89] they could row into, with a natural rock jetty inside.

'Smyth's sketch of the town [Pantelleria] *is very correct'*

> Here we moored our barge, the men landed, dined, bathed, and slept; and
> we having a portable cooking apparatus on board landed it, and made the
> most delicious dinner of our own cooking I ever ate.

They lay up for three hours in the cave, still only half-way round the
island. In the late afternoon they rowed on, and he would have liked to
gone ashore beneath the eastern cliffs to geologise, but they had run out
of time. Night fell. The moon rose.

> Headland after headland appeared and disappeared without our seeing our
> vessel's lights. At last we saw them, and arrived safely at eleven o'clock at
> night, with our men almost exhausted.

The next morning, June 24th, he called on the Governor in his fortress-
prison, and was deeply depressed by what he saw. A few prisoners were
paroled to enjoy the freedom of the island but most – galley-slaves and
political deviants all together – were held in squalid, wretched cells. The
houses and streets of La Citta were filthy, and as he returned to the *Anna*
under a burning sun he was mobbed by the townsfolk and exhausted by
their attentions. In the late afternoon, after a siesta, his sailors rowed him
to a cove about a mile away, and he took a swim in a patent bathing-
machine attached to the boat's awning and lowered over the stern 'like a
machine in England, only not upon wheels'. It was the first time he had
used it. They had to anchor in deep water. A heavy swell was coming on.

By the time I returned to dinner the swell had increased, and the evening came on gloomy and ill-looking.

As night fell, the wind got up from the north-west, the worst possible quarter for their anchorage. The Duke was nervous. They were on foul ground, much nearer the rocks than he would have liked. The bottom was flat rock, with only the odd ledge to lodge an anchor. Wilcox got the top-gallant masts and yards down on deck, and had a second, lighter anchor and chain rowed out from the *Anna*'s bow, as a precaution. Its chain, when the strain came on, snagged the leg of one of the goats that the Duke kept on board for fresh milk, and the poor screaming animal had to be put out of its misery. But Wilcox's precautions were not in vain.

In the middle of the night the most terrific squall the sailors had ever seen came in an instant, burst over us, and then shifted round to its old point, right into the harbour's mouth; so we could not stir, and had not room to run away more cable. Our last bower anchor and chain-cable were dropped under our bows, as no boat could live to carry it out … no hempen cable could stand half an hour. We hung over our lead line for only ten minutes, to see if the vessel drifted astern: it was cut in two by the rocks.

During the night it blew what the Duke called in his diary a *gregara*,[90] which generally occurs during the Mediterranean winter and lasts several days. The sea ran mountains high, and broke all around them on the black, sharp, basaltic shore. The first squall, from the south, was

Another ship – but perhaps not unlike the Anna Eliza's *situation at the height of the storm (Aivazovsky)*

furnace-hot, and those who ran out on deck thought the ship was on fire. Then the wind suddenly swung round into the north, with much thunder and lightning, and a minor earthquake in La Citta, and turned cold. Daylight revealed the full extent of their danger: they were slowly, inexorably moving towards the rocks. Their second anchor that had snagged the goat, with 60 fathoms of chain out, seemed to be holding, more or less. The first, with only 20 out now and somehow not taking the strain properly, had dragged during the night.

It was a long and anxious day. It was obvious, from marks taken on the shore, that they were losing ground foot by foot. They struck their top-masts, spanker, driver and jib-boom, and lowered all the yards to the deck, leaving only their two lower-yards aloft to take advantage of any wind that might arise to give them sea-room. All hatches and ports were secured, and although she shipped some water in the huge seas the *Anna*, sharp up front, slipped through the water without resistance and dived under the waves like a seagull. The cutter and jolly-boat, on which they might have to depend to save their lives, were hoisted aboard, and the barge, towed astern during the previous night on a long painter, was brought in close in case they had to abandon ship.

> Thus closed in the night. We, of course, did not take off our clothes, as, had our chain gone, very few minutes would have been allowed us to attempt our escape in, and we retired into our cabins with the knowledge that, had one link of a chain given way, there was no salvation for us – but in another world.

The Duke managed to get a little sleep that night, fully-dressed. He was woken between one and two o'clock in the morning by heavier lurches than usual; then the wind seemed to moderate a little, and the waves to run less high. But dawn revealed that they had drifted even closer to the shore, within a stone's throw of the rocks. Radcliffe and Wilcox came to his cabin for an emergency meeting. Radcliffe urged that they should haul the *Anna* up on her second, lighter anchor, and weigh and re-cast their first, heavier anchor farther out. Wilcox objected that it would be dangerous to disturb their one good anchor.

> There was no alternative but to try the experiment to save the vessel, as it was evident that what we now had out could not hold us. I therefore desired the attempt might be made.

The *Anna*'s crew worked with outstanding steadiness and courage, especially Carphy, the boatswain and Trafalgar veteran, and Michelson the carpenter. A young seaman called Seymour had already distinguished himself during the height of the storm by taking a flying leap into the barge to save their stern-light buoy, which was being washed away. They winched the *Anna* slowly forward to above their first anchor, and weighed it, only to find that it was useless. Its iron stock had sheered clean off. So they weighed their sheet anchor[91] too (the last to be dropped beneath them when the storm began, and the heaviest of all) and bent the chains of the broken bow-anchor to it, and winched the *Anna* farther forward to a position almost above their good anchor (which providentially held), and shot the sheet anchor and a third stream anchor either side of the bow. Then they veered away, and the *Anna* held by three chains, all bearing an equal strain. They seemed to be safe.

On the morning of the 27th, having lasted for three nights and two days, the storm blew itself out. They surveyed the damage. Part of their steering-gear had been washed away, and the rudder-head had split in the violence of the storm.[92] Michelson secured it with an iron hoop and wedges, and made it as strong as ever. But most frightening of all, when they weighed the light bow anchor which was all that had held them during the height of the storm, was the discovery that it had lost its fluke to within seven inches of its crown.

> By this stump, which must have got jammed into a cleft of the rock, we have held, and to this we owe our safety. The wooden stock must have helped to hold us, as it came up sprung and torn to pieces ... It took us five hours to get up our rigging and anchors, and repair our damages, before we could get sail upon the vessel, when we left this wretched island, as I hope, never again to see it.

CHAPTER FOURTEEN

Ponzese and Sards

The Duke probably wrote his travel diary with an eye for publication – or at the very least to be read by his family and intimates – and there are occasions when he could be accused of self-dramatisation: his audience with George IV; the sinister stranger behind the pillars at Paestum; the armed galley-slaves in the cave at Segesta; and so on. But his account of the Pantelleria *gregale* carries absolute conviction. It had been a truly terrifying two days. As the *Anna* sailed back to Naples round the north-west corner of Sicily, there can hardly have been a soul on board who wasn't suffering from delayed shock, and thanking God for their deliverance. The Duke himself was badly shaken, and may well have been thinking at this time[93] about sending the *Anna* home without him.

They found Naples, in whose Bay the *Anna* moored just before night-fall on June 30th, in a state of panic. There had been some sort of armed uprising of carbonari in Calabria and a simultaneous, foiled plot to assassinate the king as he walked in a religious procession through the capital's streets. The roads were picketed with gendarmes, the towns were full of spies. 4,000 soldiers had been embarked for Salerno, the centre of the discontent, where the castle was said to be in rebel hands. King Francis I, in the best and bravest traditions of the Neapolitan Bourbon royal family, spent two nights sleeping on board a government frigate in Naples Bay, ready for immediate flight. In the event, the insurrection turned out to be a fairly minor affair: 45 banditti led by an old man, one-time carbonaro and a member of the Neapolitan parliament, who had been intolerably harrassed by the king's secret police.

The Duke heard this news only at second-hand when he first arrived, because the *Anna* was held in strict quarantine on her anchorage at Castellamare, in spite of the fact that he'd been assured by the Neapolitan ambassador at Malta that Pantelleria was in pratique with Naples.

The general opinion is, that I have been kept out of the way, purposely, of hearing of the risings in Calabria. They never can get rid of the idea that we are cruizing in these seas for a political object, and I really believe they fancy I want to become king of Naples.

He put his enforced idleness on board to good use, however, by dealing with correspondence from home. To Thomas Fremantle, who sat in his interest as MP for Buckingham, he wrote: '*On my return to this anchorage from Malta and Sicily I found letters and newspapers detailing the late events connected with the government … My health is quite good. I hear that Louisa has given you another girl. I rejoice to hear that she is safe – give her my best love. Emma Wilson is* slowly *recovering. But she is still very weak, and it must be a long while before she gets quit of the consequences of her rash imprudence.*'[94] On July 26th Fremantle answered, perhaps rather tactlessly, that he would be '*assisting at the slaughter of your partridges at Stowe the first week in September, where Chandos means to take the field with a regiment of double-barrelled fowling-pieces*'.

What on earth was the 'rash imprudence' of poor, pretty young Emma Wilson, wife of his acting chaplain? Was she tuberculous? Or had she, in the Duke's view, unnecessarily exposed herself to some sort of deadly, summer, nocturnal marsh-gas (of which the Duke, as his diary makes clear, was always mortally afraid), and caught malarial fever? The Wilsons seem to have remained behind, anyway, at Naples during the Duke's cruise to Malta and Pantelleria, probably because of her illness.[95]

> I answer my letters from England. The late changes appear so extra-ordinary, and the conduct of the Duke of Wellington so arbitrary, that I must pause before I can support a Government so formed – especially as the Catholic balance is entirely destroyed. I, therefore, write to my friends to beg that they will remain neuter.

In fact the Duke of Wellington was coming round to the emancipationist point of view. That very July, in Ireland, Daniel O'Connell had been elected MP for Clare, but was disqualified from taking his seat in the House of Commons because he was a Catholic; and the Iron Duke, in his practical, commonsensical way, had begun to realise that unless something was done about Catholic emancipation, there would be an Irish civil war which could spill over into England. Wellington spent the rest of 1828, and the spring of 1829, trying to change the mind of his over-my-dead-body King, who kept quoting his Coronation Oath; and of an equally-intransigent Church of England. In the end he got his way:[96] the Catholic Relief Act, which ended all Catholic disability in the United Kingdom except that of the Sovereign marrying one, received royal assent in April, 1829.

He wrote also to his favourite uncle, Thomas Grenville, describing his near-shipwreck. Thomas wrote back affectionately on September 9th: '*Your letter from Castella Mare, my dear Duke, gives a most fearful account of your danger at Pantalaria* [sic], *though followed by the welcome details of your Providential escape. I therefore sincerely rejoice to find that your marine travels are, soon after this time, to be exchanged for those of chaise and horse, and that the yacht is to swim home again ... Come back to us soon, my dear Duke, and take care of yourself to return well.*'[97]

July 3rd. This evening we got pratique. The excuse now made is, that they mistook Pantelleria for Lampedusa! – that the former is in pratique with Naples, and the latter is not. Now, in the first place, it is not likely that such

'a last splendid view of Vesuvius' (the Duke)

Gaeta, where the Duke taunted a sentry by waving his hat at him

a mistake could happen; in the next, Lampedusa is uninhabited, except by rabbits – so there could be no question of quarantine or pratique with an uninhabited island.[98]

To add insult to injury the Neapolitan Board of Health, on July 9th, sent him a large bill for the time they had kept him in quarantine. He sent the bill on to Sir Henry Lushington, the British ambassador to Naples, with a note saying that he positively refused to pay up, and gave orders to Wilcox to prepare the ship for immediate departure. He had already taken the precaution of having his passports 'visé', as he called it, by the appropriate foreign embassies of the places he intended to visit.

> At one pm I got under weigh. The wind at first was scant, but it soon freshened into a lovely breeze, carried us across the Bay of Naples (whose beauties I bade adieu to), under the brilliant hues of an Italian sunset, which gave me, also, a last splendid view of Vesuvius, and the delicious coast of Baiae. We rounded Cape Misenum, went between Procida and the main, and steered a straight course for Mola di Gaeta.

He would never see Naples again. In view of his outstanding bill with its Health Board, it was probably just as well.

❖   ❖   ❖

The seaport of Gaeta, said by Virgil to have been named after Aeneas's wet-nurse, lies a little over 20 miles north of Naples on the Italian mainland, crouching beneath Monte Orlando on the southern headland of the Gulf of Gaeta. It would be the scene, in 1860/61, of the final stand of Francis II, last of the Neapolitan Bourbons, against the United Italian forces of Garibaldi. The withdrawal of the French fleet made bombardment from the sea possible: King Bomba, this time, was on the receiving end.

The *Anna* anchored within its mole at 9 am on July 10th and was given immediate pratique. Its governor, the Duke of Milan, sent him civil messages of welcome. But the Duke declined to land. His time was limited, and he preferred to explore along the coastal cliffs in his barge. There was a fortified battery on top of one of the cliffs, and the proximity of his barge threw its sentry into a paroxysm of rage.

> He capered, and screamed, and made signs, then took off his shako, and shook it; then threw three stones at us; and then, finally, pointed his musket at us. But all his antics had no effect, and we pulled off our hats to him, and left him still screaming … The beauty of the scene is very great. The mountains are clothed half-way up their sides by orange trees and ilex; and the sea-shore is studded with farm-houses and villas, and ruins of Roman piscinae and baths. Here stood Cicero's Formian villa … A tower stands on the spot where he is said to have been murdered, as he was coming down to the sea.[99]

On the afternoon of July 12th, in calm weather, they anchored in the little, well-protected harbour of Ponza, about 70 miles west of Gaeta and the biggest of the five volcanic islands in the Pontine archipelago. Today, the ferry from Formia on the Italian mainland takes about three hours, and as you approach Ponza it looks like a range of mountains rising out of the sea. In fact it's only one mountain thick: the long, thin crescent of an extinct volcano's rim.

> The appearance of the island is very picturesque. At a distance much appears like chalk cliffs, ribboned down with different coloured strata. The whole is trachite[100] and grey-stone, consequently volcanic.

On the bookshelf in his cabin he kept a copy of George Poulett Scrope's[101] *Considerations on Volcanos*, which dealt at length with the Pontine islands, and the Duke was keen to test Scrope's observations at first hand. First, though, the Governor sent a boat out to him with presents of fruit and fish, the latter very welcome because no fishing, other than for the gubernatorial table, was allowed on the island, and there were no fish for sale. The island – yes, yet another Bourbon political prison[102] – was home to 400 inmates, who were allowed to roam its nine-mile-by-one-mile volcanic acres but were denied access to any boat.

In return the Duke gave the Governor, who turned out to be a civilised, humane major in the gendarmerie and an amateur archaeologist, some of the Birmingham cutlery he'd brought with him. In the evening he took to his barge and, on the north side of Ponza bay examined some *scogli* (monolithic, upright rocks) which reminded him of Staffa and the Giant's Causeway. He detached and brought on board a natural rock arch, about two feet across the span, which seemed to the Duke a perfect specimen of prismatic trachyte, with a very high content of glassy, tar-coloured pitchstone.

The next day he circumnavigated the island in his barge, this time travelling clockwise. Along the way he sketched the Grotta di Pilato, not far from the port: three intercommunicating caverns in the cliff-face, with marble steps leading down into crystalline water 15ft deep, and carved niches for bathers to lie on. There was a local myth, almost certainly produced by a confusion of names, that Pontius Pilate had governed Ponza after the Crucifixion, and had lived in a villa adjoining the caves. The caves are thought, in fact, to have been used by Roman augurers

Roman baths on the island of Ponza

who opened the stomachs of eels, not birds, in order to forecast the future. The augurers are supposed to have looked through a hole cut in the cliff-face (it still exists) to assess for their magic the configuration of Draco and the Great Bear.

On the south side of the island, before we came to La Chiaja della Luna,[103] we saw in a bay some excavations; and, landing there, found galleries and vaulted chambers in the rock, evidently of Roman work. In one of these was a well of fresh water. Before it were the ruins of a building evidently Roman, and in one the apartments were the remains of an altar, on the front of which was a rude image of Christ crucified. It was no 'Christ' of Catholic times; it was evidently as ancient as the house, which clearly was of Roman work. From all the circumstances of its locality, from the huge vaults into which it opened, with the well within it, I have scarcely any doubt of its having been one of the prisons of the Christian martyrs, who were sent here either to pine in hopeless banishment, or to be privately made away with. The image, rudely sculptured, and defaced by the weather, I carefully brought away with me, as one of the earliest remains of Christianity – a very few years, indeed, subsequent to our Saviour's death.

The Duke may not have been so far off the mark. During the 303-AD persecutions, which flushed out Christians by the simple expedient of requiring every Roman citizen in the Empire to make a public act of worship to Diocletian as a God, 300 Christians were abandoned on the neighbouring uninhabited island of Palmarola, and left to die. This image of Christ (if that's what it was) that the Duke took away with him (its present whereabouts, even if it still exists, are unknown) could have been very old, perhaps even older than the extraordinary head of Christ, on a ground of the Chi Rho symbol and flanked by two pomegranates, that was discovered in a floor-mosaic at Hinton St Mary, Dorset, in 1963[104], and which has been dated to sometime in the fourth century after Constantine made Christianity an official religion of the Roman Empire in 324 AD.

On the east side of the island they came across a freshwater spring gushing out of the trachyte cliff, and saw the remains of a three-mile aqueduct that Caligula had built to take the spring-water to Ponza town. The aqueduct followed the windings of the cliffs, with gaps where the headlands, over the centuries, had been eroded away. They landed in one of the bays. The Duke discovered to his delight something that Scrope had missed: a small, still-active volcanic fumarole surrounded by hot sand, sulphur, iron sulphate and rock-arsenic.

In the evening, as they returned to the yacht, they stopped to watch on the shore a spontaneous country-dance.

Cagliari – 'as we sailed in we saw the fleecy cloud of malaria ...'

We saw a party of country people, men and women, dancing the *tarantella*, to the sound of a tambourine and a sort of violin, played with a bow, consisting of three strings, and held something like a violoncello, between the knees. The tune was nothing but a simple modulation of see-saw to mark the time, but the dance is light, airy, and graceful. It consists entirely of the dancers setting at each other; then, with graceful movements of the arms, and with castanets moving round each other, alternately approaching and retreating. It was a very moderated, decent fandango. One woman dances until she has tired herself, then she sits down; another occupies her place immediately, and thus the dance is continuously kept up.

At sunset on July 17th the *Anna* dropped anchor in Cagliari roads, at the heel end of Sardinia and in one of the Mediterranean's safest anchorages. Not that safe, in the Duke's opinion.

As we sailed in, in a lovely summer's evening, we saw the fleecy cloud of malaria and intemperia creeping over the whole island, carrying certain death within its bosom to any – especially strangers – exposed to its influence.[105]

They were now in a different kingdom, that of Piedmont, ruled from Turin by the Savoyard king, Carlo Felice, via his Viceroy on the island. This Viceroy was a very different type from the pleasant archaeologist of Ponza: pompous and formal, and a great stickler for etiquette. One of his rules, of which the Duke was quickly made aware after being given pratique, required the *Anna* to salute first, with her guns, the Piedmontese flag. After some negotiation, the Duke agreed to do this, with 21 guns, returned gun for gun; then 17 for the Viceroy, again returned (this in fact a compliment, not part of the original deal). The next morning, he and Wilcox, dressed up to the nines as if they were calling on their own king, made an official visit ashore and the Viceroy received them with great ceremony and gave them the freedom of the island and of his carriage. The word had gone round that he was the King of England's father, and the whole town turned out to see him in the street. Later, the Viceroy wished to be presented to the rest of the Duke's party.

> But it is expressly intimated to them that they must go full-dressed, and in knee-breeches. Several have them not; but the English Consul, accustomed to cut short such difficulties, kindly offered to borrow breeches for them. I shall be charmed to see how this difficulty is to be solved … .
>
> The costumes of the local people are most singularly grotesque. The lower orders are usually in a thick leathern jacket sitting tight to the shape, a red cap hanging behind in a bag, an undressed sheepskin capote, and sometimes a wollen cloak over all with a hood, trowsers half-way down the leg, and leathern gaiters buttoned close down to the heel, the hair hanging in long, uncombed, unshorn locks, and many with thick beards. Thus equipped they march through the country generally with a long gun, or a pike, with the thermometer at an average of 86 deg … They boast that they don't rob: they only assassinate. That they do the latter is well known; that they do not do the former is not quite so clear. The higher orders literally scarcely ever stir out. There are not more than twenty carriages in all Cagliari. The only means of travelling is on horse-back, except on one road[106] newly made from Cagliari, which is the wonder of the world.

On July 22nd he dined with the Viceroy, and after dinner they rode out in his carriage to Quartu, a village about four miles from Cagliari to the east. Their route lay alongside muddy salt lakes, just a few inches deep. The Duke was anxious about their 'unwholesome exhalations', as he called them, but what he saw on the salt lakes provoked one of the loveliest descriptions in his diary.

> On all these lakes there are, in the water, myriads of swans, geese, and water-fowl of every description, and, above all, of that beautiful bird, the flamingo. They migrate thither from the coast of Africa. They fly in large bands, like wild geese, and preserve exactly their order of march like them. When they first appear they look like lines of fire on the horizon, their red plumage glittering and flashing in the sun. The moment they see the lakes of Cagliari, their accustomed haunts, below them, they form spiral concentric circles, screaming, and wailing, and at length alighting in regular lines upon the mud or in the shallow waters, stand mid-leg deep, like miniature lines of soldiers, dressed in scarlet. They are very difficult to approach.

At Quartu they were welcomed into the home of a rich Sard peasant-farmer, the owner of 500 sheep and 40 cows, and entertained with fruit and wine and country-dancing. The local priest thumped enthusiastically on a little piano, to the accompaniment of a mountain shepherd's pan-pipes.

> Their dance is *en ronde*, holding each others' hands, and making steps forwards and backwards like the *chassé* and *en avant* of a modern quadrille, and they slowly move round ... the musician is a shepherd, who came in from the mountain, with a long leathern case like a quiver at his back, filled with cane reeds of different sizes.

The Duke bought a set of pan-pipes to take away with him.

> Having dined with the Viceroy, I had my star and ribband [the Garter] on and a military laced loop in my hat. These attracted the old man's attention, as he could not guess what they meant, and desired leave to look at them. The laced loop he turned his nose up at, and exclaimed, 'Bagatelli!'. The English consul did the honour of the rest, and made the most of the highest order, the noblest, &c, &c, in Europe! The old man looked at them also, turned up his nose, and again exclaimed, 'Bagatelli!' and returned to his chair – a good comment on human greatness. But the young ladies did not view li bagatelli quite in so contemptible a light as the old father did, and that consoled me.

On July 25th the *Anna* was at sea again, to explore up Sardinia's west coast. The Viceroy heard he intended to take on water at Pula, on the south side of Cagliari bay and with a bad reputation for malaria, and insisted he used the viceregal cisterns without payment: an honour not given even to British ships of the line. The wind was against them. They were all day beating out of Cagliari's roads, and Captain Smyth's charts and soundings proved less reliable here than in Sicily.

> There is a large bank in mid-channel, with less than three fathoms upon it, which he does not lay down, and a passage on the Pula shore, on the other side of it, equally unlaid down. This is unpardonable in a roadstead so much frequented, and so important, as that of Cagliari. The fact is, I suspect, that Mr. Smyth was rather afraid of the malaria, and trusted more than he ought to have done to others.

On the 26th they doubled the huge granite headland of Cape Spartivento, the southernmost point of Sardinia. Beyond were vast gloomy forests[107] of evergreen oak, beech and chestnut on the slopes of the mountains, and, because of the prevalence of malaria, very little sign of humans. A stench of seaweed, rotting in the marshes along the shoreline, made the environment seem especially unsafe.

> Added to all this, the dews fell heavy like rain at night; today, for instance, although the sun was so hot that the thermometer, in the coolest part of the ship, stood at eighty-four degrees, the damp was such in mid-day that some of us were drawing upon deck, and we found that our colours would not work, but ran into one another, and did not dry.[108]

They came to the Isola di Sant' Antioco, once an island but now connected to Sardinia by a causeway that the Carthaginians began and the Romans completed. The *Anna* stood off a healthy distance from Sant' Antioco town – five miles away – and sent in the cutter for supplies, but it was refused permission to land, or to make any purchases.

> Upon being told this – as I had an order from the Court of Turin, and another from the Viceroy of Sardinia, directing that my vessel should be treated as a man-of-war – we weighed anchor, to run up to the town and enforce our demands.

Fortunately, about two miles from Sant' Antioco, they ran into a boat containing the English vice-consul and the port's health officer, both Sards, who said the whole thing had been a mistake on the part of ignorant soldiers. They were given immediate pratique and permission to land.

So we merely shewed them that we had shotted our guns, and were able to bring the town to reason, and then we became good friends; and I sent them off for provisions, fruit, &c, and a party went on shore sight-seeing.

In 1816, only 12 years before, Tunisian pirates had raided the town, and carried 800 inhabitants off into slavery, including the wife and family of the English vice-consul, whose house they'd plundered and destroyed. The English flag had been torn down. The vice-consul's family was successfully ransomed three months later, and in August of the same year Sir Edward Pellew, C-in-C Mediterranean and one of the legendary captains of the Napoleonic era, led a flotilla of five ships-of-the-line and five frigates against Algiers and bombarded the Dey into abolishing Christian slavery in his territories. All the other surviving captives from Sant' Antioco were subsequently released.

On August 1st, about half-way up the west coast, they anchored in the Bay of Oristano, which seemed to the Duke one of the finest natural harbours he'd yet encountered in the Mediterranean. But a foul smell was coming off the shore, denoting pestilence and death, and they didn't contemplate landing. The next morning he sent off a boat with orders not to land, only to buy provisions on the beach and alert the British Consul. The boat was met by local people who said that the whole coast as far north as Alghero was a charnel house of malaria. They implored them not to risk their lives by coming ashore. The consul was ill in bed, and expected to die. They would prepare provisions on the shore, and hoist a black flag in the evening when all was ready to be collected. They should anchor for the night well out in mid-channel, and move on as soon as possible in the morning.

The Duke took them at their word.

Alghero – 'the hand of God is against this fine country'

The hand of God is upon and against this fine country. It quite made us melancholy to see it. The worst of all this is that the damps fall so heavy that we all shiver below in these beautiful nights quite as much as if the weather was bad, and the thermometer in the great cabin never stands at less than 84 deg.

On August 4th they anchored in Alghero bay, and watched coral fishers snagging red coral with iron bars dragged over the seabed in about 60 fathoms of water. On the evening of the 6th they moored in the next bay to the north, beneath the white limestone cliffs of Punto della Caccia which appeared to the Duke like a giant Egyptian mummy lying on its back. The mountains behind were covered with majestic forests of ilex and chestnut, full of wild boar, deer and wild sheep called *muflone* – or 'muflong' as the Duke called them in his diary.

> August 7th. Some of our gentlemen went with their guns to see if they could find any game; a party, armed, went on shore to cut wood; and I passed the day in surveying Punta della Gallera and the adjacent cliffs, and shooting wild pigeons. I was fortunate enough to wing and bring down a small eagle, two or three of which accompanied our sport to pick up wounded birds; but this poor devil miscalculated his distance, and fell a victim to his temerity. It is a beautiful bird, very rare everywhere but here; and, having only his wing broke, although very high up, I shall endeavour to keep him alive.
>
> The shooting party on shore had no sport. The wooding party executed its duty; and in order to facilitate its object by clearing away the palmetto from the ground and leaves off the bushes, set the wood on fire, which ran like fury all over the mountain opposite, that was in a blaze in a minute. I was frightened out of my senses lest any houses should be scattered over the mountain's side; but, fortunately, none were in the line of fire, and we were told afterwards, by some country people, that we had done them good, by clearing away land for their sheep next spring, a thing which they were not permitted to do themselves. The fire lasted until night, and then – probably meeting a ridge of rocks – gradually died away.

The next day, August 8th, he set off round the cliffs of Capo Caccia to explore the Grotta di Nettuna, one of the world's most beautiful limestone caves, where stalactites drip into crystalline lagoons and rock-pigeons flutter in and out to sip fresh water caught in crevices in the walls. The cave's entrance was too low, and the surge too dangerous, to row the cutter straight in, but they managed to drag it inside with a rope, and their guide and six sailors lit up the interior with 100 candles. The Duke, like a king in fairyland, took up a position on an alabaster rock in the middle of a vast Gothic hall, and settled down to paint a watercolour. His bugler played, blue lights were lit, and all agreed that the effect was beyond imagination.

August 10th. We hove-to this morning off Cape Negretto, and Signor Donati went on shore to geologise ... I took the opportunity of bathing in the barge – in no bottom at 900 fathoms of line! We had calms and extreme heat all day until after Divine service, when a breeze sprung up and carried us round the Isle of Asinara, the northern point of Sardinia ... We got wild boars and partridges, and we broke up a wreck which we found on shore for firewood ... I went geologising in my barge ... In the evening we got under weigh for Ajaccio.

Neptune's Grotto – 'I had brought my bugle player with me.' They lit the grotto with 100 candles

CHAPTER FIFTEEN

Corsica

They had come to the source of Europe's pain, the birthplace of the 'Corsican monster', as Queen Maria Carolina of Naples used to call him. The year of his birth, 1769, in Ajaccio, was also the date of the death of the 14-year-old, independent Corsican republic, murdered by French troops at the battle of Ponte Nuovo over the Golo river. Corsica has been French ever since, except for the years 1794 to 1796 when the British were effectively in charge. They were ejected by a French expeditionary force led by the young Corsican artillery officer who would later conquer Europe. The house where he was born in Ajaccio in the Rue St-Charles overlooks a small, tree-lined square, Place Letizia, where there is a bust of him as a child.

Ajaccio – 'the reception of me is a struggle between the Bonapartists and the Royalists'

To the Duke, anchored in Ajaccio Bay and waiting for the pratique boat to row out and clear him for disembarkation, first impressions of the island were favourable. The mountains surrounding the bay seemed higher, more serrated, and more Alpine than those of Sardinia; their sides, covered in woodland, had been neatly terraced to high levels to make fields and farmhouses. The climate felt cooler too.

> It is impossible not to see the existence of a better and more liberal government exemplified by increased and improved agriculture, good houses, and the employment of capital in agricultural labour … Active improvements are going on in the town, old houses pulling down, and new ones erected and building … A fine market-place, and public promenade with trees, and a fountain in the midst, has been opened, and has a clear and good effect.

No pratique-boat arrived, however. In the end he grew tired of waiting. The *Anna*'s cutter was sent ashore to find out what was going on.

> [It] was met by a harbour-master or master pilot, who saluted it with what he thought a sailor's blessing – 'God d____ your eyes! Go back to your ship! We will be on board immediately.' In about an hour a boatful of French doctors came alongside, who, instead of giving us pratique, put us into five days' quarantine, because we last came from Cagliari, into which port, four months ago, an Algerine vessel had been chased by a French brig. The port being a neutral one, the Frenchman could not attack the Algerine, but blockaded her. The Sardinian government put guard-boats round the Algerine to prevent any communication with the shore, and would not give them water or refreshments. The Algerine sailed out in the face of day, out-manoeuvred and out-sailed the Frenchman, and escaped. The Frenchmen, enraged at missing their prize, went into Marseilles, and, out of pure sulkiness, told a lie, that the Algerine had communicated with Sardinia, and had it put into quarantine without any notice to its government, or, as I believe to anybody, as the French consul at Cagliari assured me that I should have immediate pratique at Ajaccio.
>
> All this we pleaded, but the doctors were inexorable, saying it was 'leur devoir'. I told them that it was 'un trés sot devoir' … but all this did not take us out of quarantine.
>
> August 16th. Got pratique this morning. I have reason to believe the reception of me is a struggle between the Bonapartists and the Royalists – the latter having shewn me such very marked attention, sending me fruit,

refreshments, &c, in profusion, and the commandant having taken no notice of me. They are very proud of being inhabitants of the place which gave Napoleon birth, and are very much surprised that I do not land to see his house, the room where he was born, &c.

The manner of his reception had, not for the first time, offended the Duke. He flatly refused to go ashore and pay his respects to the commandant. Instead, with deliberate discourtesy, he had his sailors row him in his barge in the opposite direction, to the Pointe de Sette Nave on the south side of the entrance to Ajaccio Bay: a dangerous reef of seven large rocks that seemed to him, from a distance, like ships under sail.

The sea breaks over them with immense fury ... The other side of the bay is guarded by a group of rocky islets, called les Isles Sanguinaires. A party went from the ship geologising – granite of different colours, jasper, and quartz.

August 17th. Visits all day; and crowds of people to see the vessel. Amongst others, the serjeant-majors of the garrison. I gave them a bottle of wine. They were very thankful, and in great glee; insisted upon carrying off Serjeant Mehan and the état-major of the vessel with them, to shew them the barracks &c ... Just as I was at dinner the commandant called upon me, and went away in high-dudgeon because he was not received. The fact was, that I meant to mark my sense of his incivility. The serjeant-majors have been parading all round the town, telling everybody of my reception of them.

On the 19th, at three o'clock in the morning, while the town was still fast asleep, the Duke finally slipped ashore at Ajaccio. An hour later a strange, picaresque procession, armed to the teeth, left the town on the new road (at that date the first proper, made-up road on the island) to Bastia, some 100 miles away to the north-east. The Duke led the way in a cabriolet, a two-wheeled, two-horse carriage, with one of his Manton double-barrelled shotguns between his legs, and his travelling-pistols stuck into his belt, all loaded and ready to shoot. His cabriolet reminded him of an English butcher's cart. It was about as comfortable. Its seat had no back-support, just a rail that cut into his loins, and he was forced to sit bolt upright throughout his entire journey. Donati and two of the *Anna*'s crew followed on horseback, each armed with pistols and a sabre.

Donati's pistols were astonishingly large, and clanked against the geological instruments and hammers suspended from his saddle and over his shoulder. The Duke's *lacquais de place*, Giovanni Gandolfi, also mounted, was wearing jack-boots and a night-cap. He carried a blunderbuss, and was followed by Sharp, on foot, armed with a blunderbuss and a cutlass. A local gendarme went ahead as advance guard, another marched beside the cabriolet, and a third brought up the rear beside their baggage-cart. They were nine in all – 11 to begin with, for two officers of the Corsican Rangers regiment had offered to guard them on the first, most dangerous stage of their journey: a miniature army setting out across the interior of an island with one of the worst reputations for blood-feuding and banditry in the entire Mediterranean.

On the whole – or so the Duke had been led to believe – parties of strangers were left alone. Most murders involved a family grievance that could go back years, generations even. But if trouble occurred, they were ready to confront it. The biggest danger was if one of their party became separated from the others. Stragglers were a favourite target for the less scrupulous *banditti*.

One of their gendarme guards told him a hair-raising story about a terrorist he'd shot dead three years before. The man had killed someone from Ajaccio, cut off his head and went around with his severed ear as a trophy in his pocket. In the end his own family had given him away. The gendarme ambushed him at a spring he was known to visit in the mountains, and put two quick shots through his body from his carbine. The man was eating as he walked along, with his gun over his shoulder. He suspected nothing.

> He fell without a groan, only biting his fingers to the bone with fury as he dropped.

Turning the corner of a square as he left Ajaccio, the Duke saw a tall, elegantly-dressed woman, heavily veiled, kissing her hand to him. He gallantly returned the salute, and passed on. The day before, a tame young stag had been brought to the *Anna* with a mysterious note signed 'Une dame d'Ajaccio'. The stag was a present to 'L'ami des Bourbons'. He found out that his *incognita* was the wife of an officer in the Corsican government, whose husband was in Paris, and he wrote her a note back saying that he couldn't possibly come ashore after his discourteous reception, and that she would have to be satisfied with his thanks from a distance. He was anyway, he confessed, more than 50 years old.

The veiled lady was the only person in the street at that early hour, and the Duke suspected she was his correspondent. On board, the young stag proved a great success. Of a darker brown than an English red deer, it fed out of hand and followed them around like a dog. Most of the time it preferred the officers' quarter-deck, but at mealtimes it went forward and begged biscuit and potatoes from the sailors. They christened it Boney.

Their route took them up the valley of the river Gravona, between high mountains covered with gum cistus and arbutus, and forests of elm and chestnut. At first the valley was wide and well-cultivated, with little evidence of livestock. In the August heat, the Corsican cattle, sheep and goats were mostly pastured high up in the mountains, for green grass and to escape the flies. The few shepherds they met on the road were all heavily armed. By breakfast-time, they had covered over 20 miles and were in sight of the little mountain village of Vero, high up on their left hand and supposed to be the lair of Corsica's principal bandit. Here on

Monte della PovFeri – the bandit's lair

View from the Inn: they 'stopped to rest, eat and bait the horses.' And sketch

the roadside there was a gendarme post and a small public house, and they stopped for an hour or more to rest, eat and bait their horses. In the distance, away to the north east and at the end of the valley up which they were climbing, they could see the rocky, 7,600-ft-high, granite pinnacles of Monte d'Oro, part of the mountain spine, a continuation of the Alps, that bisects Corsica from north-east to south-west. Their route to Bastia, on the other side of the island, lay across a high pass on the flanks of Monte d'Oro.

Beyond Vero they crossed to the south side of the Gravona by a single-span granite bridge, recently-built.

> It is a very good piece of masonry, and indeed the whole road does credit to the engineer who has executed it.

The river was fast-flowing now, through pastures and chestnut-woods, and they saw several little water-mills working busily, and groynes diverting water into irrigation-channels for riverside fields. The mountains, pressing in on either side, reminded him of the Pyrenees and the days, in 1814, when he'd led his Buckinghamshire Yeomanry to join Wellington's victorious army in the last days of the Peninsular campaign, before the battle of Toulouse.

At the end of the first day, at the foot of Monte d'Oro, they came to the small town of Bocagnano, some 25 miles from Ajaccio, and put

'the road does credit to the engineer'

up in a little inn that the Duke thought fairly wretched, yet palatial compared with some of the lodgings he'd encountered on the road in Sicily. They'd brought their own provisions and beds, and Giovanni cooked them an excellent dinner. They were all tired, but proud of their day's progress.

> The craggy heights of Monte d'Oro rise just before our window, and the streams, which gush out everywhere, are as cold and pellucid as ice. In some of the crevices of the mountains snow is still to be seen ... .

> August 20th. Started at four o'clock this morning. The rogue of an innkeeper had the modesty to charge me 186 francs – we having only had beds, a piece of mutton, two pigeons, and some milk. I insisted on his putting the bill, according to the laws of France, in writing, and declared I would take it to the Préfet, who was in the town. He then came down to 100 francs. I insisted on my bill. He than had it written out, and reduced it to 50. I gave him 40 francs, which was twice as much as he ought to have had.

At the top of the pass, at a height of nearly 4,000 feet, they emerged out of the chestnut forest onto a granite mountain-side bare of vegetation except for the odd, scrubby evergreen oak. Monte d'Oro towered above their heads. Then the road began to descend in zig-zags through a forest of pine, chestnut and beech, with an understorey of arbutus, myrtle, tree heath, common fern, and sticky-leaved gum cistus: perfect bandit-country and the haunt, in fact, of a notorious robber that the authorities had been after for some time.

> On entering it our gendarmes unslung their carbines, and one went on as advanced guard. We did the same, and kept together … After we had gone through about four miles of the thickest forest imaginable, we came up with a party of men at work on the road, who informed us with the greatest glee that this terrific personage had been shot close by, the evening before, by the Voltigeurs de la Corse; and shortly after we met Le Juge de Paix of the Canton going to view the body, and make his *procés verbal*, accompanied by one of the voltigeurs who had killed the brigand.

It turned out that some shepherds had given him away. They'd seen him climbing the previous day amongst the crags of Monte d'Oro, perhaps to ambush a straggler either of the Préfet's party, or of the Duke's, and two voltigeurs, sent out to look for him, had come across him sitting in the open on a rock and sharpening his stiletto.

> They crept up towards him; but from some stone which fell from under their feet, he discovered them. They cried out to him to surrender; he instantly caught up his double-barrelled gun which lay beside him, and fired at the voltigeurs, but missed both shots; one of them fired and wounded him, the other killed him dead.

By breakfast-time they had emerged from the forest and arrived at Vivario, 13 miles from their overnight stop, with views to the west of Monte Rotondo, at 8,500 ft the second highest mountain in Corsica. They were also emerging, geologically speaking, from the western part of the island composed of crystalline rocks (granite, gneiss, diorite) into the eastern, sedimentary side (schist, slate and shale). Donati was busy with his hammer. In one outcrop he found some dark, glassy obsidian.

Beyond Vivario, they crossed the river Vecchio by another fine single-span bridge whose engineering the Duke much admired – it was thrown over a deep gorge – then skirted the eastern flank of Monte Rotondo on a vertiginous corniche. Their three-man guard of gendarmes left them now, for the remainder of the road was considered safe. But every shepherd they met was still heavily armed.

In the evening they came to the town of Corte, having covered a distance of 26 miles during the day. Corte had its brief moment of glory during the days of Corsican independence: it was proclaimed the island's capital, and Pascal Paoli founded Corsica's first university there in 1765. The old town sits up on a high buttress of rock, at the exit of the Gorges du Tavignano. Both the town's inns were on top of the cliff, unapproachable by carriages of any kind, and the final approach had to be made on foot. The Duke sent a courier on ahead, to order dinner at five francs a head, and struggled up, tired, hungry and out of breath, to the lower of the two inns. Their rooms were good – airy and clean – but dinner was a disaster. A party of French army officers had eaten there before them.

> After waiting for two hours, in came une pinçée of vermicelli swimming in an ocean of oil, as soup; then came three trout, of three quarters of an inch each in length (for I measured them), and three cotelets and an omelet, with apologies for sauce from the landlord, that he had *calculated* on getting some gibier for my altesse, but had failed, and that vraiment Messieurs les Officiers had ate up everything in the house.

The harassed innkeeper suggested a cheaper price for their meal.

> I told him that it was not reduction of price but increase of dinner that we wanted, and I desired him to send out and get some more meat. Alas! None was to be got. The weather was hot, meat would not keep, and so there was none, and we had no more dinner.

They were on the road the next morning by 4 am, on the last leg of their journey to Bastia, 43 miles away (the Duke put it at 46). Their route lay down the Golo River. It was hard going all the way, over a road that was little more than a mule track; the Governor of Corsica was a native of Ajaccio, and all the money allocated for the island's first proper highway had been spent on the southern end of the road. They stopped for breakfast at 8.30 am at the Ponte Nuovo, where Corsican independence had died in 1769, and pushed on through dense, evergreen, shrubby maquis. The Duke correctly identified its main constituent as the winter-flowering strawberry tree (*Arbutus unedo*) with its glossy green leaves and reddish-brown bark; and recognised that he'd left the granite behind in the mountains, and was now in a land of schist and shale. Five miles from the sea, not far from where Bastia airport now stands, they turned north for the final 13 miles of their journey, up the coastal plain and alongside a long brackish lagoon, the Etang de Biguglia (now a nature reserve), the haunt of cormorants, purple herons, flamingoes, marsh tortoises, and – in the Duke's day – malarial mosquitoes. They reached the old Genoese port of Bastia after dark. They were exhausted. They had covered nearly 100 miles in three days, through scenes that very few people, especially Englishmen, had ever witnessed. The *Anna* was waiting for them in the harbour.

> An immense crowd assembled to see us, and attended us to the water's edge. The streets got narrow and winding; the mob increased and grew noisy; all the night-capped population assembled at the windows, and that part which was dressed came into the streets to see what was the matter, and could not quite make out whether I was some hero enjoying an ovation in a cabriolet, or a criminal carrying to the galleys in a cart. However, I was thus conveyed to my barge, and the mob thanked me for the sight I had afforded them by cheering me when I pushed off from the shore.

> August 22nd. The English Consul came to me. Bad news of quarantine at Genoa, and at all the Mediterranean ports, in consequence of the illness at Marseilles called the small-pox, which is spreading its ravages. The Collector of the Customs called and offered every civility. The Mayor and Prefect did the same. In short, my reception here forms a strong contrast with that at Ajaccio.

The *Anna* was beset by boatloads of sightseers. Pretty Emma Wilson proved an added attraction.

> I allowed all well-dressed persons to come on board … But a boatful of brigands hung round the ship, peeped through the quarter-deck ports, and laughed and made faces at Mrs. Wilson on the deck. They were desired to go away, but would not; said it was their port, and they would do as they liked. Our men were ordered to force them off, which they did; and the Frenchmen went swearing on shore, and threw stones, but, on a musket being pointed at them, ran away. I sent off to the police, who in a twinkling seized the boat and the men, and put them all into prison, when the Mayor sent me a world of excuses, &c, and issued an ordinance to prevent a repetition of such impertinence … The crowds of ladies who come on board to see the vessel are incessant. We have not a moment to ourselves.

From the deck of the *Anna* they watched the youth of the town daring each other to jump off the 40-ft-high Lion Rock, feet-first into the sea and crossing themselves before they jumped. A Corsican singer with a fine bass voice came on board. He was married to a modest, well-mannered Englishwoman whose father had ruined himself in Paris, and the Duke, impressed with his singing, gave him a letter of introduction to Lord Burghersh, British ambassador and musical impresario at Florence. The singer was all for leaving for Florence at once. On the evening of the 28th the *Anna* herself left Bastia, heading south along the coast in light airs. The Duke wanted to explore the archipelago of grey granite islands in the Straits of Bonifacio, between Corsica and Sardinia; in particular a little islet[109] which the Romans were supposed to have used in classical times as a granite quarry. The Straits, a maze of low, rocky, windswept islands overlooked by the white limestone cliffs of Bonifacio, are nowadays a magnet for summer tourists and yachtsmen. Since 1992 they have been given some protection by being declared an international marine nature reserve.

They put in for the night in what turned out to be the very sheltered roadstead of Porto Vecchio, after a nasty moment in late afternoon when a sudden squall caught the *Anna* unawares and layed her on her beam-ends. They had to double-reef the sails, and were nervous because they could see reefs about them on every side and had no charts of the Porto Vecchio roadstead.

> In the midst of all this pother we found the vessel answer the helm, as we thought, very ill; and, on examining, we found that the blessed remains of Mr. Stebbing's iron-work, in his patent steering apparatus, had flown like glass, and we were obliged instantly to unship it all, and fix the iron tiller.

The town of Porto Vecchio was more or less deserted at this time of year, because of the threat of malaria. Between it and the sea was an area of marshy ground covered with heath and arbutus. Going ashore was out of the question. The next night they anchored in the Golfe de Santa Manza and admired the white limestone cliffs of the Rocchi Bianchi; but not a house, hut, shepherd or living being could be seen anywhere along the coast. The only sign of life was a French brig laden with firewood which her crew were stealing out of the woods that grew along the shore.

On August 30th he set out in his barge to look for the ancient quarry that had supplied the granite, it was said, for the Pantheon at Rome. He landed first on the low-lying Ile Lavezzi on which he found some miserable goats and horses shipped over for its meagre summer grazing from the Corsican mainland; and four fishermen. They directed him back on his tracks to the uninhabited Ile Cavallo, now an exclusive island with luxury villas and its own airstrip and signs along the shore forbidding you to land.

On a small islet separated from Cavallo by a very narrow strait, we found the object we were in search of. Immense blocks of granite lay all over the islet, *ébauché*[110], and partly worked, and signs of immense quantities being carried away. A large column lay on the ground rudely rounded off, as it came from the parent rock under which it lay, sound, and compact, and ringing like a bell. It was 29 feet in length, and 3 feet 6 inches in diameter … Amidst all these rocks and ruins we took our dinner. The causeway, or inclined plane, formed of blocks of granite, and along which these immense masses were rolled to be embarked, is quite visible, and perfect down to the water's edge; and a large mass, probably intended for part of an entablature, is now to be seen at the extremity of the causeway close by the water, raised upon its granite supports, ready to be hove into the boat waiting for it … I cannot find that upon any of these islands there is fresh water.

On the evening of the 31st they weighed anchor and set a course for Genoa, some 200 miles away to the north. It would be the Duke's final voyage aboard the *Anna Eliza*.

CHAPTER SIXTEEN

Path to Rome

September 3rd, 1828. This morning I dropped my anchor in the harbour of Genoa, and here ends my voyage. Instead of finding quarantine, we obtained pratique immediately, the quarantine being confined to Marseilles and the land communications across the Rhone. The illness at Marseilles is not the small-pox ... Nothing can be finer than the situation of Genoa, covering the side of one of the lower roots of the Apennines, with its white houses, marble palaces, and churches.

'I dropped my anchor in Genoa and here ends my voyage'

The Duke had made up his mind to send the *Anna* back to England without him, and pay off his crew in their home port, Southampton.[111] The costly alternative was to keep her and her crew moored up at Genoa until the spring or summer of 1829. As for himself, he wanted to spend the winter and spring at Rome with his sister, then return home overland across the Alps and down the Rhine.

On the 4th, he paid an official call in full dress at the Palazzo Doria, and was civilly received by the Queen Dowager of Piedmont and Sardinia in a huge room with such a slippery floor that he had to be careful how he moved about. He found her a mild-mannered, respectable old lady, with little of the usual Austrian hauteur. She avoided politics and asked him politely about his travels, especially in Sardinia.

On the 5th he explored in the *Anna's* barge eastwards along the coast.

> Nothing can be more beautiful than the Bay of Genoa. In some respects it is finer than that of Naples. The Apennines rising high immediately behind the town; the *luxe* of marble palaces, and houses of every degree, colour and form, interspersed with orange and olive groves, and vines, covering the mountain's base, and swarming up its side; the bold outline of the walls and fortified positions crowning its summit, present a picture not to be equalled anywhere … To the eastward is the Lazaretto[112] and Dockyard, where three large frigates are on the stocks. Here the English were to have stormed the works, upon their eastern flank, in 1814. Wilcox was to have commanded a party of seamen upon this service; but the town capitulated that evening.[113]

At anchor in Genoa. Here he was received by the Queen in a huge room with a slippery floor

On the 8th Mr Arundel, the brother-in-law of his sister Mary, arrived on the steamboat from Naples on his way home for treatment in England. He'd been crippled at Rome by a chill caught when he'd been hot. He had a paralysed leg and walked with crutches, but bravely kept his spirits up. The Duke made a point of entertaining him on board, and taking him sightseeing in his coach round Genoa. It seems probable that Arundel sailed home with the *Anna*.

On the 13th September the Duke gave a farewell party on board for his crew.

> The embroidery and gold work here are famous. I have bought some for those I love best. I have given Carphy and Michelson a silver coffee or punch pot each, in token of my approbation and thanks, and a silver snuff-box to Ford. They are delighted beyond measure. To Donati, who takes leave of me here, I have given a gold snuff-box, ten pounds to carry him home to Naples, par diligence, and a letter to Sir Henry Lushington, requesting him to advance Donati fifty pounds sterling, to pay him for his time. He is sorry to go, and I am equally so to lose him, as he has been a very active, quiet, unassuming companion, and has been of great use to me. I give my ship's company a supper and bowl of punch as a leave-taking. They were very uproarious and jolly, and the quiet harbour rung with their cheers until eleven at night.

> 14th. Wilcox and Radcliffe take leave of me – I believe highly pleased with all that I have done with respect to them. I have certainly every reason to be satisfied with them both …

> September 15th. This morning I took leave of the 'Anna Eliza'. My crew parted with me; I believe, also, with regret. They fired a salute and cheered loudly. I went to the Wilson's lodgings, where my carriage was, packed, and, after many vexatious delays, got off from thence about twelve o'clock.

The *Anna* had been the Duke's home for over a year. She had enabled him to visit places, and see sights, that few travelling Englishmen had ever witnessed, let alone recorded. It must be admitted that, when she left for home, a certain magic and glamour departed with her: he became, in a way, just an Ordinary Tourist, like all the others who went on the Grand Tour in the 17th and 18th centuries. Now he planned to make a month-long, autumn excursion by private coach into the Alpes Maritimes, to the foot of Mont Blanc.

The Wilsons preferred to remain for the time being at their rented lodgings in Genoa – Emma Wilson, it seems, still hadn't fully recovered from whatever illness had afflicted her at Naples. So now just three of them remained to travel in his four-horse calêche: the Duke, his *lacquais de place* Giovanni, and his other personal servant, Sharp. A fourgon (baggage-carrying mule-cart) followed behind. Beyond Voltri, where they changed horses for the first time, they looked back from higher ground to the white city of Genoa and its azure bay.

> We saw the 'Anna Eliza', with every sail set on the breeze, gaining an offing under her royals, and making her way to dear, distant England.

Their route took them along the coast road as far as Nice, over the high mountain passes of the Colle di Tenda to the Piedmontese capital of Turin, then up the valley of the river Dora through Aosta to the foot of Mont Blanc. The Duke had his usual altercations with rogue couriers, idle postilions, fraudulent post-masters, and rapacious innkeepers. In the Alpes Maritimes, where the road, lacking a parapet, was cut along a dizzying precipice, their muleteer abandoned the two lead mules for regular swigs from a bottle hanging behind the carriage. His mules plodded on, sure-footed and regardless, but the Duke threatened to shoot him dead unless he stayed at his proper place beside their heads. Near the village of Cormayeur, with Mont Blanc in sight now, they came to a sharp turn over a deep ravine.

In sight of Mont Blanc, a picnic breakfast of mutton chops

The road was torn up by a torrent, so we got out; and well we did, as our rogue of a postilion took too sharp a turn and all but overset the carriage down the precipice. Had we been in the carriage I think we should very likely by our weight have carried it over.

Mont Blanc was rather a disappointment: barely visible, by no means picturesque. The weather was bad, with much rain, and the mountain had its head in the clouds. Their best moment occurred in an Alpine meadow shaded by walnut trees: a delicious open-air picnic-breakfast of mutton chops cooked with the aid of his canteen, and brief glimpses of the summit of Mont Blanc, over the top of another mountain, before clouds blotted out the view. By October 5th he was back in Turin, at the town's second-best hotel where, according to Giovanni, none but voituriers ever stayed. The bad weather had filled up the smarter Hôtel de l'Europe, whose proprietor had put his prices up accordingly. But the three rooms he hired in the lesser inn were clean and well-furnished, and gratifyingly cheap.

> October 7th. My landlord, in spite of having made a contract with me, sent in a ridiculous bill. Got my passport visé, and my order for post-horses, and set him at defiance – telling him that I would pay his contract, and not a sou more. He angry, more so at my laughing at him.

On the road back to Genoa, on the flat Piedmontese plain five miles south east of Alessandria, he visited the battlefield of Marengo where, on June 14th, 1800, Napoleon had achieved one of his more improbable victories: the battle lost at five pm, and won back again at seven. Napoleon marched his Army of Italy over the Great St Bernard pass from Dijon to halt Austrian expansion in northern Italy, then was caught by surprise, with his forces scattered, at the village of Marengo by the main Austrian army. The battle raged all day, and by five o'clock his exhausted and outnumbered troops were in full retreat, and the elderly Austrian commander, Baron Melas, returned to his headquarters in the belief that victory had been won. He left his chief-of-staff behind on the battlefield to organise the mopping up. In the evening a fresh French corps under General Desaix, to whom at one o'clock Napoleon had sent the brief, panic message: 'Revenez au nom de Dieu!', arrived by forced marches and launched a ferocious counter-attack which caused surprise, then panic among the Austrians, and turned the day. The Austrians lost 9,500 men in the battle, and all Italy south of the Mincio. By February 1801

Austria was out of the war and Britain stood alone against revolutionary France.

> Thus was the victory torn out of Melas' grasp, and the destinies of Europe for many years wholly changed … The whole battle was fought upon plain and even ground, like a bowling-green – not a tree nor an irregularity to hide a man behind. It was all fair, downright fighting, without maneouvring of any kind. It is singular that two fields, so bloody and so important in their consequences as Marengo and Waterloo, should thus have been fought on plain ground, where there was not the power on either side to maneouvre, but when everything depended on the courage and firmness of the parties engaged … The army which was strongest in cavalry ought to have won the day, and the advantage was clearly on the side of the Austrians.

On the 9th, during an overnight stop at the town of Novi Ligure, he found himself in the middle of an earthquake.

> This morning at half-past three o'clock, as I was lying in my bed awake, I felt a great shake in my bed. My first idea was, as there was an archway into the inn under my bedroom, that a heavy carriage coming in had run against the side of the house; but in a moment I found it was an earthquake. The bed cracked, timbers of the room groaned, and the floor heaved like the waves of the sea. I jumped up and ran under the arch of the door of my room, knowing that under an arch I was safest. I counted four regular heaves from west to east. The house literally bent like a willow, and overhung the street. I expected the last heave would have thrown it down – two seconds more I am convinced would have done so. I think the shock lasted about nine or ten seconds. The furniture of the room flew against the wall and fell down: the noise was tremendous. But how much was occasioned by the earthquake itself, and how much by the clashing of glass, the cracking of beams, and the clatter through the whole house, I of course could not tell. Those, however, who were out of doors said that the roar and rushing of a subterranean wind were very awful.

As soon as the shocks ceased, he rushed to the window and threw it open. Outside it was a clear, calm, starlit night; nothing untoward; nature apparently at peace with itself; no sign in the sky of what had just occurred. But there was pandemonium in the streets: women screaming, men shouting, dogs howling, the drums of the town's garrison beating the call to arms, soldiers running about half-naked, citizens arming themselves against looters and putative invaders.

I went out of my room to see if the house was injured or any one hurt, and the whole interior population of the inn was assembled in shirts and chemises on the staircase, some praying and all screaming. One fat Frenchman in his shirt, and with stockingless, unslippered, and dirty feet, with a red nightcap on his head, as I opened my door, fell down in a fainting fit. The house had several cracks in it, but no mischief was done, and I went to bed again; the clamour in the streets and on the inn stairs continued all night, and defied sleep.

In the morning, when he got up, he found that some chimneys had fallen down, and houses cracked, but there had been no significant destruction of buildings or widespread loss of life. Some travellers who came in on the coach from Milan described the earthquake as coming from that direction, and later that day, as he headed south in his coach towards Genoa, he was able to trace its route through all the towns and villages through which he passed. The earthquake seems to have affected the entire north Italian plain, especially Turin, and passed under the Apennines.

That evening his four-horse calêche negotiated the final steep, slow, winding descent into Genoa, and entered the town at a fast canter along the harbour walls. Genoa had also been badly affected: two steeples down, many houses cracked, everyone sleeping out on the streets. But the Duke was glad to see his friends the Wilsons again. He'd been on the road for more than three weeks, with only his two servants for company.

October 10th. Last night there were three small shocks, and one of them has cracked Mr Wilson's lodging, in which I am. The alarm here is excessive. The English and many of the natives have left the city, or are leaving it. Great nonsense this, as the visitation is so extensive, one place within a day's journey of this city must be as dangerous as another. I remain, and shall abide it. The priests are taking advantage of the convulsion, and are filling the people's heads with all sorts of superstition.

About 30,000 Genoese, according to his calculation, slept out in the open that night, and every horse in the city had been taken by fugitives into the countryside. Capuchin and Franciscan friars, of whom the Duke had a fairly low opinion at the best of times, were preaching at every corner that the end of the world was at hand.

They prophesied that last night Genoa would be destroyed. If any mischief had happened they would have had the credit of truly prophesying; it has not, and now they say the danger was averted by their prayers – so they are right either way. The people were singing the 'De Profundis' and the 'Miserere' all night. Many slept in carriages. My courier – whom I believe to be a veritable poltroon, but has more sham courage than I ever saw in a man, evinced by eternal talk and boasting – slept, I find, in my calêche, and did the honours of my fourgon to a married couple of his acquaintance, who passed the night in it, stretched at length on their bedding, which they stuffed into it, and then crept in as if into a hearse.

The Duke, Giovanni and Sharp set out for Rome on October 20th. Their route took them via Lucca, Pisa and Livorno, then over the hills via

Radicofani – a view from the inn of the volcano-top village

Poggibonsi and Siena to the volcano-top village of Radicofani that dominates the Val d'Orcia; then on down the Tiber valley on the Via Flaminia to Rome. Between Massa and Lucca the Duke had probably his closest shave with *banditti* in all his travels.

To reach Lucca they had a mountain to cross, and were warned at the foot of it that, only the night before, a coach had been stopped and robbed. A gendarme commandant offered him an escort if he paid for it. The Duke, shocked and angry, accused him of bargaining for travellers' blood and offering his sovereign's militia for hire, and pressed on without an escort.

The mountain is two miles in ascent; and, I must confess, that a better suited place for a sanguinary deed I never saw. A steep precipice on one side; rocks, covered with brushwood, on the other; and thick woods behind them. We were told that the banditti were four in number. The moon rose upon the scene, and cast its broad light and broader shadows across the Apennines. I never saw a more lovely, romantic scene. My postilion, and he of my fourgon, when the road became steep, got off their horses to walk up. I thought this was too good a joke, if there was any truth at all in the story. I therefore told the men to mount, and assured them that if we were attacked, and they stopped or left their horses, I would shoot them first. To raise our spirits the rascals pointed to our notice a cross, newly put up, and informed us that a courier had been murdered there not a month ago. Giovanni was on the box, with a carbine; I in the calêche, with three brace of pistols, and Sharp on the box of the fourgon, also with a carbine. Just in the darkest part of the pass the postilion said – 'Ecco excellenza – this is the very spot!' The words were scarcely out of his mouth when, about 100 yards before us, we beheld four men, in the moonlight, in the middle of the road. The moment they saw us they divided, two on each side of the road, and advanced, singing together a sort of wild chorus.

The postilion, to do him justice, flogged manfully on. I said to Giovanni – 'There they are. Do you take the right hand birds, and I will take the left.' The men advanced, singing, one before the other. I fully expected the rear man would have made a spring at the horses' bridle, and the front man at the carriage door, especially as I observed the front man tend, or swerve, in his walk towards the carriage, instead of making room for it, as a person on foot, in that situation, at night would naturally have done. The moment, therefore, the fellow nearest me came abreast of me, I cocked my pistol, and put it to his head, and, if he had put out his hand towards the carriage,

I should instantly have shot him dead. At the same moment Giovanni cocked his blunderbuss in the other fellow's ear. Upon hearing and seeing these hostile preparation the fellows ducked – 'Their song broke, the warblers flew.' They slid by the carriage, encountered Sharp, blunderbuss *en avant*, standing up, like Mars in his chariot, on the seat of the fourgon. They made another duck, and were in a moment lost in the gloom of the rocks and the road ... We were quite frightened, and so, perhaps, were they.

A week later, near the Lago di Bolsena, they met, on its return from Rome, the carriage that had been robbed in the same spot. Its voituriers gave an exactly similar description of the four *banditti*, and how they had advanced on them, two-by-two and singing a chorus, before their attack. They claimed the gendarmerie below the mountain were in league with the robbers, and probably sent a warning on to them that the Duke's party was armed.

It is clear that we had an escape, and that nothing saved us but the sight of our arms, and the knowledge that we were ready to use them.

The Via Flamina – time to walk, time to talk. Now a busy main road (Thos Jones)

They reached Rome on November 4th, having spent more than a fort-night on the road. The Duke's first, distant view of the Eternal City, like that of Mont Blanc, was something of a disappointment.

On mounting the hill above Baccano the postilions stop, and with an awful cast of voice exclaim, 'Ecco Roma!' and they look back at you to be sentimental and cry, or to be extatic and dance. I could not do the latter and I did not do the former, whereupon I was ill thought of by the postilions and my courier. In the first place, the view is nothing. The Apennine forms a fine background, but it is too distant. The Campagna is a horrid ugly, wide, wasty, weltering plain, and of Rome you behold only the misty haze which overhangs what you see is a city, and the overtopping dome of St Peter's ... As we advanced I cannot say that Rome improved.

The campagna – 'a horrid, ugly, wide, wasty, weltering plain!' (the Duke)

CHAPTER SEVENTEEN

Roman Winter

He crossed the Tiber over the Milvian bridge, passed along a filthy lane reeking of garlic and goat-dung and flanked by the ugly, jerry-built hovels of washerwomen and prostitutes, and entered the city by the Porta del Popolo. His *lasciare passare* from the papal government swept him through the hall of the custom-house into the Piazza del Popolo beyond, one of the loveliest in a city of beautiful squares. It was here that the just-arrived Martin Luther had fallen on his knees, held up his hands to heaven and exclaimed: 'Hail holy Rome, sanctified by the holy martyrs and by the blood they shed here'.

The Duke was no Luther. He hardly gave the square a second look. He was tired after his long journey. And he didn't like the baroque.

> The piazza is not noble. The two churches, with each a cupola, opposite, standing like two Brobdignag sentry-boxes, are frightful. The Egyptian obelisk of granite in the centre is very fine, but the houses round the piazza are plastery and white, and give one the idea of an English watering-place.

Three roads fan out from the far end of the Piazza del Popolo, and the two fine baroque churches that the Duke disliked so much – S Maria di Monte Santo and S Maria de Miracoli – stand in the acute angles of their intersection. The Duke's carriage took the left-hand fork, rattled down the Via dei Babuina, and came to a halt in the Piazza di Spagna, where most fashionable English arrivals ended their journey to Rome. The diary records only that he put up at an hôtel: perhaps the exclusive Albergo Londra near the Spanish Steps.

News of his arrival soon spread. The next day, November 5th, the English consul called on him early, and he had hardly finished his breakfast before his sister Mary turned up, eager to whisk him off to see St Peter's, the epicentre of her Church. It was the beginning of an intensive round of sight-seeing and antiquity-hunting during the day, guided by his sister; and socialising at night, shepherded by a Lady Westmoreland who had set herself up in Rome as a leading society hostess.

November 8th. Extraordinary woman, and sometimes mad. Very good-humoured and kind when she chooses to be so, but a violent and bitter enemy. She has taken it into her head to take me up very eagerly just now. She engaged me to go with her to the opera tomorrow, which I agreed to, forgetting it was Sunday. I recollected it this evening, and wrote her a note merely saying that I had made a determination not to break through my English Sunday habits when abroad, and that she, therefore, must excuse me, and I was sure she would not be affronted.

Lady Westmoreland sent a reply by return setting out, in four pages, all the arguments for doing in Rome as the Romans do. But the Duke stuck to his principles. They went to the opera on the following Tuesday, a production of *Othello*[114] by Rossini which he didn't much enjoy. The tenor seemed to him conceited, the prima donna a screamer.

The Coliseum, in the Duke's day an occasional quarry for Roman builders

One by one, he ticked off the important sights: the Forum, Trajan's Baths and the painted ceilings of the underground rooms of Nero's Golden House, where the guides held up candles on 20 foot long canes to enable him to see the wonderful, Pompeian-style arabesques. He spent two hours at the Coliseum, which in imperial times had seated 50,000 spectators and now served as a sort of occasional quarry for Roman builders. In the Duke's day it was like an English abbey in an advanced state of decay: mature trees grew in the arena. Before it was given a good weed in the 1870s, 420 species of wild flora had been identified in its rubble, some of them probably exotic introductions with animal feed in Roman times. He visited the Baths of Caracalla, where Gibbon conceived the theme of *Decline and Fall* and Shelley in 1819 composed *Prometheus Unbound*. The Duke, like all his generation, was familiar with Gibbon and the best-selling Byron, but there's no evidence that he'd ever heard of Shelley, other than as the eldest son of a Sussex landowning baronet; or, more especially, of Keats, who died in 1821 in his little room beside the Spanish Steps, perhaps not a stone's throw away from where the Duke was staying now. Shelley, anyway, was a member of the secret, anarchist society of Illuminists who believed in cutting the throats of all kings, priests and feudal aristocrats, and would have loathed the Duke and all he stood for.

> November 10th. I went to the Capitol. The statues of Castor and Pollux decidedly ugly. The trophies of Marius fine. The equestrian statue of Marcus Aurelius the finest thing in the world, especially the horse. Marcus Aurelius rides like a tailor. But the whole is magnificent. In the Museum the Dying Gladiator.[115] Studied it some time. Great doubts are entertained whether it be a gladiator or not.

Two days later he walked out into the Campagna, beyond the walls of Rome, to visit the delightful little Temple of Bacchus (known today as the church of S Urbano) which began its career as an outdoor pavilion of a Roman villa, and which must surely have reminded the Duke of his landscape gardens at Stowe. It wouldn't do so today: the surrounding, once-Arcadian landscape has been obliterated by modern development.

> Crossed the fields to the Temple of Bacchus. Very pretty, snug, brick temple, with Corinthian columns – now made a chapel. It stands on a brow of a small hill, at the foot of which starts the spring of Egeria, out of the side of the tufa rock, in a sort of cavern or opening in the hill, overgrown with brushwood and aquatic plants, and very delightful in summer. The water is very pure and limpid … Although this spot is close under the walls

of Rome, it is as much deserted as if it was in the depths of the forests of
Apulia ... The sedgy brook creeps along the valleys ... the snipe and water-
hen are the only inhabitants.

'close under the walls of Rome it is ... deserted'

But what really obsessed the Duke's attention, with a mixture of
fascination and repulsion, was St Peter's and the Vatican, and all the
medieval pomp and pageantry that surrounded the Triple Tiara and the
Vicar of Rome. He liked to wander into St Peter's of an evening, sit down
on his folding travelling-stool which Giovanni carried about for him, and
watch shafts of declining sunlight streaming into the cupola from high
windows, and hear the distant sound of organ and choir from a side-
chapel – and at the same time be horrified by the sight of the Catholic
devout kissing St Peter's 13th-century bronze toe; or, on a feast day, of
the Pope enthroned not beside, or behind, or in front of – *but on top of*
– the high altar.

When I was there the different persons officiating were preparing for
vespers, and choristers, singers, deacons, priests, canons, &c, were all
dressing together in public, just like a masquerade shop; and sopranos,

tenors, baritones, and bassos were all squeaking, and grumbling, and balling, at the top of their voices, making a din like people at a fair … The organ and the chant of the choristers, performing vespers in the distant chapel, faintly but entirely filled the body of the cathedral with a light but interrupted cloud of harmony … The music ceased, the crowds dispersed, but the lights in the chapel, on the high altar, and round the confessional of St Peter, remained, before which devotees were kneeling … Some English like myself lingered amongst them, and at length I remained the last man in the vast edifice.

On November 21st he attended the Vatican in full dress for a formal audience with Leo XII. It lasted three-quarters of an hour.

The Pope, in his morning-dress of white camblet, with a white cap over the tonsure, advanced from the table, where he was sitting, and received me most cordially. I bent my knee to kiss his hand, as to my own sovereign, which is the etiquette, but he stopped me. His appearance was singularly dignified, easy, pious, unassuming and gentle, and his manners quite those of a man of the world … His sentiments are decidedly liberal.

They communicated in French, and talked of European politics in general and the problems faced by English Catholics in particular. At the end of it the Duke, deeply moved by the Pope's mildness and moderation, recalled to him that his old father the Marquess, a heretic Protestant like himself, had been blessed at Rome by his predecessor with the words 'Jeune homme, le benediction d'un viellard ne peut pas vous faire du mal'.

Saint Père, [said the Duke] le benediction d'un pieux, vertueux, et auguste Souvrain à la tête de la Religion Chretienne la plus ancienne du monde, ne peut pas faire du mal à celui que la reçoit. Benissez moi, Saint Père!

The Pope took no offence at the Duke's rather oddly-phrased request.

The old man was affected, and the tears came into his eyes. He seized my two hands in his as I bent before him, and, with one hand making the sign of the cross over me, said, in evidently a tone of great feeling –
  'Je le fais de tout mon coeur. Que le bon Dieu vous benisse, mon cher fils!'
  Can I be blamed for saying that I retired from his presence as good a Protestant as I entered it, but warmly impressed with the kindness of his manner, and the sanctity of the act?

*   *   *

St Peter's – to the Duke it was a subject of fascination and repulsion

The winter turned out to be unusually cold, with ice and snow in Naples, and skaters in the Borghese gardens. The Duke attended a formidable round of dinners, soirées, balls, diplomatic receptions, tableaux vivants and poetry improvisations. He was particularly impressed by a Capuchin friar who could listen to a poet improvising on a subject plucked out of the air by the audience, then construe the lines, on the spot, into Latin hexameters. But the superficial glamour of Roman social life soon began to wear thin for him, and he disliked its snobbish, backbiting gossip. His uncles sent him letters urging his return.

> They are right. The great question[116] which is the feature of my political life is now coming to a crisis, and I owe a duty to my country and to myself to be present … But, in my state of health, the idea of a winter journey of 1,400 miles across the Alps is more than I can face with philosophy, or execute, probably, with safety.

Meanwhile, there was terrible news concerning two of his companions on the *Anna*.

> November 15th ... Poor Donati is in prison, and in great danger of his life. When he left me at Genoa he came here, where he passed some days, and then, returning to Naples, was arrested the moment he set foot on the Neapolitan territory. It now appears that he belonged to one of the Carbonari societies, and has been named by four or five of the people taken up during the late disturbances in the Neapolitan territory, as being connected with that plot. He is said to have gone into the Abruzzi before he embarked with me. At Malta, he is also said to have got into the society of some Piedmontese and Carbonari, by whom he must have been betrayed. They are now moving him to Naples, where they mean to try him. If he escapes with his life, he probably will spend the remainder of it in some prison. I am sorry for him, on account of his wife and family, who will be ruined.

> 23rd. I wrote today to Le Chevalier de Medicis at Naples, to intercede with the King for my poor friend Donati. I have received a heart-rending letter from his wretched wife. Dr Nott promised to be the bearer of it.

News of the specific charges against Donati arrived later. One of them alleged that his mission had been to enlist the Duke of Buckingham as a fellow-conspirator. The Duke wrote an outraged letter to the British ambassador, Lushington, protesting against the impertinence of his name being dragged into the trial in such a manner.[117]

> February 1st to 12th ... During this melancholy interval my poor friend, and almost daughter, Emma Wilson, is taken away from us. She died with scarcely a struggle. I saw her before I was confined by gout to the house. She was stronger on that day. The day before she died she was stronger still, and sat up in her chair. In the night, poor Wilson, who was lying by her, thought he heard some movement. She threw herself up in bed, raised her arms over her head, flung them round his neck, and expired. He would not believe that she was dead, sent for Peebles,[118] and kept rubbing the body and trying to recover her until Peebles came. Thus died in her youth this sweet, amiable, pure-hearted girl. God's will be done! We now find that Wilson understood and knew from the first her danger, communicated it to her, and prepared her regularly for death. His conduct has raised him very high in my estimation. His grief is excessive. He was at first stunned; and, when Peebles came in, he only said, 'What makes her stare so?' The eyes of the corpse were still open. He then cried bitterly, and has done so ever since.

It was agreed that she should be buried in the English burial-ground at Leghorn, which belonged to the Consulate. It was deemed quieter and less likely to be vandalised than the little Protestant Cemetery in Rome, off the Via Caio Cestio, where Severn buried Keats, and Trelawney Shelley's heart. Her body, encased in lead, set out on the long journey overland by coach to Leghorn. When it arrived there, there was a sudden change of plan. The coffin was loaded onto a ship bound for England.

> I saw poor Wilson before he set out; it was a heart-breaking scene. I am now alone. Wilson gave me a lock of her hair, and a little snuff-box thermometer and compass, which the poor thing desired me to keep for her sake. This has weighed me down very much, and affected me severely. My sister came to me directly, and sits with me most evenings.

Gout attacked him again, this time in his right hand, which made writing letters and his diary a painful chore. Then he heard he'd lost £1,100 when Cauty, an English auctioneer holding deposits for estates sold on his behalf, went bankrupt.[119] On top of all this, his *lacquais de place* contrived to get himself dismissed.

> Giovanni Gandolfi, my courier, having, at Naples, fifteen months ago, made his own contract with me, came to me this morning, in a very free manner, and wants to break it, making me pay for his lodging – a thing no courier is ever paid for, as the inn-keepers always lodge the couriers gratis. I was determined to resist this imposition, and told him that he might either go or stay as he chose, but I would not alter my bargain. He fancied I would not take him at his word and said he would go. I immediately turned him out of the room, paid him his wages, and dismissed him, to his great amazement. I gave him a fair but honest recommendation; but he will find it difficult, at this time the year, to get a place, and will regret the losing one where he had so little to do. I shall not take another, but trust to my coachman to act as courier, and take a lacquais de place at the towns where I stop. Couriers are, in general, very useless, and very imposing and expensive servants.

This was the Giovanni who had served him faithfully at Naples and in the *Anna*; who had been through the storm with him at Pantelleria; who had ridden behind him across wild Corsica; who had protected him at Segesta; who had cocked his blunderbuss against the ear of the robber on the Lucca road.

*   *   *

But there were compensations. Roman aristocrats and church hierarchs in need of money were in the habit of dribbling classical artefacts out onto the tourist art-market; some genuine, many less so. In November he bought from the Braschi collection two marble statues for his portico at Stowe: a priestess holding a sacrificial taper, and a Roman consul. He paid 440 scudi – about 80 guineas (£8,400) – for the pair.

> The consul is a beautiful statue. He holds a roll of paper in his hand, and by his side stands a triangular trunk, with a regular hasp and lock, as to a modern portmanteau, and on the top of it a sort of place let in, in which stand other rolls of paper similar to the one he holds in his hand. This, as well as the form of the sleeve of his right arm, are new, and never have been observed before in any other statue. Both, as well as a lovely little bust which I have also bought out of the same collection, were found in Hadrian's villa.

Hadrian's villa. The Duke bought 'a lovely little bust' which was found here

Later, thinking it over, he couldn't resist adding to his shopping-list all the Braschi gems, a statue of a drunken Silenus supported by two Satyrs and riding a third, and a marble statue of Apollo thought

The Duke's six columns. The two at the top are broken halves

to be – well – Hellenistic Greek. Elsewhere he stumbled across six polished, oriental, granite columns, more than nine feet high, ordered, but never paid for or collected, by the Duke of Wellington. He paid £25 each for them, in his opinion a quarter of what they were really worth.

> The connoisseurs are decided that the group of Silenus and the Bacchantes is by Michael Angelo. The prices which I have paid for them are the wonder of all Rome.[120]

At the beginning of December he sat for his bust to Raimondo Trentanova (1792–1832), a sculptor of marble heads in the Roman imperial style and now largely forgotten. Set on a dove marble pedestal, the bust cost the Duke 40 louis d'or.[121]

> December 16th. I go to Trenta Nova's. My bust is to be cast off in plaister; and the last touch was given it to-day. It is now to be cut in marble. All the world is coming to see it. The likeness is said to be wonderful; and certainly, as a bust, it is a very fine one. Trenta Nova is very proud of it; and it has already got him several new ones ordered.

In January he began an excavation in a vineyard south-east of the city and outside its walls, near the huge tomb of Cecilia Metella, the daughter-in-law of Crassus the triumvir who bankrolled Julius Caesar in his early years. The tomb sits on a hill beside the old Appian Way that leads out to Ciampino airport, and dominates the surrounding campagna. The *scavo* began well. They quickly found two burial chambers with frescoes on the walls, undisturbed by robbers, and the skeletons they contained were still intact, one of them with a coin to pay Charon the ferryman stuck between its teeth. The Duke dated it to the reign of Caracalla (211–217 AD). Then, following the lines of party walls, they uncovered an entire mosaic floor with an intricate border-motif, and an Etruscan urn represented at one end. The Duke was sure he was onto something big.

Trenta Nova's bust of the Duke – 'all the world is coming to see it, the likeness is said to be wonderful'

January 27th. Go to my scavo with party. Uncover my sarcophagus;[122] it is of full size, fluted, and handsomely worked on one side with a tablet. As appears by the inscription, the bones were those of quite a young, tall man … When the lid was removed, such a gush of azote[123] and ammoniacal gas rushed out, that the workmen and assistants were obliged to draw back until the air was purified … With great labour we raised the sarcophagus out of its vault, which was twenty-five palms deep … We open the ground towards the Via Appia.

Then, in early February, at about the time that Emma Wilson died and he received news of the bankruptcy of the auctioneer who owed him money, came another minor disaster.

I have stopped my scavo. The frost broke my mosaic pavement in pieces, to the great mortification and despair of the proprietor of the ground, who had insisted on asking me an immense sum for it. I have got the sarcophagus and all the marbles for 40 scudi.

The conclusion of this bitterly cold Roman winter found the Duke feeling lonely, gout-afflicted, and depressed. Chandos, ultra-Tory and reactionary, had been stirring up trouble amongst the farmers against Catholic emancipation, and had called a grand breakfast meeting of the Stowe tenantry at which he'd spoken ill of both his father the Duke and his grandfather, the late Marquess. Later, the tenantry had dragged him on a triumphal cart through the streets of Buckingham. On March 13th the Duke wrote letters back to England that included a stern, public rebuke to both his son and his tenantry.

Sad! Sad! Sad! I really begin to feel no wish to return home. Very low … Forbearance must have its limits, and I have reached them. I must not be afraid of maintaining my own principles because my son forgets what he owes to me and my family. I thank God that I have forborne so long. I remained at home all day and all the evening.

On March 21st he was 53 years old.

My birthday, and a wretched one! May God bless my wife, son, daughter, and grand-children. I have no further happiness in this world left for me to look forward to. In the morning called upon Lord Burghersh.

CHAPTER EIGHTEEN

Roman Spring

Pope Leo XII died in the middle of February 1829 of prostasis; an agonising, and at that date inoperable, condition involving blockage of the neck of the bladder. On February 23rd the Cardinals were due to go into conclave to choose his successor; and the Duke paid a visit to the *manica lunga* (the 'long sleeve') in the Quirinal[124] to view the preparations. He saw the little stalls along an extended, windowless chamber, with just a narrow, high-walled courtyard for exercise, where more than 50 cardinals would be shut up, along with about 150 servants, secretaries, masons, carpenters, barbers and doctors, to choose a new pope.

> The meals of all conclavisti are conveyed to them through turning-machines, like those used in convents, and each turning-machine is watched day and night by persons appointed both within and without, who take the duty by turns; and everything, even the dishes, are carefully examined, to prevent notes &c, from being conveyed to the Cardinals. Their meals are brought to them ready dressed, in heated dishes ... Here they remain until two-thirds of them agree ...

They would vote twice a day, on slips of paper burnt in a stove if the vote was inconclusive, while crowds in the piazza outside watched for tell-tale signs of smoke. No smoke signalled a successful vote.[125] Then the walls of the conclave would be broken down and a new Vicar of Christ proclaimed in Latin to the waiting world.

The Duke was fascinated by it all, and was part of the huge crowd that turned out to watch the arrival of the first 32 cardinals – the rest, coming late from abroad, would be let in through a door locked by three janitors with three separate keys. The streets on that day were lined with soldiers, for the government had got wind of a carbonaro plot to assassinate the cardinals as they walked in procession, and to overthrow the government. There had been many pre-emptive arrests.

The conclave, in the event safely begun, turned out to be a long one: it lasted more than a month, until the end of March. While Rome and the Catholic world waited, the Duke, gouty and depressed, continued his routine of exploring the city and its environs in his carriage during the day, then going out into society in the evening. One night he dined with the French ambassador, the Vicomte de Chateaubriand.

View of the Forum in Rome (H W Williams 1828)

A stupid concert, a hot assembly, and a hot supper, at which the Italians ate tremendously and pocketed more. I watched an Abbé who literally crammed his pockets not only with sweetmeats, but with more substantial fare. This lasted until twelve o'clock, when Lent began.

Chateaubriand, who had fought with the Bourbons, then attached himself to Bonaparte, was at this stage of his career a modernising liberal. He also loved intrigue. He was doing all he could to deter the three ultra-reactionary, Jesuit-favouring French cardinals from attending the conclave. But the cardinals, in spite of his warnings of bad roads, deep snow, cold weather, danger to their Eminences' health etc, were already crossing the Alps.

March 4th. Chateaubriand sent in the other day, through one of the turn-about machines, a note. On opening it by the searchers it seemed nothing but a piece of blank paper. Suspicions were excited, and it was held to the fire, when writing in sympathetic ink appeared. It was a piece of nonsense, and passed off as a joke, but some think that Chateaubriand was trying the ground ...

On March 7th he saw Cardinal Albani enter the conclave: the living embodiment of a medieval catholic hierarch.

A fine upright old man of sixty-four, looking like an old oak, untouched by the tempest of time ... The way into the Quirinal was lined on all sides by troops, and a great crowd assembled. He waited to see whether the smoke issued from the funnel, which would be the signal that there was no Pope; he then advanced on foot through the lane formed by the soldiers. He walked with his red hat in his hand, returning the bows of the people. He walked upright and firm, and so stout and fast as to distance his train. He is a Roman by family, and the people, charmed with his appearance, almost cheered him as he passed on ... Albani was very anxious to get into conclave before the new Pope is chosen, as he is fond of money; and being the senior deacon-cardinal, he will have to break the wall of the conclave down, and, advancing out of the breach, proclaim to the people the election of the new Pope, for which he gains 4,000 scudi, about £1,000 sterling.

Temple of Vesta, Rome (S Prout)

Later in the month, on the 19th, he drove out sketching for the day, then spent the early part of the evening with his sister Mary, who was going into a convent for a week.

> She is entirely absorbed in her devotions, and I fear is in the hands exclusively of the Jesuits ...

Three days later he took her out for a final drive in his carriage.

> She goes into a convent to-morrow for a week's devotion. This is a common custom with Catholics at this season. Lord Arundel goes into a monastery, I suspect shrewdly against his will.

Lord Burghersh, British ambassador at Florence who was at Rome for the conclave, had no such scruples about Lent. He petitioned the cardinals, via the Governor of Rome, for the close season for foxhunting in the campagna, in force since the beginning of February, to be waived for his own private pack. The cardinals sent him back a polite, but dusty, answer.

> Good taste this of John, Lord Burghersh, who might, with just as much tact, have asked the Government's leave to bring a seraglio with him.

Castello St Angelo, Rome (S Prout)

*   *   *

March 31st. This morning 100 guns from St Angelo announced the election of the Pope … The rain poured in torrents all day; but the crowd on the Quirinal Hill was immense. They deferred the proclamation as long as they could, in hopes of fine weather. But the heavens shone not on the new Pope. The wall of the balcony of the conclave was broken down by the masons shut up in conclave for that purpose. At half-past two o'clock, pm, Cardinal Albani advanced through the breach, and, with a loud voice, addressed the populace. Cries of 'Viva il Papa!' followed; but there was much water mixed with the wine. The people were wet through; and of all misfortunes that is the greatest to an Italian.

The new Pope, Pius VIII, was a compromise choice; an elderly Italian cardinal who had argued in vain not to be given the job. He was old and infirm, he pleaded, and subject to violent fits of temper[126]. They'd soon be back in conclave choosing his successor. But the cardinals, by now immured for over a month, had made up their minds. The papacy of Pius VIII lasted only 16 months.

The Duke wrote off for tickets for the Pope's coronation on April 5th, and was indignant to be offered only a place on the roof of the colonnade.

So I went in a plain coat, determined to obtain from the civility of others what I could not obtain from the Pope's minister.

He arrived at St Peter's in good time at seven in the morning, and persuaded the officer commanding the Swiss Guards to give him a position in front of the military, with an excellent view. An hour later the Pope was carried into St Peter's on a chair overhung by a white damask canopy embroidered with gold. As the choir sang 'Tu es Petrus', the Duke settled down on his folding travelling-stool to imbibe, like a glass of fine wine, the ancient, gorgeous ritual.

Three times … an officer appointed for the purpose put a quantity of flax upon a sort of fork, and holding it up before the Pope, set fire to it, and as the flame expired, exclaimed in a loud voice, 'Sancta Pater, sic transit gloria mundi!' …

The service inside the cathedral having been concluded, the Pope and his cardinals climbed to the outside balcony, over the South Door, from which the devout are blessed on Easter Day, and mounted a throne. Below him, the Piazza San Pietro was thronged with worshippers. The Duke estimated the crowd at up to 40,000.

> After this we had to struggle, and scramble, and squeeze – men and women altogether as they could into stands and booths formed over one of the colonnades. Here those who were lucky got seats – those less fortunate were obliged to stand. The heat of the sun bearing on our heads was tremendous; and, in addition to all the other neglects that were heaped upon foreigners, we were placed, as if on purpose, on the sunny side of the piazza, whereas had we been placed on the other side the sun would have been at our backs.

He was able to witness, though, the crowning, climactic moment when the Pope's golden mitre was removed by a cardinal, and replaced with the Triple Tiara.

> In an instant the whole multitude dropped on their knees, the troops knelt and presented arms, the colours trailed on the ground, and so perfect a silence followed the tumult of the mob, that it seemed as if a sudden spell had been cast over the noisy multitude. Every bell was hushed, and nothing but the occasional neigh of a horse interrupted the silence. The Pope rose, and, elevating his arm, blessed the whole Christian world. The effect certainly was for the moment sublime.

In the middle of April, parties of his countrymen – 'John Bull', as the Duke derisively called them – began to arrive in Rome from Naples, preparatory to their annual Easter migration back to England. From Naples, too, came palm branches. They were blessed by the Pope on Palm Sunday and handed out to Roman aristocrats, who carried them in procession round the Sistine chapel – a very foolish, uninteresting ceremony, in the Duke's view. His sister and brother-in-law, who were childless, received one of the palms. They put it beside their bed.

> [It] is to preserve the bed, and all in it, from harm of all sorts. I doubt much, however, if the palm will produce fruit.

During Holy Week, leading Catholics washed the feet of poor pilgrims in a convent, made up their beds and looked after their quotidian needs.

I fear the Arundels are included in those who practise this very foolish mockery.

His mood, since the death of Emma Wilson, was sour. He found himself increasingly irritated by what he perceived as the excessive Lenten religiosity of his sister and brother-in-law. One day he went shopping with his sister, and watched with incredulity as she bought a gross of rosaries. They would be blessed, she explained, by the Pope – with whom she had an audience the following day – then sent to the faithful back in England. On Wednesday in Holy Week he attended in full uniform, wearing his garter star, High Mass in the Sistine Chapel. As he waited to be directed to his seat, he saw a Swiss guard give a violent elbow-shove to the chest of an Italian princess that he knew, and he pulled rank to make the man stand aside and let her in. There was an hour-long wait for the Pope to arrive. He spent it in a detailed examination of Michelangelo's Last Judgement behind the altar – or what he could see of it, for much of it was hidden behind a (in his opinion) tawdry and tasteless crimson canopy embroidered with gold. He had no eyes for the Creation sequence on the ceiling above his head; at that date, long before late-20th century restoration revealed its colours, still somewhat obscure.

> Strong as my objections to frescoes are, I think this chapel is a wonderful work.

To the singing of psalms, 12 great candles on the altar and rood-screen were extinguished one by one – a metaphor for Christ's abandonment on Calvary by his disciples – until only one candle in the chapel remained alight; that of the Virgin Mary, loyal to the last. It was taken out of its socket in a high candelabrum and put behind the altar, and in the near-total darkness a single castrato began to sing the Miserere – to be joined, after a few bars, by the entire (if that is the right word) soprano choir.

> The 'Miserere' … is certainly a performance of which no one has the least idea who has never heard it … I can quite understand weak nerves being moved to tears … But a few years must terminate this style of music. Soprani are no longer made, and the present tremulous old gentlemen will have no successors.

At sunset on Easter Sunday he went to St Peter's to see the illuminations. The *San Pietrini*, as those employed for the purpose were called, flew about the cupola and façade of the great cathedral on long ropes suspended from the roof, placing *pots à feu*, filled with grease and topped with shavings, in the recesses of the stonework. They swung about fearlessly high up in space, and pushed off with their feet from pillar to frieze and cornice to position their lights. As dusk fell, their ropes became invisible and they seemed to the Duke like jackdaws wheeling about a crepuscular roost.

The great bell of the cathedral tolled one hour after sunset[127]. As its vibrations died away, the chief of the *San Pietrini* waved from the summit of the cupola's cross a torch of silver fire.

> In the same instant five hundred other torches are seen flying about the dome, cathedral and colonnades, borne by men swinging from the ropes, and running along the roofs, and in one instant lighting hitherto unseen *pots à feu* … The effect is magical, and from all the hills of Rome the sight of this immense silver dome, studded with gold and diamonds blazing in the air, is awfully fine.

But the Duke's Roman interlude was coming to an end. All England seemed to be on the road. On the night of Easter Monday alone 300 post-horses left Rome, and every day he saw couriers and heavy carriages rolling out of the Piazza d'Espagna bound for home. But the city's energy had somehow, in spite of his melancholy, pierced his heart. He loved Rome now. It suited him. He was loth to leave.

He met La Guicciola, Byron's mistress, and made friends with John Taafe, the Irishman resident in Italy who was a Dante scholar and had been a close friend of the poet. He found La Guicciola pleasing in conversation but less pretty than Byron had described her. She had fine features and a mass of blonde hair, but a poor figure: shorter standing up than sitting down, he thought. Taafe told him that Byron had treated her very badly – in effect, ruined her. She and her family were now kept under surveillance by every monarchist police force in Europe.

On April 28th Chateaubriand gave one of the last great receptions of the season: an open-air *déjeuner à la fourchette* for 300, starting at noon, at the Villa Medici in honour of the Grand Duchess of Russia. It was a disaster. As the guests began to arrive, an uninvited *ouragan* (cyclone) came too, from the Apennines. It blew over the glass-domed pavilion specially erected for the occasion. Table-decorations, bronzes, glasses, cutlery, food, porcelain – everything except heavy tureens of hot soup –

went bowling away through the garden, pursued by the French embassy staff. Chateaubriand put the Russian Grand Duchess off for two hours, and arriving guests were herded into the Villa Medici to admire the statues.

> The whole force of France in Rome was sent in moveable columns all through the town, to beg, borrow, steal, and buy up all the breakfasts, and all the dinners, and all the soup, fruit, pastry, glasses and dishes, that they could collect.

In the end some sort of order was restored – but, in the confusion, the number of guests had subtly swelled to 400. There were too few tables, and most of the men had to stand up, plundering for food from wherever they could. The Duke was given charge of a table seating a dozen ladies and a child.

> While helping my ladies, I constantly saw a brown hand with a diamond ring upon it introducing itself under my arm, and cribbing and stealing first my bread, then wine, and whatever it could fix its claw upon. At last, strawberries being a rarity, I was helping my ladies out of a solitary plate which we got, and a brown hand tried to take my plate from me. I then spoke loud and sternly, and desired the owner of the diamond ring to go to the servants if he wanted anything. He began to grow saucy, and I told him distinctly that if I caught him again I would send for the gendarmes and turn him out. In the confusion of the morning all tickets had been forgot, and all people gained admission, and at these entertainments an Italian invited to eat always stays to steal.

The Grand Duchess of Russia, he noticed, was never less than gracious and charming.

In the second week of May, he made a last sketching excursion outside the city, to the Alban hills some 14 miles south-east of Rome. The hay harvest was in full swing in the Campagna: waggons being loaded, hay-ricks stacked, the scent of wilting grass. Near the Lake of Nemi he found an abandoned chateau and woodland park belonging to the Gighi family. He entered it through an old iron gate beside a fountain. The neglected park, with its overgrown rides impenetrable to a horse and rider, was difficult to explore; you needed an axe and billhook (or, in the Duke's case, be preceded by a man with an axe and billhook) to get through. But it somehow suited his mood. Perhaps it reminded him of his park at Stowe, which he hadn't seen for nearly two years.

'a last sketching excursion', to a Roman tomb on the Via Appia

By the lake of Nemi he found an abandoned park

The family come down perhaps for one day in the summer, and they pass it in walking – not in their lovely park, enjoying its crystal waters, its embowering shades and extended prospect – but in parading up and down the hot street of Albano and dining at the inn; and this they call enjoying the country.

By the middle of May the summer heat was coming, and with it the dangers of malaria. He knew it was time to leave. On the 14th he bade farewell to the new Pope, who said to him, with great simplicity: 'We Catholics think we are right; you Protestants think that you are ... He alone must judge between us. In the meantime it is our duty to feel and entertain charity towards each other.' Then he called on the Secretary of State, Cardinal Albani, whom he found bizarrely dressed in a flannel morning-gown, and brown trousers with scarlet stockings and scarlet shoe-buckles. His face and chest were covered in dirty snuff.

> The best figure I ever saw ... He apologised, over and over again, for his appearance.

He went to take a last look at St Peter's, and sat beneath its cupola, silent and thoughtful, for more than two hours.

> May 16th. Left Rome with great regret ... While ascending the hills above Rome I stepped aside and looked back at the Eternal City for the last time.

'I stepped aside and looked back at the Eternal City for the last time' (S Prout)

CHAPTER NINETEEN

Going Home

He headed north-west from Rome, on the Via Aurelia towards Civitavecchia and the Tyrrhenian Sea. Lucien Bonaparte, Prince of Canino, had invited him to come and see his Etruscan dig on the western fringes of the Apennines near Canino. It gave him a perfect excuse to avoid the main route north, the Via Flaminia up the Tiber valley, and its parties of homeward-travelling John Bull.

The Duke's unlikely friendship with Lucien Bonaparte (1775–1840) had begun in Rome. Lucien had been a Jacobin firebrand in his youth. It was his bravado that saved the day for Napoleon during the Brumaire *coup d'état* in 1799 when, mounted on a horse, he'd galvanised the wavering grenadiers by pointing his sword at his elder brother and threatening to run him through if he ever betrayed the principles of the Revolution. Later, of course, Napoleon did exactly that and Lucien, in disgust, went into voluntary exile in Italy. He was created a prince by Pope Pius VII, and now lived in rural retirement, farming and writing books. He and the Duke were brought together by their common interest in archaeology.

The Duke reached Tarquinia on the evening of May 17th. Two of Lucien's gamekeepers guided him the next morning to Canino, four hours away over rough tracks: along the sea shore at first, across a plain of flowering broom, cistus, roses and myrtle; then up into the hills through thick forests of ilex, oak and thorns; in the end coming out onto a plateau, the Piana del Diavolo where, some ten years before, an Etruscan necropolis had been discovered by a bullock putting its hoof through the roof of a tomb cut deep into the tufa rock.

> I found myself at the door of a shepherd's hut, built of straw and wattles, like an Indian wigwam, but very large and comfortable, where Prince Lucien and the Princess received me. We were in the middle of excavations

of numberless tombs, out of which hourly vases of the greatest beauty, of what is called Etruscan manufacture, are found. He has already discovered above 2,000, and more were brought in, in greater or less degrees of entirety, during the whole day.

At Rome, back in March, the Duke had been shown by the Princess, Lucien's wife, part of the astonishing royal hoard her husband had already unearthed: a gold chaplet of laurel, with two golden ram's heads, beautifully worked, hanging by silver wires on either side; golden vine-leaves, probably embroidered into a burial-shroud long since perished; golden rings, earrings and necklaces; ivory spoons, dice and sword-hilts; a magnificent golden breastplate for a robe.[128]

> After passing the day at the cabin we returned to the Casino, where the Prince and his family reside, preferring it to the old rambling château of Canino, which is three miles from the excavations. The Casino is an old house, formerly an hospital of the Knights Templars; it is now made very tolerably comfortable. It is beautifully situated, in an amphitheatre of forest formed by the hills of Canino.

Early next morning Lucien took him to see his flock of sheep being milked for cheese, and they looked round a straw-and-wattle wigwam, just like the cabin at the excavations, with a fire in the middle, where 30 shepherds had passed the winter. In June, the shepherds would drive their flocks out to the high mountain pastures to avoid the heat and flies.

> Yesterday the Prince affixed my name to a tomb, which was opened this morning in my presence. He attaches the names of his friends to the different excavations. In this case luck attended my name, for a very fine vase, entire, and in perfect preservation, was found, of large size and beautiful painting, which the Prince gave me; and another smaller one – both representing Bacchus and his worship – also was turned up at the same time, which he also gave me. In the larger vase two small lachrymatory vases were also found.

It rained all afternoon, and he whiled away the time examining Lucien's remarkable collection of Etruscan vases in his Casino, and chatting to him about the old days in revolutionary France. Lucien told him several things that surprised him. Lucien himself had been devoted to Marie Antoinette. His elder brother, egged on by Talleyrand and Bernadotte, had certainly been guilty of the murder of the Duc d'Enghien. When the disgraced Queen Caroline of England, wife of George IV, was staying as Lucien's guest at his Roman palazzo, a writing-box containing valuable cameos and gold medals mysteriously vanished from the library to which she had pleaded to be given access.

They parted the next morning with many expressions of friendship and regret – a Grenville, ancient enemy of republicans, saying goodbye to a Jacobin who had once styled himself Brutus.

His road lay north-east now, across the Apennines, towards Assisi and Umbria. The hedges were scented with wild roses and honeysuckle,[129] and in the Vale of Terni he saw silkworms stripping mulberry trees of their leaves, and the creamy spikes of wild mignonette growing by the wayside.

> The valley extends to the furthest limit of vision, fertile, loaded with corn, wine, and oil, full of timber; the whole scene lovely, joyous, plentiful, quiet, and serene.

The climb up to Spoleto was so steep that four oxen were required to pull the baggage-carrying fourgon that followed behind his caleche. At Trevi his little pug-dog ran out of his rooms for a moment, and disappeared, and his servants whistled and called for it around the inn, then around the town, without success. The Duke blew for the innkeeper.

> I told him my dog was stolen, and by some one in his house – I knew not and cared not by whom – but that unless he was restored to me within five minutes, I should apply to the police and have the house searched, and every soul in it taken up and examined … The five minutes expired, and no dog. With a loud voice I sent off a servant to the police, begging their immediate attendance, and retired to the balcony of my window, from which I had the pleasure of seeing my dog brought into the inn in the arms of one of the waiters, who also took St. Salvador to witness that he had seen the dog in the possession of a little boy in the streets.

At Assisi he entered the Basilica di San Francesco at its bottom level, the crypt where St Francis is buried; then ascended via the Lower Church, where he admired Cimabue's simple painting of the saint and the stained glass in the windows, to the Upper Church, whose stalls, inlaid with marquetry, caught his eye. But of Giotto's masterpiece[130] – his cycle of 28 fresco panels that make up the Life of St Francis here and in the Lower Church – hardly a word. His taste for narrative painting, unguided by a Ruskin or a Berenson, tended towards 16th and 17th-century artists like Guido Reni, Domenichino and Annibale Carracci; painters nowadays largely dismissed.

Altogether the mass of frescoes, and the gloomy richness of the heavy decorations, pleased me very much; although the frescoes, taken separately, are of course, from their date, stiff in drawing and faulty in colouring.

Beyond Perugia, he was pleased to exchange the shovel-hatted Jesuits and loitering friars of the Papal States for the pretty, straw-hatted women of Tuscany. He hurried on to Florence, trying to catch up on time overspent in Rome and Etruria. He arrived there on the evening of May 27th.

You see nothing of the city until at the turn of the corner round one of the hills the whole north of Italy bursts upon your sight, with the distant but distinct line of Alps as a barrier. Below you lies Florence with its dome and towers, the neighbourhood thickly studded with white houses and villas, the lovely Arno winding in a thread of silver through the plain, the Apennines towering to the right, and Fiesole, dear to every reader of Milton, overtopping the minor hills clustering round its base.

'Florence with its dome and tower ... the lovely Arno winding in a thread of silver' (J D Harding)

KNIGHT JEWEL.
(441.)

The Buckingham Knight – not the Renaissance jewel he believed it to be

Florence seemed to him pretty and neat, but much less exciting and energetic than Rome. The style of the Duomo was 'that sort of bastard Gothic which belongs to the twelfth and thirteenth centuries … the effect of the whole very gloomy, especially to those whose eyes are full of St Peter's'. He preferred Santa Croce. In the Museum of Natural History he saw a horrifying depiction, in wax, of bodies infected by the plague in varying stages of decomposition, and inspected, in the Loggia dei Lanzi, the white marble lions from the Villa Medicis that were the originals of his lead lions at Stowe. He spent a day in the Uffizi, then went shopping, and bought a little pendant jewel, about four inches high, of a mounted knight – later known as the 'Buckingham Knight' – to wear on a chain from his neck on glittering social occasions. It was sold to him as a Renaissance jewel; in fact it was a contemporary fake.[131]

On June 6th he drove out to Fiesole.

I … went up the steepest and most rugged road ever carriage ascended. None had ever appeared there before. I put four horses to my carriage, of which my coachman was very proud; but, unfortunately, he went on too far without inquiry along a narrow road, and, being obliged to turn, overturned me. My carriage was a caleche. Fortunately, it being very hot, a lady who was with me had only a quarter of an hour before desired to have the head of the vehicle put up. This saved us from, perhaps, being killed. As it was, nobody was in the least hurt, and the carriage not broken. I fell undermost, and saved the lady …

He declined invitations to go out into society, but made an exception for a lively opera written by Lord Burghersh and put on at his home.

Some of the music was exceedingly good, and did him credit. The symphony was too loud and noisy. It was meant to represent a battle, and, to be sure, no battle ever made greater clatter.

His health had improved, and he didn't want to risk it in hot rooms. Anyway, Florence bored him.

June 13th. Don't like Florence. The society is confined, but gossipy to a degree. Everybody's concerns are known, and publicly talked about. A lady is ill-looked upon if she has no lover, and women go with their lovers publicly and avowedly … The English women don't improve by their communication with foreigners.

Ponte Sta Trinita, Florence (J D Harding)

On June 14th he was on the road again, heading for Venice. As he approached Bologna he saw beautiful waterlilies flowering in the road-side ditches. In the city it was the feast of Corpus Christi, with bells and processions beginning at daybreak, so he escaped to nearby Modena, 'a quiet, clean, cool town, where I can but have the gout, without my head being cracked with the noise of bells'. The Grand Duke of Modena, whose father he remembered visiting Stowe in 1786, entertained him to a formal dinner, and he had a long talk to a Professor Amici, who was investigating, under a microscope, sap-circulation in plants; and, with a 12-inch reflecting telescope, the satellites of Jupiter. His inn-keeper at Modena demanded compensation for a burn hole, caused by a knocked-over lamp, in a carpet in the Duke's room, and threatened to tell the Grand Duke (who owned the inn, shared the profit and had a reputation for meanness) if he didn't get it. The Duke, himself normally no pushover in these matters, had no option but to pay up.

On the 29th, in a heavy thunderstorm, he crossed the Po at Rovigo, north of Ferrara. The ferry, accessed by a rickety loading-ramp and a narrow, slippery causeway across the mudflats, didn't inspire confidence, and the river was running fast. But his carriage crossed safely to the other side. He was concerned to push on as fast as possible, for he'd heard that a cabinet courier from London had been searching for him throughout northern Italy with important letters, and now awaited him at Padua. He worried about the welfare of his family.

The moment I arrived the sight of the man, bearing a letter with a red seal, and my son's signature, put me out of that pain, and I was soon put out of all other by finding the packet contained nothing but a long, frothy letter from my son, and letters from my wife, &c, on the subject of Chandos's misconduct to me, and my public letter.[132] These epistles Chandos, in the plenitude of his magnificence, had sent out by an extra messenger from the Secretary of State's office, at an immense expense, and for no one object but to alarm me. He will never learn common sense.

Venice, the Rialto (S Prout).
The White Lion where the Duke stayed is to the right

On July 10th his coach carried him down the banks of the Brenta, and a Venetian government boat met him at Mestre. Six stout gondolieri stowed his baggage and rowed him the five miles to Venice, to the steps of the 'White Lion',[133] a fashionable inn not far from the Rialto bridge.

Venice at dusk, at the time when the gondolieri lit their lanterns, seemed to him a city of silence; although beautiful in its melancholy. The piazzas were deserted, the facades of the palaces crumbling or boarded up. There were very few English tourists about. In the cool of the evening, he sat out on his balcony overlooking the Grand Canal, and heard distant music, but that was more or less the only sound beneath the stars. The gondolieri, it seemed, had forgotten how to sing.

The next morning the Vice-Governor called, and offered him every civility. The English consul was away, but sent word that his private gondola was at his disposal. Beneath a broiling July sun the Duke made, just as he used to do in his barge round the Italian islands, a preliminary *tour d'horizon* of as much of the city as he could explore by gondola, along the whole length of the Grand Canal.

> Came home and dined. In the evening went out again. A gondola the most luxurious boat in the world.

The city may have been deserted, but he saw many swimmers in the water, even in the dirty, stinking side canals. One man in the Grand Canal was swimming with his hat on, and smoking a pipe. His Roman acquaintances, the Taafes, were staying at the White Lion too, and John Taafe told him that Byron's favourite way of getting around the city was by swimming. After dining out, he would peel off his coat and waistcoat, throw them into his gondola, and dive into the water. His gondola followed him home. At night, he had a little lantern attached to his cap, to stop other gondolas running him down. One day he swam to the Lido and back, a distance of about 11 miles. The Duke visited the Lido, and found it just as deserted as when Byron and Shelley had gone for rides together along its deserted strand.

Shelley's *Julian and Maddalo*, written in the autumn of 1818 at Este, commemorates those Adriatic rides.

> *I love all waste*
> *and solitary places, where we taste*
> *the pleasure of believing what we see*
> *is boundless, as we wish our souls to be.*

* * *

After ten hot days of sight-seeing – the Accademia, Armenian manu-scripts in a convent on the island of San Lazzaro, Arsenale, Bridge of Sighs, Doge's Palace, pigeons of St Mark's, Rialto – the Duke had had enough.

The Doge's Palace in Venice (S Prout). The Duke's son Chandos had collected many items from the palace on his visit 12 years earlier

Upon the whole, Venice very interesting for a short time, but a most *triste* residence.

On July 20th he departed from the White Lion in a large gondola that carried a sail. Halfway across the lagoon a sudden storm blew up, and they had to go to the rescue of a water-carrying barge that was in difficulties. The barge had more or less sunk by the time they got to her, and was only kept afloat by air trapped in her water-barrels. One of her crew had already drowned; the other, up to his waist in water, was pulled aboard. The Duke was relieved to reach the mainland, and the safety of his caleche.

He travelled quickly now, via Padua, Vicenza and Verona, and put up for the night at the little town of Desenzano, close to the shore of Lake Garda. In the morning he hired a boat and landed at Sirmio, the isthmus where Catullus had lived. When his brother died he wrote one of the saddest threnodies ever written: '*Frater, Ave atque Vale*'. In 1883 Alfred Lord Tennyson, just like the Duke, hired boatmen to row him out to olive-silvery Sirmio.

> *Row us out from Desenzano, to your Sirmione row!*
> *So they row'd, and there we landed – 'O Venusta Sirmio!'*
> *There to me through all the groves of olive in the summer glow,*
> *There beneath the Roman ruin where the purple flowers grow,*
> *Came that 'Ave atque Vale' of the Poet's hopeless woe,*
> *Tenderest of Roman poets nineteen-hundred years ago …*

He pushed on, via Brescia, to Milan, where he sought advice about maps, and the state of the roads into Switzerland via the Splugen and Little St Bernard passes. On August 2nd, he made a day's excursion to Monza, some eight miles away, to see the little iron crown of Lombardy with which Napoleon had been crowned. The crown, said to have been hammered out of a nail of the True Cross, had once belonged to the Emperor Constantine. It stood encased in a silver crucifix in Monza's Duomo.

> An immense crowd in the church to see me, besides a dead man, who wanted to be buried, but was obliged to wait until the priests had handed mia altessa about the whole church, and shewed me all the relics … Then they let me go, and buried their dead man. I returned to Milan.

At eight o'clock in the morning of August 4th he embarked his carriage on the steamboat at Como, sailed north up the lake, past the Villa d'Este where Queen Caroline of England had sported with her ex-servant and lover, Pergami, and disembarked at Riva. At Chiavenna, at the foot of the Splugen, he had difficulty hiring post-horses, and appealed to the provincial governor, who quickly set things right. Then he set off up the mountain, through forests of chestnut and fir. Falling cataracts made rainbows of spray beside the road.

Lake Como (S Prout)

The pastoral scenery below, the chalets dotted about along the mountain's side, the dark forest of pines, and the eternal snow above all, formed a beautiful prospect, especially when, looking back into the gorge which you have left, the eye plunges into Italy.

The road, built only eight years before, passed through a series of galleries cut into the rock; on exposed sections, it was roofed with timber to shoot avalanches off into the valley below. Then he crested a high ridge, followed a stream that was one of the sources of the Rhine, and descended, over a bridge covered with a wooden gallery, into the village of Splugen. He was in Switzerland.

August 6th. We stopped, baited our horses, and ... slept. Fresh snow fell on the Splugen this night.[134]

Epilogue

At 5 o'clock in the morning of August 30th, 1847, a party of bailiffs, led by a Mr Smythson, smashed in the glass of the great north door at Stowe, and forced their way into the hall. Simultaneous dawn raids were made on Wotton in Buckinghamshire, Avington Park in Hampshire and Buckingham House in Pall Mall (where the bailiffs found 6,000 bottles of wines, fortified wines and spirits laid down in the cellar). Chandos, the second Duke, 'Bucky' to his cavalry friends, had gone spectacularly bankrupt. His net debt amounted to over a million pounds (perhaps £100 million today). The great dynastic adventure of the Grenvilles that had begun with such stellar promise in the late 17th century, and astonished 18th century England with its talent and ambition, had finally run its course: in a misery of writs and counter-writs, of ledgers in copperplate, of sneering clerks and lawyers, of moralising leaders in *The Times*,[135] of forced auction sales. Their loss of Eden seemed irreversible. They had been cast out of Paradise.

The 1848 sale of Stowe's contents, which attracted intense public interest but, on the whole, disappointing bids, lasted 40 days. At the end of it the great palace lay desolate. The Chandos portrait of Shakespeare, the Van Dykes and Domenichinos, the furniture, tapestries and carpets, the great collections of majolica ware and Dresden china, the Worcester Service, all the statuary, the Silenus carried by satyrs and the consul standing by a trunk, the silver, the books, the coin collection, even the Buckingham knight and the lock of Mary Queen of Scots' hair – they were all carried away in chaises or on carts. A solitary housekeeper patrolled an empty husk of a house that nobody wanted to buy or lease.[136] For 13 years Stowe remained abandoned. Ivy and valerian opened cracks in the walls of the Temple of Ancient Virtue. Nettles, thistles and ground-elder usurped the flower garden where, in 1827, the Duke and his Duchess had shed silent tears. The Elysian fields became a jungle of brambles and adventitious weeds.

In 1861 a minor miracle occurred. Paradise was regained – after a fashion. On what the first and second Dukes would have considered a shoestring, Stowe was reopened, by the third and last Duke, Richard,[137] at whose week-long christening gala back in 1824 his father's Buckinghamshire Hussars had been paraded, and re-paraded every day for a week. He was as practical and business-like as his father had been otiose. By working hard at jobs[138] that his father and grandfather would have turned up their noses at, and by frugal living and shrewd investment in the railways, he scraped together enough money to re-open Stowe and restore the family's pride and respectability. But the great days of glory had departed. The swans, as it were, had flown the Eleven-Acre Lake.

Perhaps the first Duke should have the last word. Twenty years earlier, on July 11th, 1827, the day before he left Stowe for the Mediterranean, he wrote in his diary:

The Grenville mausoleum at Wotton where the Duke lies (Buckler)

This is a very heavy day with me, people pressing me on all sides with business, and my heart longing to be alone. God's will be done! – but my mind is very low, and I cannot look at the scene of my childhood, manhood, and age, for perhaps the last time, without a very, very bitter pang. Some feelings, too, of sorrow swell in upon me and help to overwhelm me. But although I have cause for regret, I have none for self-reproach. My country and my neighbours have been the better for my money. No unworthy pursuit has consumed it. With a little management and the blessing of God, I may yet recover and pass what age God gives me in comfort.

God gave him 11 more years. He died in January 1839, aged 61, and lies in the family mausoleum at Wotton. Anna Eliza, who predeceased him in 1836, preferred, as always, Avington[139] as her final resting-place. Their only son Chandos, the second Duke, bankrupt and divorced, was pensioned off by his son in his final years to live in rooms in the Great Western Hotel that overlooks Paddington station. Perhaps the patterns formed below him by the steam expresses as they arrived and departed from one of the capital's great termini reminded him of his beloved yeomanry, and their complicated mounted drills. He died in 1861, and, like his father, lies at Wotton, whence the Grenvilles had first emerged, like dog-foxes, to sniff the dynastic air.

The strangest irony, in a story full of irony, is that Stowe and its landscape gardens may have survived in their original form because of, not in spite of, the improvidence of the first and second Dukes. There was no money around in the latter half of the 19th century, or early 20th, to modernise Stowe or give the gardens a Victorian or Edwardian gloss. What we see today is *sui generis* and time-specific: a breathtakingly beautiful early Georgian landscape. On a July evening, as the sun goes down over the Octagon Lake, it is easy to imagine the first Duke and his Duchess making their farewell carriage-drive round Stowe gardens. What they saw then, and what we see now, has hardly changed.

Select Bibliography

Primary Sources, unpublished
Centre for Buckinghamshire Studies, Aylesbury: Stowe MSS Fremantle
  MSS
Huntington Library, San Marino, California: Stowe-Grenville Papers
  (STG)
Public Record Office, Kew: Register of Ships

Primary Sources, published
Aspinall, A (ed.), *The Letters of King George IV 1812–30* (Cambridge
  University Press, 1938), 3 vols.
Blessington, Countess of, *The Idler in Italy (London*, Colburn, 1839)
Brydone, P, *A Tour through Sicily and Malta* (London, Strahan and
  Cadell, 1776)
Buckingham and Chandos, Duke of (ed), *Memoirs of the Court of
  George IV 1820–30* (London 1859), 2 vols.
Buckingham and Chandos, Duke of (ed), *The Private Diary of Richard,
  Duke of Buckingham and Chandos* (Hurst and Blackett, 1862).
Clarke, G B (ed) *Descriptions of Lord Cobham's Gardens at Stowe,
  1700–1750* (Buckinghamshire Record Society, vol 26, 1990).
Craven, Elizabeth, *Memoirs of the Margravine of Anspach* (London,
  Colburn, 1826), 2 vols.
Eden, William, Lord Auckland, *Journal and Correspondence* (London,
  1860–62)
Fox, Hon Edward, *Journal 1818–30* (London, Thornton, Butterworth)
Fulford, R and Strachey, L, *The Greville Memoirs* (London, 1938)
Greig, J. (ed), *The Farington Diary*, by Joseph Farington RA, 5 vols
  (London, Hutchinson, 1923–4).
Hampshire Chronicle.
Hirst, Joseph, *Memoir and Letters of Lady Mary Arundel* (Leicester,
  1894)

Maxwell, H (ed), *The Creevy Papers* (London, John Murray, 1904), 2 vols.

Murray, E C G, *Young Brown* (London, Smith, Elder and Co., 1874).

The Times

Scrope, George Poulett, *Considerations on Volcanoes* (London, 1825)

Swartz, H M and M, *Disraeli's Reminiscences* (London, Hamish Hamilton, 1975)

Wellington, 7th Duke of (ed), *Wellington and His Friends* (London, Macmillan, 1965)

Secondary Sources

Beckett, John V, *The Rise and Fall of the Grenvilles 1710–1921* (Manchester University Press, 1994)

Bevington, Michael, *Stowe House* (London, Paul Holberton, 2002)

Hibbert, Christopher, *George IV* (London, Allen Lane, 1973)

Hibbert, Christopher, *The Grand Tour*, (London, Weidenfeld and Nicolson, 1969).

Hussey, Christopher, *English Gardens and Landscapes, 1700–1750* (London, Country Life, 1967)

Lambert, R S (ed) *Grand Tour: A Journey in the Tracks of the Age of Aristocracy* (London, Faber and Faber, 1935)

National Trust, *Stowe Landscape Gardens: A comprehensive guide* (London 1997)

Rodger, N A M, *The Command of the Ocean, A Naval History of Britain, 1649–1815* (London, Allen Lane, 2004)

Sack, J J, *The Grenvillites 1801–29* (University of Illinois Press, 1979)

Notes

1   *The Private Diary of Richard, Duke of Buckingham and Chandos*, Hurst and Blackett, 1862, Vol i, 138

2   The family's preferred educational route was Eton and Christ Church. This may have had something to do with it.

3   *Journal and Correspondence of William Eden, Lord Auckland*, London 1860–62. Sheffield to Eden, Nov 22, 1788, II, 244

4   Demolished in 1908. The RAC club now stands on its site.

5   In the preface, p viii, to *The Private Diary of Richard, Duke of Buckingham and Chandos*, Hurst and Blackett 1862, edited by his son Chandos.

6   This Brown has no apparent connection with Lancelot 'Capability' Brown who worked at Stowe, Blenheim, Chatsworth and Kew, and who died in 1783.

7   They arrived two days later, on July 7th. They would probably have been green sea turtles, *Chelonia midas*, imported in tubs of sea water from the Caribbean. Early voyages to, and exploration of, the New World were largely enabled by green turtles, which the sailors kept live for long periods on board and used as protein, lack of which could make a man's gums suddenly grow over his teeth and send a corpse a day over the ship's side. Green turtles could measure up to five ft. over the carapace, and weigh a huge 240 lbs (although most were much smaller). The flesh is said to taste somewhere between veal and lobster.

8   The ancient king of Connacht.

9   A 600-acre estate near Burnham in southern Bucks, bought by William Grenville (he was created Lord Grenville in 1790) in 1791. His eldest brother George, the first Marquess, helped him buy it. His sinecure, after 1791, was the Auditorship of the Exchequer (fixed at £4,000 pa). In 1806, as First Lord of the Treasury, he found himself in the embarrassing position of having to audit his own accounts.

10   tipped

11   The Duke's stomach, and his cousin Charles Wynn's squeaky voice, were favourite targets of Canning's biting wit.

12   On the 28th December, 1825, at 4.30 pm, the king wrote to Lord Liverpool from the Royal Lodge: 'I forward to you the extraordinary inclosure, which I have only just now recd. from the Duke of Buckingham. It is not necessary for me, I am sure, to add any comment or observation of my own upon it, further than this, that I consider it a very indelicate & improper communication to me, both as to its matter, as well as to the mode in which it has pleased the Duke of Buckingham of stating that matter to me … I must state to you my opinion that I think it is quite impossible to suffer so very strange a paper, as it is, to pass entirely *sub silentio* & without some sort of notice & reply.'

The Duke had been pitching for the Viceroyalty of Ireland or the Governor-Generalship of Bengal, and had hinted that, if he didn't get either job, he might withdraw the support of his members in the Commons. It must be admitted that, unlike his sharp old uncle William, he was a fairly clumsy political operator. *Letters of King George IV, 1812–1830.* A. Aspinall (CUP 1938), 3447, p 453.

13   *Memoirs of the Court of George IV 1820–1830*, by the Duke of Buckingham and Chandos, Hurst and Blackett 1859, Vols I and II.

14   For a brilliantly researched and written account of the Duke's twists and turns in these years in the pursuit of office, see *The Grenvillites 1801–29*, James Sack, University of Illinois Press, 1979.

15   The coppering of the ships of the Royal Navy, first introduced in the 1770s, once the problem of electrolytic corrosion between the copper and its iron fastenings had been overcome, gave them a significant sailing advantage over French ships of the line during the Great Wars. They could stay at sea for much longer, and outsailed their French opponents, slowed down by barnacles, by about a knot. For a full account of coppering and its significance, see Professor N A M Rodger's remarkable naval history, *The Command of the Ocean*, Allen Lane 2004.

16   See her registration certificate, July 31st, 1827, Southampton. Kew PRO, BT 107, ref. 193, entry 22.

17   Her planking was flush, not overlapping (clinker-built).

18   *Private Diary* Bk 1, p 52.

19   Wide-bore, short-range guns, often filled with grape-shot with

deadly scatter-effect. They take their name from the Stirlingshire town, Carron, where they were first made.

20 Where the Itchen flows into Southampton Water

21 The first commercial steamship in Britain was Patrick Bell's Comet (1812). Paddle steamers were introduced in the mid-1820s on European rivers and short sea runs. It was not until the late 1830s that the marine propeller was developed, and quickly adopted by navies throughout the world. For Fontara's steam kitchen, see *The Diary* Bk 1, p 79

22 Captain William Henry Smyth (1788–1865) was a naval hydrographer who surveyed the Mediterranean during and after the Napoleonic Wars. His charts were still in use during WWII. He became Vice Admiral Smyth, Vice President of the Royal Society and a noted astronomer, and in 1844 brought out his *Cycle of Celestial Objects*, a classic description of double stars, star clusters and nebulae. A lunar sea, Mare Smythii, was named after him. He was Baden-Powell's grandfather.

23 According to the *Hampshire Chronicle* of August 13th, the bill exceeded £16,000. This, in modern money (perhaps £1.6 million), seems cheap for a yacht of the *Anna*'s size and specification.

24 It was not until 1829 that the club was invited, by an Admiralty warrant, to fly England's most beautiful flag, the white ensign with red St George's cross, and Union flag top left, that had flown from the forepeaks of Nelson's ships of the line at Trafalgar.

25 The gun salute is said to have originated as a sign that the saluter had discharged his weapons, and was therefore unarmed. Traditionally, salutes were odd-numbered (even numbers were considered unlucky). In the early 19th century, all merchant vessels at sea were required to salute British Royal Navy warships with seven shots, firing first. 21 guns were accorded to royalty or heads of state, 19 guns to commanders of national armies or navies. The lowest salute, five guns, was given to vice-consuls and consular agents. In British India, the King-Emperor received a salute of 101 guns.

26 He was the first Commodore of The Yacht Club and introduced the Prince Regent as a member. The Duke himself was a founder member.

27 The 40-day period (from the French *quarantaine*) during which a ship might be detained at a lazaret – a floating hulk or an island –

before its crew or cargo were allowed to go ashore. Originally a defence against rat-borne bubonic plague (which disappeared from England, but not from continental Europe, in the 1660s), quarantine (also known as *pratique*) was used in British ports until the end of the 19th century to deter cholera and yellow fever. In Buckingham's day it was still a feature of Mediterranean travel, and ships with foul bills, especially from suspect ports in the Levant, ran the risk of being burned or sunk by the authorities.

28 Buckingham Villa, in Buckingham Close off Buckingham Street, still stands on the beachfront at Ryde. The house has been converted into flats and its gardens divided into building plots.

29 August 4th, 1828. *The Journal of the Hon Edward Fox* 1818–1830. London, Thornton Butterworth.

30 *Memoir and Letters of Lady Mary Arundel*, Joseph Hirst, Leicester, 1894, Ch 1

31 Centre for Bucks Studies, Aylesbury. D 54/15

32 As a very rough rule of thumb, one pound in the early 19th century was worth between 75 and 150 times what it is worth today. Like-for-like costs varied hugely, depending on item.

33 In 1747. Andreas Marggraf, a German chemist, published an account of how to extract sugar (hitherto obtainable only from sugar cane grown in the tropics) from plants indigenous to Europe, especially beetroot and carrots. The first hybrid sugar beets were introduced to France in 1775, and the first sugar-extracting factory set up in Silesia in 1802, when the price of West Indian sugar was at an all-time high. Napoleon gave every encouragement to the new crop and set up institutes for its culture, to sabotage the English trade. As the Napoleonic wars drew to a close, West Indian sugar prices were on the floor and planters were going bust. Today, nearly half the world's sugar comes from sugar beet.

34 Thomas Grenville, for instance, received an annual allowance of £600; half what his brother had given him before his death in 1813.

35 *The Rise and Fall of the Grenvilles*, by John Beckett, Manchester Unversity Press 1994, pp 151 ff.

36 PD 1,246. Arriving at Naples, he discovered that '*Rothschild, who has a house here, was sending off a courier with gold for England. I sent Mr Lunn to him, and he readily took 1,000 sovereigns, giving me a credit on his house at the par of exchange of the day, and charging no commission.*' A sovereign was a gold coin, worth 20

shillings or £1, bearing a full-figure portrait of the monarch and first struck in the reign of Henry VII. From 1817 until 1914 (when it went out of circulation) it was made up of eleven/twelfths pure gold and one twelfth copper alloy. The Duke's 1,000 sovereigns would have weighed about 7.5 kilos in ballast in the *Anna*.

37　He was an admirer, for example, of Sterne's *Tristram Shandy* and Richardson's *Sir Charles Grandison*, Jane Austen's favourite novel. PD iii, 224/226.

38　The German geologist Abraham Werner (1750–1817), for the Neptunians, argued that the rocks of the earth, such as granite, were aqueous in origin, formed as crystalline precipitates of some ancient, primeval ocean. James Hutton (1726–97), for the Vulcanists, was a landowner and doctor from Berwickshire and the founder of modern geology. He understood, correctly, that heat was an important agent in the formation of land masses, that rocks like granite were igneous in origin, that many millions of years were required for their deposition and denudation, and that the earth was therefore a great deal older than most people thought. *Hutton's Theory of the Earth, with Proofs and Illustrations* was first published in 1795 – to general incomprehension, for his style was both prolix and obscure. It wasn't until 1802, and the publication by his friend John Playfair of the much more reader-friendly *Illustrations of the Huttonian Theory* that the Vulcanists began to gain ground.

39　In the Huntington Library collection in California.

40　The original manuscript is in the Huntington Library collection.

41　*PD* I, 19, entry for July 16th 1827: 'Nothing would please her but my joining the Tories.'

42　A West Indian sugar heiress, she was certified insane in 1791, and died in 1813. From 1791 her daughter Anna Eliza was cared for by guardians.

43　Half a century later, in the 1870s, Eustace, whom the Grenvilles had managed to palm off with a job as British consul-general at Odessa, published a *roman à clef*, in three volumes, about his mother's relationship with Buckingham, who became in the book the Duke of Courthope and Revel.

44　STG Correspondence, 382/69

45　Madame de Genlis (1746–1830) was a French writer and educationalist who wrote more than 80 books. A governess to the French royal family, she was exiled by a Revolution with which she largely sympathised. Her estranged husband, the Marquis de Sillery, was guillotined in 1793. She supported herself in Switzerland and Germany by writing and painting until Napoleon welcomed her back to France, and gave her a state apartment and a pension of 6,000 francs. She lived to see her old pupil, Louis Philippe, installed on the throne of France. Her English translations were best-sellers, and Jane Austen was a fan, albeit rather a prim one. In 1807 she wrote of *Alphonsine* and its references to sodomy: 'We were disgusted in twenty pages … it has indelicacies which disgrace a pen hitherto so pure.'

46 Hardy, against whom Buckingham had fought his duel, was a fellow member of The Yacht Club.

47 Which gave rise to the saying 'As safe as the Rock of Gibraltar'.

48 For a brilliant account of the Royal Navy's rise to world dominance, see Professor N A M Rodger's *Command of the Ocean, A Naval History of Britain*, 1649–1815 Allen Lane 2004.

49 The floating batteries, specially designed by the Academie Française, mostly caught fire and sank.

50 Priesthood.

51 ie lieu-tenant.

52 At 201 Corso Pisani, on the south side of Palermo. A large building, with a street-frontage of about 75 metres, it seems to have been used as a military prison, but is now boarded up and abandoned. Over the main door is the legend: *Humanitate et munificentia monumentum perenne anno* 1824.

53 Lord William Bentinck (1774–1839) was a liberal Whig, the son of the Duke of Portland, who, after service in the Peninsular War, was appointed commander of British troops in Sicily. His attempts to create a constitutional government for the island – attempts which alienated King Ferdinand and his reactionary queen, Maria Carolina – eventually ended in ignominious failure, and he was recalled in 1815. He later became Governor General of India.

54 The creation of Prince Ferdinando of Palagonìa, who died in 1789. Goethe thought the monsters hideous.

55 The flying buttress at the promontory's tip is gone now, eroded by the sea.

56 Port or sherry with hot water, with sugar and spices added. It is said to have been invented by Colonel Negus, in the days of Queen Anne.

57 Suffering from Wertherism, a condition that derived from the title of Goethe's novel *Die Leiden des jungen Werther* (1774). Werther was a highly-strung, melancholy social misfit engaged in a hopeless love-affair: the prototype of the 'interesting' young man.

58 Most of old Messina was destroyed by an earthquake in 1908, considered one of the ten biggest in history. It killed perhaps 100,000 people, and was accompanied by a seismic tidal wave that swept many out to sea.

59 Prime Minister to King Francis I, King of Two Sicilies.

60 Through the worst storm that Nelson had ever experienced. The Neapolitan royal family and court went to pieces, prostrated by terror or seasickness, and Sir William Hamilton cowered in his cabin with a loaded pistol, ready to blow his brains out if the ship went down. Emma Hamilton rolled her sleeves up, and was everywhere, nursing, comforting, cajoling. It must have been one of the reasons why Nelson loved her so.

61 The controversial affairs of the Naples forts, and of Commodore Caracciolo:

Three forts dominated Naples, St Elmo, Nuovo and dell'Uovo, and by the time Nelson's fleet arrived in the Bay of Naples in June 1799 their rebel occupants – soldiers and collaborators of the Parthenopean Republic – had agreed with the Bourbon commander on the ground, Cardinal Ruffo, to march out with colours flying and safe passage guaranteed to Toulon. As soon as the rebels were embarked in 14 poluccas, and the forts occupied by British marines, Nelson reneged on the deal, and handed over about 4,000 Neapolitan Jacobins (2,000 in the poluccas and as many more ashore) to summary justice. The King and Queen of the Two Sicilies had given him strict orders never to negotiate with rebels. In February 1800 Charles James Fox thundered his indignation in Parliament: [Naples] 'has been stained and polluted by murders so ferocious, and by cruelties of every kind so abhorrent, that the heart shudders at the recital.' He accused the British of bad faith, although he did not dare to mention Nelson by name.

Commodore Caracciolo had served alongside Nelson, in the Tancredi, in 1795. After the royal flight to Palermo in 1798, he got permission from King Ferdinand to return to Naples to save his property from being confiscated. Back in the city, willingly or unwillingly, he switched sides and took command of a flotilla of republican gunboats. In June 1799, five days after Nelson's arrival at Naples, Caracciolo was hauled on board Nelson's ship and immediately handed over to a kangaroo court-martial convened by the Sicilian commander Count Thurn. Its sentence, after two hours' deliberation, was death. Nelson, who loathed Republicans and all their works, had Caracciolo hanged that evening from the yard-arm of the Neapolitan frigate, *La Minerva*, then dropped over the side with shot attached to his legs. His bloated body is said to have been seen by King Ferdinand that night, bobbing past the stern-cabin of his ship. It gave him a terrible fright.

62 She was guillotined on 16th October 1793, nine months after her husband, Louis XVI.

63 Two years later she married instead, and much more satisfactorily from everyone's point of view except perhaps the Emperor of Brazil, the King of Spain.

64 These muzzle-loading, double-barrelled English flintlocks were the Bosses or Purdeys of their day. They had slender, polished, walnut stocks specially fitted to the Duke's reach and shoulder, and their twin-triggered hammers were filed into graceful curves and the actions engraved with fine scroll patterns. They were as light, well balanced, elegantly finished and fast handling as money could possibly buy. We know that his gunmaker's bill in 1820 was £153, perhaps paid out for these very guns. Compared with a modern shotgun, however, they suffered from two major disadvantages. The hammer-flintlock ignition system caused a puff of powder to blow back and blacken your face, temporarily blinding you. And the guns were muzzle-loaders: they had to be ramrod-filled, with powder, wadding and shot, which took time and trouble. Breech-loading shotguns, employing cartridges with copper percussion caps – all later innovations by British gunmakers – did not arrive on the sporting scene until about the 1860s.

65 An opera in three acts by Giovanni Pacini (1796–1867). Its first performance was at the Teatro di San Carlo in November 1825.

66 One ducat, according to the Duke (*PD* ii, 37), exchanged at the rate of 3s 2d – about £16 in modern money (x 100). So his piano for a month would have cost him about £3,200.

67 Lunn married a naval captain's daughter in 1837 and died in 1839, aged only 43.

68 See Francis Lunn, *Alumni Cantabrigienses*, and *Clerical Guide* 1829.

69   At the battle of Navarino, October 20th 1827, an allied squadron of British, French and Russian warships, commanded by Sir Edward Codrington, C-in-C Mediterranean, annihilated the Turco-Egyptian fleet of Ibrahim Pasha, and won independence for Greek insurgents struggling to throw off Ottoman rule. It was the last recorded occasion in history that two fleets under sail (they were in fact anchored among each other at the time, in a sort of Mexican stand-off) met in conflict. The bay of Navarino (the modern Pylos) is on the west side of the Peloponnese.

70   In 1833 the caretaker of the Duke's 'poor little cottage' at Ryde on the Isle of Wight was dismissed. He threatened blackmail. The Duke paid £150 to stop him publishing the following cryptic lines:
Duke Richard's love and lullaby
On the Ocean, or the brigand the
Beauty in the bay of Naples. To which
Will be added innocence tempted with
Gold in the Temple, the meeting at a
Cottage near the sea, the false oath,
And 15 years in Bedlam.
The final four lines refer to an unfortunate affair of Chandos; the first three to some sort of intrigue by the Duke in the Bay of Naples. STG Correspondence, boxes 368/37, 375/46.

71   See chapter 19.

72   Centre for Buckinghamshire Studies, Aylesbury. D104/109

73   He was wrong. It was the AD 79 eruption that blew the top of the mountain off, leaving two peaks, the slightly lower Monte Somma and Vesuvius proper, with the main fissure in between.

74   *Greville Memoirs* 1814–60, Lytton Strachey and Roger Fulford ed (Macmillan 1938), Vol 1, pp 449/450

75   Centre for Buckinghamshire Studies, D-FR139/8

76   In 2005 the National Lottery Fund announced a grant, via the Stowe Preservation Trust, of £50 million for the restoration of Stowe House. The Landscape Gardens are owned by the National Trust.

77   Once an Aragonese fortress, now the Museo Archaeoligico dei Campi Flegrei

78   It would be another half-century (1880) before Alphonse Laveran, a French military doctor performing autopsies in Algeria, identified the causative agent for human malaria as a protozoan parasite

which he christened *Oscillaria* (now *Plasmodium*) *malariae*; and 70 years (1897) before Sir Ronald Ross, a British military doctor in India, showed that Anopheline mosquitoes were the vectors of the killer disease. They both won Nobel prizes for their work.

79   Casalmicciola has the hottest spring on the island, Terme Rita, which comes out of the ground at 180°F. It contains much iodine. Many of the Ischian springs are radioactive, and require a doctor's certificate. Casamicciola was flattened by another earthquake in 1883, which killed 7000.

80   According to the diarist Charles Greville, at Naples in 1830, a carlino was worth 4d. English (*Greville Memoirs* 1814–60, Strachey and Fulford edn. Vol 1, p 448) – or (x 100) about £1.66 in modern money.

81   Mary Anne Arundel, née Lady Mary Grenville (1787–1845) had been a Catholic convert since 1806. In 1811 she married James Wardour, 10th Baron Arundel. He was a fairly penniless Catholic aristocrat from Wiltshire, and seems to have resented his brother-in-law. See the Journal of Edward Fox 1818–30 (Thornton Butterworth 1923), entry for August 4th 1828: 'He [Wardour] does not disguise his dislike for his fat brother-in-law, the D of Buckingham, of whose meanness he seems quite aware, tho', as is sometimes the case, it is wedded to the greatest and most expensive ostentation ... Some years ago [in 1815] when Ld A was poorer (even than he is now), as it was before his father's death, the Duke pressed them very much to spend a few months with him at Paris, to which they unwillingly consented. At the end of the residence Ld, or as he was then, Mr Arundel found to his great dismay that the Duke intended to pay half the house accounts, which, in consequence of the large dinners his Grace had given, were much more than he could well afford.' Fox, however, is a scathing, bitchy witness, without a good word for the Grenvilles. He continues: 'Of the Orange violence of her nephew, Lord Chandos, which he has inherited from his mother, who was brought up with a horror for the religion of her mother, the old Duchess of Chandos, Lady A can hardly speak without temper.'

82   George Grenville, Baron Nugent (1788–1850)

83   Muir was one of his servants or sailors on board, probably the former, judging by Anna Eliza's knowledge of, and concern for, his wife.

84 So called by John Julius Norwich.

85 Januarius (Gennaro), the patron saint of Naples, was bishop of Benevento. Not much is known about him. He is thought to have been martyred during the Diocletian persecutions of 305 AD. The liquefaction of his blood, first recorded in 1389, is supposed to occur three times a year: on the first Saturday in May, and on his feast-days of September 19 and December 16. But the saint is unpredictable, and sometimes doesn't oblige – in recent memory when Naples elected a Communist mayor – to the intense irritation and anger of his adherents.

86 The temple of Hera 530 BC, of Ceres 500 BC, and of Neptune (the biggest, and one of the most complete Greek temples in Europe) 450 BC. The Tomb of the Diver, with its famous frescoed slab, was discovered half a mile from Paestum in 1968.

87 The old town was flattened by bombing in May 1943, in preparation for the Allied invasion of Sicily, and rebuilt in concrete. It's the least attractive part of the island today.

88 See note 22.

89 Perhaps the Grotta delle Sirene.

90 Transcribed thus in the 1862 edition. The gregale or 'Greek' wind, blows, in fact, from the north-east.

91 An additional anchor carried in larger ships for security in case the bower anchors failed to hold. Hence the term 'sheet anchor' meaning security in general.

92 The Duke blamed defective iron in Rubie the boatbuilder's anchors, and in his steering gear. *PD* ii,146.

93 See his Uncle Thomas's reply in September to the Duke's letter from Naples (p 161).

94 Centre for Buckinghamshire Studies D/FR/139/8/6

95 *PD* ii, 151. The king's favourite, Grindorge, a Neapolitan shop-keeper, was the Wilsons' landlord at this time. Grindorge brought news to the King about the revolt in Calabria, and a tin of English pickled salmon. The King took the tin, locked his door, and ate the salmon; then found the time to ask Grindorge (who told the story later to Wilson) what was going on. The old carbonaro, ringleader of the rising, had so far evaded capture. The King told Grindorge he sympathised with the old man, because of his treatment by the police, but if he was caught he'd have to hang him.

96 Thomas Grenville wrote to the Duke of Buckingham about it on

April 14, 1829. The King 'is fonder of abusing his Ministers than of changing them. For a few hard words cost him nothing; but a great political change could not be made, if at all, without much more trouble, fatigue, and worry to the King than he will like to expose himself to.' *Memoirs of the Court of George IV*, Duke of Buckingham and Chandos, ii, 395.

97 *Memoirs of the Court of George IV*, Duke of Buckingham and Chandos, ii, 378–380.

98 Nowadays Lampedusa, part of the Pelagie archipelago, and the southernmost point of the Italian Republic, has about 4,000 inhabitants. It is an ecological disaster.

99 On December 7th, 43 BC, 21 months after Caesar's murder. Cicero tried to save the Roman Republic and was proscribed in Rome by his old enemy, Mark Antony. At the time of his murder he had a ship waiting at Formia, near Gaeta, in which to escape, but is supposed to have returned to his villa saying: 'Let me die in the country which I have often saved.'

100 Trachyte is a volcanic rock with a total silica content of between 55 and 60 per cent. In the Palaeolithic era, Ponza exported obsidian, a silica-rich and glassy volcanic rock, to Cuma for the manufacture of tools.

101 Scrope (1797–1876) was a distinguished geologist and political economist, and a fellow of the Royal Society. His *Considerations*, published in 1825 and partly based upon his observations of the great eruption of Vesuvius in 1822, was the earliest systematic textbook of vulcanology, and a big influence on the geologist Charles Lyell.

102 In Roman times, too. Nero, as a foetus or as an infant, and Caligula's sisters, all did time here, and Augustus confined his nymphomaniac daughter Julia on the smaller, neighbouring island of Ventotene (Roman name Pandateria). After Italy's liberation in 1944, Mussolini was held on Ponza for six days.

103 The aptly-named Moonlight Bay, immediately opposite Ponza on the other side of the island, less than a mile from the port and within easy walking distance. Its lovely crescent beach, beneath 300-ft-high cliffs, shines when the moon is up.

104 Now in the British Museum, and the earliest known representation of Christ in Britain, if not in western Europe. It was discovered by the local blacksmith digging a post-hole for a stable. He was

prevented from digging through it by a Victorian waterpipe than ran just inches above it. When he cleared round the pipe he revealed part of the floor-mosaic, which occupies a considerable area.

105 After WWII, the US Army, with money from the Rockefeller Foundation, eliminated the anopheles mosquito, and malaria, from Sardinia and Corsica. Its work enabled tourist and other development of the *stagni* (lagoons) along their coasts.

106 Begun by King Carlo Felice, not without opposition from local inhabitants, in 1821. When completed, it ran from Cagliari to Sassari and Porto Torres on the north coast. It's still called the Carlo Felice highway.

107 Almost all destroyed, alas, later in the 19th century. Today Sardinia is more or less deforested. Only pockets remain of the great swathes of holm oaks, cork oaks and pines that once covered the island.

108 The implication, here, is that the Duke himself was engaged in painting a watercolour.

109 The Duke gives it no name. It was Ile San Bainsu.

110 Sketched out.

111 In August 1833 ownership of the *Anna Eliza* was transferred by mortgage indenture to two City of London businessmen, Sauter and Pope, who sold her on to George Morgan, a citizen of Southampton. When he died in 1841, his widow sold her (still described as square-rigged, with a standing bowsprit) to a Kentish merchant called Edmund Read. She was last heard of in March 1846, in Bombay, probably in the carrying trade. (PRO BT 107, Ref 84, November 12th 1841, entry 411).

112 Place of quarantine

113 Backed by English assurances of independence, Genoa rose against the French in 1814. But a secret clause of the Treaty of Paris, confirmed later by the Congress of Vienna, gave it to the Kingdom of Sardinia. Republican discontent at Genoa produced Joseph Mazzini, and the abortive rebellion of 1848.

114 It was premièred in 1816

115 Now known as The Dying Gaul.

116 Catholic emancipation.

117 *PD* iii, 55.

118 An English doctor with a practice in Rome.

119 *PD* iii, 68/9.

120 *PD* iii, 43.

121 It was sold out of the family in the 1848 auction, but returned to Stowe School in 1983.
122 It was shipped to Stowe, and used as a mausoleum for the Duke's dead dogs.
123 An old name for nitrogen.
124 Where papal elections were held until 1870, when the Sistine chapel began to be used.
125 When the move was made to the Sistine chapel, the procedure changed: damp straw, black smoke, no pope; dry straw, white smoke, pope elected.
126 The Duke had an audience with him on May 14th, and found him a 'shrewd, sharp-eyed, active-minded, old man'.
127 Equivalent, according to the Duke, to our eight o'clock in the evening.
128 PD iii, 105–6
129 The Duke called it woodbine.
130 Giotto's frescoes in the Upper Church were terribly damaged by an earthquake in September 1997. They were painstakingly restored, and reopened to public view in 2002.
131 Sold in the 1848 auction for £16 5s 6d, it passed into the Rothschild collection, and was auctioned by Sothebys in 2003 as a 19th-century reproduction, with a modest estimate of £6,000 to £8,000. After the restoration of the Bourbons, there was a fashion for Renaissance jewellery. Limited supply encouraged fakes.
132 On February 21, 1829 Chandos held an anti-Catholic meeting for the hundreds of Buckingham, Ashendon and Cottesloe. He was escorted by 300 mounted gentlemen and farmers, and his coach was pulled through Buckingham by a crowd estimated at 3,000. He had already presented 97 anti-Catholic petitions to the House of Commons, with 7,000 Bucks signatures. The Duke wrote a public letter to the hundreds condemning his son, and their support of him.
133 Converted from a 13th-century mansion and now the three-star Locanda Hotel Leon Bianco.
134 The Duke's published diary takes him as far as Geneva. The remaining 52 pages of the original diary, unpublished and, because of the Duke's poor handwriting, largely illegible, are in private hands in England (photocopies available at the Centre for Buckinghamshire Studies, Aylesbury). They take him down the Rhine through

Germany and the Low Countries until his embarkation, three months later on November 4, 1829, on the Lord Liverpool steam packet for England, where he was met by his son Chandos.

135 On August 15, 1848, in *The Times*, Lord Macaulay pulled the stops out: 'In the midst of fertile lands, and an industrious people, in the heart of a country where it is thought virtuous to work, to save, and to thrive, a man of the highest rank, and of property not unequal to his title, has flung all away by extravagance and folly, and reduced his honours to the tinsel of a pauper and the bauble of a fool.'

136 Professor John Beckett (*The Rise and Fall of the Grenvilles, 1710 to 1921*, Manchester University Press, 1994) contends that the real saviour of Stowe was Anna Eliza, the first Duchess. In 1828, while the Duke was in Italy, she foresaw which way the wind was blowing for the family, and resettled her Chandos estates accordingly, by a private Act of Parliament. Her trustees were forbidden to sell Chandos land to pay unsecured Grenville debts, but sales were permitted to buy equivalent land marching with Grenville estates in Buckinghamshire, or, in effect, to pay off Grenville mortgages. After her death in 1836, Chandos played fast and loose with her trust and its trustees, and it was touch and go in 1848 whether his son Richard, who had forced his bankrupt father to hand over to him the running of the family's affairs, would be able to retain any land at all. Stowe House and estate was offered for sale privately after the great auction of the house's contents, but there were no buyers. In the end, because of the Duchess's foresight in 1828, there turned out to be enough capital tied up in unencumbered Chandos land to take Stowe off the market, satisfy the Grenvilles' principle creditors, and train about 9,500 acres in Buchinghamshire. *Op. Cit. pp* 149–281.

  Richard was helped by one further factor. He married, in 1851, Caroline Harvey of Langley Park near Slough, who was fairly well off. The second Duke disapproved of his new daughter-in-law. She was only a baronet's daughter and therefore 'derogatory to me'.

137 He died in 1889, and the Dukedom of Buckingham and Chandos died with him.

138 He was chairman of the London and North Western Railway from 1852 to 1861. It doubled in value under his stewardship. His father, 'Bucky'. was disdainful. 'To think that a son of mine could be a clerk in a railway booking-office,' he once remarked.

139 Avington Park was sold in the fire-sales of 1848 (which only Wotton survived with its contents intact). The buyer was John Shelley, younger brother of Percy Bysshe, the renegade poet and member of the Jacobin secret society of Illuminists who, back in the early years of the century, had advocated cutting the throats of all kings, priests and aristocrats.

Index of Names and Places

Monday April 2nd 1827

Received a letter as soon as I was up from Theresa informing me that the account which Holmes gave her was untrue and that nothing is settled. Canning the Warrender so bad myself & the old latter pressed the former about me and India, he said? "dread an army in the present state of things?" and wondered how Clanw or I could suppose he felt any thing like unkindness towards me. I walked all about the grounds and remained upon my legs all day. My Wife means to live very much here if Sir J. India. Looked over the Library and take out a good many books for the library at Avington. Mary, Catherine & Daniel Maxwell dine here today. Looked over the Kitchen Garden which is in good order. During dinner I received my letters & News papers from London, with one from the Duke of W and an account from Chandos of his interview with him. The Duke very kind & expressing himself with that. I was in Cabinet. As to India he could not interfere unless he came in his way and was referred to him, he disre= stated his anxiety to serve me. Bold in his Con= = rather however and in his letter he has fallen